Philosophical Imagination and Cultural Memory

Appropriating Historical Traditions

DUKE UNIVERSITY PRESS

Durham and London 1993

© 1993 Duke University Press

Printed in the United States of

America on acid-free paper ∞

Typeset in Berkeley Medium

by Keystone Typesetting, Inc.

Library of Congress

Cataloging-in-Publication

Data appear on the last printed

page of this book.

Contents

Acknowledgment

The essays in this volume are the product of a National Endowment for the Humanities Summer Institute held at Clemson University in 1990. The authors served as faculty members of the Institute or contributed as participants. Some essays were originally presented as public lectures for the summer program. The aim of this book is to extend and continue that inquiry. The authors and editor gratefully acknowledge the financial support provided by the National Endowment for the Humanities, which has made the publication of this volume possible.

Introduction

"What's past is prologue."—THE TEMPEST (2.1.261)

What task remains for philosophy?

It often has been observed that we find ourselves at the end of this century amid the husks of pragmatism, the rubble of analysis, and the regular litany of moribund pronouncements on the practice of philosophy. So what could be the future of philosophical activity? What remains of the philosophical enterprise that has not become terminally introverted, wholly effete, or alarmingly indistinguishable from other sorts of enterprises?

The essays in this volume exhibit one set of answers to these questions. Each exemplifies an exercise of the philosophical imagination on some dimension of human history. "Philosophical imagination" is a term coined by Alasdair MacIntyre for that ability by which the best of philosophers can provisionally or temporarily inhabit alien philosophical systems. As the title of this book suggests, the authors in this volume provisionally or temporarily inhabit some situs of cultural memory. Another way of describing what these authors have in common is to say that all of them are engaged in the philosophical appropriation of historical traditions. Among such historical traditions are literature, art, scientific projects, social theories, and cultural practices as well as philosophical systems. These traditions may have been handed down in the past and yet not perdured in cultural memory per se. They are called "historical traditions" here to emphasize that they no longer necessarily bear their original associations and meanings in current cultural contexts. For the authors of this volume, both the search for original meanings and the metamorphosing of what is handed down provide significant tools, or focal points, for ongoing philosophical inquiry.

In short, then, here is the suggestion of this volume: the inquiries, narratives, and past events held in cultures and in some way handed down are providing the pith of some of the most provocative exercises of current-day philosophical imagination. For the philosophical thinkers in this volume, history is not limited to past figures who have participated in the genealogy of problems of ultimately Platonic ancestry. Neither do these authors seek merely to excavate uncodified meanderings of previous moments of civilization. Rather, their implicit view is reminiscent of the ancient Dionysius of Halicarnasus's characterization of history as "philosophy by examples."

To take historical traditions as illumination or inspiration for philosophy is hardly innovation. Paragons of philosophizing from historical traditions are ancient: Theophrastus, Aristotle, Diogenes Laertius. But the contributors to this book are emerging from the postmodern philosophical crisis as a vanguard. What is emerging with them is the enormously rich and increasingly complex and compelling business vaguely referred to heretofore only as the "history of philosophy."

This book is not unique in its ostensible purpose. Other efforts have been made in recent years to uncover new directions for philosophy in the wake of the meticulous self-refutation of analysis, empiricism, certain modes of moral theorizing, and absolutist metaphysics. Indeed, philosophy's recent progress along a sort of *via negativa* of self-definition has prompted several volumes intended to anthologize the remaining viable candidates for future philosophical inquiry. Typically cited as potential areas for study are hermeneutics, the philosophy of literature, and the philosophy of science. The history of philosophy is occasionally cited as a source of a direction and as a prescription for future philosophizing, but the suggestion is not always helpful since the precise nature, purpose, and results of that history still seem to evade complete definition.

But while much remains to be said about what it is to study philosophy's own history, and about why and to what extent this should be done, such a study is not the purpose of this book. Rather, the chapters that follow are meant to suggest, and test, a more definitive rubric. Prosaically named "the philosophical uses of historical traditions" and alluded to as "philosophical imagination and cultural memory," this rubric takes more than philosophy's history into retrospective view, and it must not be confused with the philosophy of history. This new enterprise not only takes all dimensions of human history to be potentially revelatory for philosophical reflection, it also reflects on the varying shapes of the many human traditions as well as on the fact of history itself.

The suggestion that many of our most important contemporary philosophical thinkers have turned their attention to cultural memory does not entail the supposition that this is a monolithic movement. The present volume calls attention to multiple inflections of the enterprise. We are familiar with finding assorted modalities within the study of the history of philosophy. Many thinkers have observed that distinct genres have crystallized in this area. For example, Richard Rorty finds at least four distinct historiographical genres for the study of philosophy's history. These include

(1) rational reconstruction: the process of attempting to translate, without anachronism, a past philosopher's views into present idiom; (2) historical reconstruction: the attempt to interpret a text strictly in its historical setting and in its own terms; (3) *Geistesgeschichte:* the edification of a present philosophical position by constructing a teleological narrative for a selective historical audience; and (4) doxography: what Rorty calls the "bloodless procession" of canonical lists of problems, figures, and texts. This list of genres cannot begin to accommodate the philosophical uses of historical traditions. The sheer volume of continuing historical accumulation, together with renderings—philosophical and otherwise—on this accumulation, suggest that the potential levels and modes of philosophizing from historical traditions may surpass anything we have managed to catalog. In this regard, these essays are offered as prototypes.

It is a venerable philosophical activity to investigate philosophy's own nature. Collecting these essays under one cover is meant to abet such self-examination. This volume documents a turn toward historical traditions by some of today's most influential thinkers, many of whom were originally trained in the analytic tradition of philosophy, which is supposedly liberated from any manifestation of cultural memory. These revisionist thinkers join a notable group of philosophers who never aspired to be free of historical tradition.

Accordingly, the significance of philosophy's return to historical traditions should be confronted. Especially when we wonder whether philosophy can survive postmodernism, we must take account of this new wave of philosophical thought that recurs to something akin to *pre*-modern modes of philosophical inquiry. What can we observe or conclude from the fact that a group of contemporary philosophers with enormously disparate backgrounds can now be seen to share an interest in cultural memory? What exactly is this new/old philosophizing from traditional texts trying to accomplish? Can the enterprises called philosophical uses of historical traditions account for these philosophers circumventing logical analysis and postmodern relativism? Indeed, does postmodernism somehow prescribe a recurrence to tradition in spite of itself? These are the questions that this book means to raise for the reader's consideration.

Philosophy and cultural memory

The following essays use cultural memory as a source of philosophical ideas and inspiration, as a backdrop for defining current situations, and as a vantage point from which to gain perspective on today's endeavors. They are collected under one cover to document an undercurrent in recent philosophy. But just what are the philosophical commitments informing this pro-tomovement? Is this work simply an exercise in antiquarianism? Or is it another strain of romanticism or, indeed, conservatism?

The emphasis on tradition unavoidably associates the book with the position known as conservatism. But such an association is uninformative and misleading. Conservatism, at least in its classical incarnations, is defined by its emphasis on tradition rather than human reason as the actual and legitimate cement of society. These essays do not contradict the conservative hypothesis, but neither do they underwrite it. None of them makes any claim for tradition as against reason; none has an express political theory; none prescribes or defends any particular form of government.

What most of these essays do attempt, however, is to explain and defend certain sorts of human attachments to traditions and institutions. These explanations are as multiform as the uses of historical traditions that are being discovered or practiced. But none of them represents the rehearsal of an established conservative agenda in either its classical, romantic, or skepti-cal guises. That is to say, none of these essays simply expresses a hostility to radical social change, nor any particular view of human frailty, irrationality, or perfectibility.

Instead, the present collection emphasizes the profound relationship be-tween philosophical reflection and cultural memory. The first two essays show how cultural memory and philosophy are by nature intertwined. George Allan's "Traditions and Transitions," which explores the nature of tra-dition, shows that cultural memory must define the form and provide the content of any philosophical inquiry. By Allan's thesis, the postmodern philo-sophical preoccupations of antifoundationalism and loss of individual mean-ing will prevail for as long as this relationship eludes understanding; these same symptoms of postmodernity, in fact, have perennially accompanied the failure to comprehend the relation between philosophy and cultural memory.

The symptomatic preoccupation of postmodernism is actually as old as philosophy itself. It is generated by the following reasoning. Without foun-dations, human knowledge seems to collapse into mere opinion; every knowledge claim is liable to be discredited and replaced. We crave the obverse state of certitude where our knowledge is stable and reliable, the outcome of our purposes predictable. Yet a particular foundation—which would be a sine qua non for certitude—can never itself be insulated from indictment or replacement. This reasoning has seemed to entail a host of contraindications to philosophy: any claim to objectivity is sheer pretension; there can be no objective reason for preferring one moral view over another; there are no thought-independent truths; we cannot reliably distinguish meanings from facts; there are no secure modes of reference.

Allan's view of the significance of cultural memory, in effect, responds to these charges. There are indeed foundations, and they are called traditions. Allan understands tradition to be that complex of interpretations of the world that happen to have been shared by many people over an extended period of time. As a framework for interpretation, tradition focuses our responses to things and thereby renders them meaningful. As a base of schemata, tradition guides and habituates and gives meaning to action and thought.

Accordingly, traditions make human interaction possible. Most obviously, discourse itself presupposes a shared commensurating framework of meanings. People need to share a certain platform of interpretation in order to be intelligible to one another, indeed, even to recognize one another. We also need an interpretive framework to exhibit individuality, to be distinctive selves in relation to other selves.

But this raises the exigent question: is it possible to arbitrate between two traditions in conflict? Allan's point is that, where there is a dispute, there must be an underlying framework for the dispute that is shared in common. In other words, there must be a deeper stratum of tradition undergirding the layers of tradition in conflict. This stratum would constitute the horizon of the intelligible world and could not be explicitly evoked. But it could, and does, function in conflict arbitration as a bedrock of tacit ideals that have the potential to be actualized in new ways.

The second essay, Donald Phillip Verene's "Two Sources of Philosophical Memory: Vico Versus Hegel," exposes some of the foregoing dimensions of cultural memory in a multilevel exercise in philosophical imagination. "Philosophical imagination," as noted, is the name coined by Alasdair MacIntyre for that ability by which the best of philosophers can provisionally or temporarily inhabit alien philosophical systems. But the term also aptly names Verene's philosophical method, a method which is not only integral to, but is also determined by, the philosophical position he uses it to deploy.

Verene's text is on memory; it is itself memorial; and it calls on the reader to partake in cultural and philosophical memory. Verene intends to make an equation between philosophy and memory, so his method of philosophical imagination is an exercise that completes the meaning of its text. He revives what really must be considered as two traditions: the Roman-Italian of Vico, and the Greek-German of Hegel. Continuing these traditions as a participant, he philosophically intertwines them.

Verene's inquiry into the nature of wisdom in Vico and Hegel finds wisdom's form to be complete speech that says all there is to say about a subject and that begins and ends in what we know. His remarks on this circularity link it to narration, which because of its circularity is the natural form of memory. Verene's notion is not simply the keeping of the past; philosophical memory, as he conceives it through Vico and Hegel, includes the power to alter and to arrange the things that it holds. All of these memorial powers must conspire to discover truth, namely, a complete narration of the whole of things that gives account of their cyclical order. The true and complete narration that is the goal of philosophical memory grasps the providential order of all things. Thus, philosophical imagination and cultural memory, which are initially engaged to provide access to one another, will ultimately come together to yield that truth which philosophy seeks: the iteration of philosophical memory.

Philosophical imagination and the history of philosophy

As part of the broader project of the philosophical uses of historical traditions, the exercise of philosophical imagination can actually be made to buttress the study of the history of philosophy in just those places where the history of philosophy is weak. The study of the history of philosophy is not necessarily either self-contained or self-justifying. The study of the history of philosophy makes certain presumptions about what philosophy's history has been and what reflection upon it can realize. Such presumptions are not simply expressed by whatever historiography the study of the history of philosophy produces. Historiography, the art of recording history, expresses in its various genres only a further set of commitments concerning philosophy's nature and past. According to genre, the inclusion of what counts as philosophy varies, as does what weight any particular contribution should be given. In addition, what counts as a good reason for deciding upon inclusion and for assigning weight may vary from genre to genre.

Philosophy considered as a discipline with a discipline-history further complicates these commitments. The discipline-history of philosophy is clear but short, dating only from the nineteenth century. Its antecedents belong to a broader tradition in which the overlap between philosophical and extraphilosophical inquiry may have been more significant than their delimitations. Philosophers who study the history of philosophy typically view their project as different from that of intellectual historians with mere antiquarian interests. They study the history of philosophy as what they consider to be either a mode or a method of philosophizing in itself. It is not clear, however, as is often the case with any particular philosophical method, how this study can be internally justified. That is, adherence to the study of the history of philosophy may rest on doctrines that themselves are not derived from the history of philosophy. Although the history of philosophy cannot necessarily either defend the selection of its subject matter or justify itself as a method of philosophizing, many of its commitments can be articulated, and certain of its commitments can even be legitimated, by the activity of philosophical imagination upon the history of philosophy when it is taken as one thread in the fabric of cultural memory.

The three essays in the volume's second section exemplify this process. One issue that all three essays address by means of this process is internally unresolvable by the standard history of philosophy kinds of inquiry. That issue concerns the nature of history itself. The question of the nature of philosophy's history polarizes the standard study of the history of philosophy. At one pole is the position that tradition is ahistorical, that philosophy really has no history, that philosophical traditions are synchronic rather than diachronic. Associated with this ahistorical pole is the view that there are timeless problems to which there can be timeless solutions, and that the solutions would be tantamount to absolute truth—a truth that convention is powerless to modify. On the opposite pole is the position known as historicism. On this view, every philosophical problem is temporally and culturally entrenched; as a consequence, the problems of one age are irrelevant to those of another age. Accordingly, problems can be addressed only by considering their place in history and their role in historical development. Associated with historicism are the multiform and unsettled issues of progress, the accessibility of history itself, and the nature of truth.

These two exaggerated positions of ahistoricism and historicism—artificial though they are—implicitly define the points of departure for philosophies of the history of philosophy found in the second section of this book. Amid its complex set of themes, Alasdair MacIntyre's essay includes a view of history that is partisan to neither of the two traditionally incompatible positions. MacIntyre views philosophy's history as temporal and progressive, and yet as potentially yielding something akin to absolute truth. As it is adumbrated in "Are Philosophical Problems Insoluble? The Relevance of System and History," MacIntyre's position is not simply Hegelianism. The history of philosophy is a history not of insular problems or texts, but of historical philosophical "systems." From the standpoint of some particular system, it is possible to view the history of philosophy as making rational progress. Indeed, it is possible for one system to manifest rational superiority over all others, thereby mediating the intellectual and cultural conflicts they represent. An encounter between two rival philosophical systems, each with an internal conception of rational justification, can be mediated without appeal to some external, theory-independent standard. The more adequate of the two rival systems will have just these properties: it will excel in internal coherence and resourcefulness, and it will have terms in which to comprehend the theses of its rivals and to account for their failures and inadequacies.

From this monumental thesis follows another: insofar as philosophy can successively formulate superior accounts and progressively more satisfactory systems, so far is it socially justifiable. This inclusion of a "social dimension" is one of the striking innovations of MacIntyre's philosophy of the history of philosophy. Many philosophers have suggested—Plato most trenchantly—that philosophy bears an ineluctably ambivalent relation to society. Philosophy requires an established social order for it to complete its critical activity and it depends upon society to provide the leisure necessary for its pursuit. Yet philosophy engages in nothing that society can recognize as useful; it seeks to criticize the established order and to insist on its own intrinsic value at the same time that it bakes no bread. Thus, philosophy can never "apologize" for itself: it can never justify itself to society.

MacIntyre approaches the relation of philosophy to society in a wholly different way. In his analysis, the philosopher's questions are those that are posed, and in some way answered, by everyone. So when the ideals of rational adequacy of a philosophical system are reformulated, it is the continuing questions of the prephilosophical public that receive increasingly satisfactory answers in successive formulations. Thus, philosophy may be seen as discharging its responsibility to the world at large.

J. B. Schneewind's "Modern Moral Philosophy: From Beginning to End?" engages historical traditions in a way that places the history of philosophy in quite a different light. In this "case study," Schneewind focuses on the notion of the equal distribution of moral autonomy. The notion that all normal adults possess equal moral competence is central to modern morality itself; belief in moral autonomy is held in common by all of modernity's most influential moral theories. Schneewind's question is, how did the modern belief in equal moral autonomy arise? The genesis of what he calls "a central aspect of modern self-understanding" emerges as he traces the history of this belief.

In Schneewind's view, the case study method is the appropriate vehicle for reflecting on the nature of the history of philosophy. Since there is no single kind of relation between the past and the present, there is bound to be more than one purpose for historical philosophical study. There is bound to be more than one sort of product as well, for what emerges as a useful result in one case study may not be valid as a general rule. Accordingly, Schneewind here does not embrace the goal of comprehensive system-building for the history of philosophy. Instead, he suggests that philosophical understanding requires retracing the rational steps that have led thinkers from some particular position or system to the adoption of another one at some later time. But there is no reason to suppose that such an internal explanation will be self-contained and exhaustive. Neither is there warrant for supposing that these steps will converge at one theoretically decipherable point.

The views of the two previous essayists are effectively amplified in "Refutation, Narrative, and Engagement: Three Conceptions of the History of Philosophy," in which George R. Lucas, Jr., juxtaposes three distinct philosophies of the history of philosophy; he describes these as refutation, narrative, and engagement. The first two have well-established adherents; Descartes, Reichenbach, and Moore, for example, implicitly view the history of philosophy as history distinct from histories of other disciplines and as a series of decisive refutations and entirely new beginnings. By contrast, Aristotle, Hegel, Vico, Augustine, and Collingwood exemplify philosophers who conceive of philosophy itself as constituting an all-encompassing and totalizing historical narrative in which the strengths and limitations of rival standpoints are acknowledged, sympathetically interpreted, and finally included and transformed within some convergent master narrative. Lucas takes up this dilemma by addressing contemporary adherents to versions of each of these two views: namely, Arthur Danto and Alasdair MacIntyre. Lucas argues that the larger conceptual sweep of the history of philosophy escapes both of these categorizations.

He further suggests that the history of philosophy can best be understood if it is viewed as analogous to the histories of art and literature in this respect: it proceeds in waves of passionate engagement with a variety of issues rather than as a rational and orderly series of ideas. When passion and interest in certain problems wane, then (to paraphrase Hegel) a "shape" or episode of philosophy's own history crystallizes, grows cold. No definitive or justificatory reasons ever can be given for the replacement in history of one philosophical movement by another. Indeed, most philosophical movements and authors have never been either refuted or absorbed in posterity; most have simply been abandoned and forgotten.

In sum, then, the three essays in the second section identify one outpost of cultural memory for which the imaginative philosophical enterprise is preeminently essential. In order to identify participants in philosophy's history, in order to articulate what the history of philosophy is the history of, in order to defend the history of philosophy as a medium of legitimate philosophizing, the philosophical imagination must avail itself of cultural memory as such. It is only by temporarily inhabiting a diversity of cultural or philosophical systems that philosophers can begin to form any meaningful self-definition, self-justification, or self-understanding.

Perspectives on the significance of cultural memory

For most of its history, philosophy has sought to be both the foundation and the capstone of all other inquiry. Aristotle expressed this desideratum by calling philosophy "the first and last science." There are certain questions that belong to philosophy, questions that cannot be addressed from within other sciences, that nonetheless apply to all the other sciences. Yet some mastery of the other sciences is presupposed by serious philosophical inquiry.

With the genesis of the culture of academic disciplines in the nineteenth century came an additional role for philosophy. The queen of sciences now had to function as the mortar for all other sciences. As a discipline, it was to seek a systematic unity of all other disciplines. The suggestions that philosophy was not an autonomous academic discipline and that its program had come to an end roughly coincided with this new role.

As a discipline, philosophy has been conspicuously divided over its history. Some philosophers, as noted, have embraced philosophy's history as its self-definition; other philosophers have been eager to rid themselves of history as they have claimed to supersede or repudiate it. Some philosophers have elevated the tradition to an ontological category; other philosophers have expressed doubt whether such a thing as a tradition exists. How does this situation compare with that of other disciplines? Why is the practice of philosophy so divided with respect to its history? Is this just part of the dialectical armature of philosophy, of a piece with conflicting positions and the absence of consensus concerning method?

The essays in the book's third section contribute to this inquiry as they prescind from the narrow, standard, disciplinary categories of debate. Some helpful questions are raised when philosophy and its history are considered in comparison with other areas of study and their histories. Just what is the relation between art, science, religion, and their respective histories? Are the academic disciplines that represent these areas divided—either in theory or in practice—over the role of their history for current endeavors? What is, or what should be, the relation of these other histories to philosophy's history? Does philosophy align in revealing ways with these other areas in either aspiration or in attitude with respect to history? Can we generalize about the significance of cultural memory for all areas of study?

These essays take as their point of departure the common notion of Modernism, that peculiar constellation of symptoms of the Zeitgeist being generally thought to be either the source or the result of a particular view of history. These symptoms of Modernism are familiar: the quest for certitude; the infatuation with progress, which dubiously refers either to progressively better insight into the natures of things or to incessant novelty; the effort to separate facts from values, subject from object, and narrative from explanation; the valuation of an individual freedom unqualified by any points of reference. Possibly as cause or effect, these symptoms accompany the nihilistic renunciation of history itself. They seem to issue in that equally familiar postmodern malaise, antifoundationalism and loss of individual meaning. The essays in this section consider the relationship of cultural memory to Modernism and postmodernism from the perspectives of art, science, and theology.

Art's history would seem to be a useful vantage for reflecting on history, the history of philosophy, and Modernism for the following reason alone: art's history is palpable, prized, and preserved. It lingers in museums. It is restored and maintained. Its originals are unanimously valued over simulacra, and the value of an original often increases with its age. Arthur C. Danto suggests, however, that this museum-case milieu for art is a manifestation of the ahistoric turn of Modernism.

In "The Shape of Artistic Pasts, East and West," Danto compares the narrative of Western painters from Giotto to Jacques-Louis David (roughly 1300–1800) with the situation of Chinese painters of that same period. For those five centuries, the Chinese artists practiced in a tradition that was nearly uniform; as Danto says, this history was "vectorless." Western painting of this period, by contrast, was a progressive discipline par excellence; periods spawned and transcended one another "in a way that pointed a progressive vector." Danto richly illustrates how the different internalized narratives of East and West determined the respective modes of influence from the past that were available to the artists of each tradition.

In this vectorless period of the East, the concepts of imitation and influence were themselves idiomatic. The artist sought what his masters had sought for centuries; imitation was simply a means to this end. And influence, we must see in retrospect, was actually mutual. Concurrently, the Western tradition unfolded a series of three narratives. The Renaissance related to the past as a narrative of recovery, and the Enlightenment took its history as stages and growth. These two narratives were taken over into Modernism, whose hallmark is to repudiate the past.

On Danto's analysis, Modernism in art distinguishes itself from every other phase in art's history precisely by its refusal to find some positive way to appropriate past traditions. To be modern, says Danto, "is to perceive the past as the locus of only negative messages." The work of Modernism is the dismantling of past narratives. The style of Modernism is historical dismissal. The legacy of Modernism continues to be the loss of faith in the relevance and in the defining narrative of one's own culture.

Danto's essay is insistent about the consequences of this legacy. What is to be said about historical causation in art when what Modernism means to bequeath are effects without causes? Shall we agree that there is no such thing as art, only individual artists? And, most significantly, how do we account for the modern turn as such? How do we understand, to use Danto's poignant illustrations, the abandonment by Van Gogh and Gauguin of their own past in favor of what were ultimately their chimerical views of the traditions of other cultures?

Danto's insights suggest that an ambivalence about art's history surfaces in the light of postmodern historical reflection on the modernist turn. The essay by Lynn S. Joy shows an interestingly parallel ambiguity for science when modern science is illuminated by historical reflection. Science, in the form of the contemporary academic disciplines of natural and physical science is not, of course, in conflict over its history. The consensus of scientists consists of the cumulative development of true theories and the progressive overcoming of past mistakes. Contemporary scientists know better than their predecessors. Science has made progress in understanding the world, and its past is simply the record of trial and error leading to present insight. The past has disproved itself. No contemporary scientist believes that this past ought to be studied for science's sake. And anyone who believes, say, in a fluid of heat called caloric, or in humors and the practice of bloodletting, would not be recognized as a member of the contemporary scientific community. Likewise, no scientist believes that any other aspect of history ought to be studied for science's sake. History has no particular relevance for what must be established empirically.

It has not always been the case that those who study nature or medicine have eschewed the study of history. Lynn Joy's "Humanism and the Problem of Traditions in Seventeenth-Century Natural Philosophy" shows how this is a peculiarity of the new science that is actually internal to its empiricism. Joy shows, moreover, how the new science and its peculiar antihistoricism were engendered in part by the diligent treatment of historical texts by late Renaissance natural philosophers. Old science sought truth by attending to two masters: the natural world of sense experience and the wisdom of ancient authority. In the hands of the Renaissance natural philosophers, the interpretation of historical texts did not interfere with, but enhanced, the empirical content of science. Both texts and sense observations were thought to require interpretation. Joy shows how this interpretation became a fruitfully reciprocal affair, with texts interpreted by aid of observation, and experience interpreted in the light of historical texts.

Such allegiance to historical texts brought the problem of competing traditions to the fore. Joy interprets Pierre Gassendi's response to the problem of competing traditions as a portent of the new science. Gassendi argued for atomism as the necessary basis for an empirical science. Epicurean atomism had suggested to him the causal mechanism of sense perception, which served as the link between the natural world and ourselves. Thus, sense perception began to supplant the ancient texts as the justifier of truth. And so the way was paved for the new science's mechanistic atomism and its practice of justifying theories by reference to experience.

Lynn Joy's analysis issues in the marvelous irony that it took historical arguments and the appropriation of ancient texts to give birth to the premise of the new science, while the new science, in turn, has tried to sequester itself from the study of its own historical genesis and from consideration of the history of ideas.

Has modernity folded philosophy into a shape with convolutions similar to those of the new science, or has it stranded philosophy with the *nunc aeternatatis* of modern art? This section's next essay suggests that the conveyance of modern art and the ambitions of modern science become supremely self-defeating when they are practiced by philosophy. When philosophy is viewed from the standpoint of theology and theology's history, it becomes conspicuous that philosophy's modern career has represented both a progressive departure from true human needs and a serial evacuation of philosophy's human categories. According to Robert Cummings Neville in "The Symbiotic Relation of Philosophy and Theology," philosophy does not need to rekindle its own history as much as it needs to reacquaint itself with originary concerns. To redress its excursion into modernity, philosophy needs theology. A reversal of the handmaiden role is particularly called for in our time because theology is the reigning steward of some of the most basic motifs embodied in our general modes of thought. Neville argues that the elementary motifs of human connections with one another, with institutions, and with material life itself must, in postmodernity, be recovered from historical theological traditions.

Neville carries out a particular case study that calls for this compensatory symbiosis: it is the collapse of the modern themes of power and narrative that he finds will require theological redress. He traces the concept of power from the inception of its modern form, i.e., as divorced from notions of value in nature, to Renaissance mathematical physics. From physics, power quickly gets extended to conceptualize the human will, whence it is readily appropriated by political theory. In modern political theory and ethics, power enjoys a heyday. Freedom in modernity gets defined in terms of the prevailing metaphor of inertial power; justice becomes the balance of power for everyone to seek his or her own interest. Neville views the political and moral efforts on behalf of power equalization as unsurprising failures—

unsurprising, because the power metaphor preempts the articulation of what true or valid self-interest can be.

The modern concept of narrative has endured a similar fate. The concept of narrative was vital when Luther and Calvin recovered Augustine's *Confessions,* but it reached its denouement with Freud and Marx. Narrative was abandoned by theology because of the problems of theodicy, and it was sublated by the concept of power in the social sciences: a person's story-form identity was replaced by a vector sum of "forces." Thus, in Neville's analysis, power and narrative live and languish together in modernity and leave morality in need of rehabilitation.

Neville finds an agent for this rehabilitation in a deep, basic cultural motif preserved in the theological tradition—the covenant. As an alternative conception of the human social condition, Neville proposes that people are related by an ontological covenant. The covenantal motif reorients not only class analysis but also *praxis.* History ceases, in this conception, to have a cosmic narrative, so moral action becomes altogether localized, piecemeal, and perspectival. This conception connects a contemporary philosophical problem with "the historical depths" of the Judeo-Christian past, and it is also "more realistic about the human condition than other themes of modernity."

Cultural memory and textual interpretation

The volume's final essays exemplify different modes of arriving at philosophical insights through the medium of traditional texts; each of the four chapters can be viewed as a prototype for a distinctive genre of the exercise of philosophical imagination on traditional texts. But there is something unique about these essays as a group. Without reducing philosophy to interpretation (as do some strains of reigning postmodern thought), these essays use a text or a received textual tradition to show that interpretation must really remain the doppelgänger of philosophy. Although it can be made to reveal features—and limits—of philosophy, interpretation is no more than a specter of any attempt at a full expression of rational reflection on human enterprises.

The section's first essay, "The Six Silences of a Grecian Urn," lies on the periphery of traditional philosophy, along the border between philosophy and literature. Eva T. H. Brann's meditation on Keats's poem begins as literary criticism but becomes an excursion that shapes philosophy itself. Brann has what might be called a chiaroscuro technique of philosophizing, where philosophical speculation and introspection are shaded off against literary analysis. Unlike metaphilosophy, which typically tries to say what philosophy can and cannot do, Brann's inquiry from philosophy's edges shows its contours and its horizons. The results of this mode of inquiry appear to be immune even to the charges of the twentieth-century critics of Western metaphysics.

Silence is not a canonical category in philosophy. On reading Brann's study, one finds simultaneously why this is so and also that such a category is not superfluous. She actually creates silence as a philosophical category. In Brann's interpretation, the urn contemplated by Keats both represents and enjoins silence; Brann goes on to discover and elaborate six significant dimensions of this silence. The philosopher's intransigent response to this silence is the desire to speak for it. Philosophy, which has traditionally overprized the verbal element of thought, will want to fill the silences with speech. Philosophy's hypersensual realm is traditionally made into the intelligible realm, which is never devoid of words. In Keats's poem, however, the silences ultimately replace invisible word with speechless picture. Beautiful things like the Grecian urn can "tease us out of thought." Keats holds the visible and its silences before us as truer than speech and reason. In the end, Keats makes beauty and truth convertible, even identical. Brann's study addresses the philosopher's question to this identity: How can Keats subordinate speech to sight when speech is the poem's vehicle for conveying the message of that subordination? The answer that is developed is subtle in its implications for metaphysics: There is a temporality in speech that is surpassed by the poet's visible image. Thus, philosophy, which has always supposed that the really real is whatever is eternal and unchanging, has the philosophical suppositions about the meaning-fixed word, its eternality and its truth, illuminated by poetry and imagery.

The next essay exhibits yet another genre of philosophizing from traditional texts. George L. Kline's "Changing Russian Assessments of Spinoza and Their German Sources (1796–1862)" exemplifies the consummate scholarship that is salutary for any philosophical use of historical traditions. If, on the one hand, it is supposed that the genesis of an idea in history is the key to its truth, then the philosophical task is to reconstruct history from all records and all products of human institutions. If, on the other hand, it is supposed that a view or doctrine must be able to sustain itself in the face of all rational criticism within any climate at all, then the philosophical task is to elucidate a doctrine, articulate its implications, and possibly take heed of the consensus that the doctrine receives.

Both philosophical tasks depend on incisive scholarship. Without it, the first sort of philosophical task is likely to confuse argumentative and rational considerations with external contingencies, and the second sort is apt to find itself arguing against positions that nobody ever held, while missing the views and arguments that thinkers actually expressed. Without scholarship, the history of philosophy easily reduces to straw man polemics; and for polemics, history quickly proves to be dispensable. For all the contributors to this volume, the philosophical use of historical traditions depends on accurate (or at least only self-consciously prejudiced) history, which depends in turn on scholarship.

Kline's essay, a double-sided example of this point, uses an exercise in good scholarship to detail a period of poor scholarship. Kline interprets Spinoza's thought as it passed through two cultural lenses: first, its German academic interpreters; second, the Russian appropriation of Spinoza's thought received through German sources during the middle of the nineteenth century until 1886—during the period, that is, just before Russian translations became available. Spinoza's works had been published in Latin nearly two hundred years before they appeared in Russian translation and received responsible Russian scholarship. In the interim, even the Russian poets who were contemporaries of Goethe, Schiller, and Lessing seemed to have no interest in the thought of Romantic pantheism. Kline reconstructs the story behind this situation with his discovery of the few brief passages on Spinoza by nonacademic Russian thinkers and the harsh criticism of Spinoza by German-influenced Russian historians of philosophy. Some of the commentary of this period represents, more than simple animadversion, rank pseudoscholarship. The story Kline unfolds shows how finally the stage was set for the integration of Spinoza's thought into proper Russian scholarship.

The third essay directly addresses the displacement of tradition as a casualty of modernity and then discovers a paradigm for its reinstatement in a modern literary technique whose source is, itself, a particular traditional text. That text and technique belong to James Joyce. In John S. Rickard's reading of Ulysses, Joyce effects an elegant rapprochement between modernity and tradition. Rickard's essay, "Tradition and Intertextual Memory in James Joyce's Ulysses," locates Joyce squarely in the modernist dilemma between the verdict on the one hand that traditional cultural paradigms have ceased to be able to give meaning to modern life and the realization on the other hand that our lives have been shaped by those paradigms in ways that elude not only our control but even our explicit awareness.

Ulysses embodies a response to this dilemma in a device that Rickard calls "intertextual memory." Ulysses is replete with allusion. Echoes of historical texts are so deeply layered that no reader could consciously register them all, even after more than one reading. These textual resonances, in Rickard's analysis, mimic the unconscious memory; they color the interpretation of events and yet do not heuristically yield univocal meanings. The result in Ulysses is a modern text that does not try to repudiate traditional structures and begin anew, but neither is it moored to the past in a definitive way. The text remains involved with antecedent traditions and narratives in continuous response to the reader's orientation.

The final essay, Stanley Rosen's "Plato's Quarrel with the Poets," epitomizes Rosen's ability to seduce a text into complete self-exposure. Here is philosophical imagination in its prepotent form. Rosen uses traditional texts in ways that are similar to those manifested in the other essays in this group. But his studies always simultaneously and self-consciously reveal something about the nature of philosophy, some crucial aspect of the meaning of the text under discussion, and something about the metaphysical situation of men enmeshed in historical traditions.

A remarkable feature of Rosen's method of inquiry is his acute sensitivity to what might be called self-implication. When one carefully follows Rosen's way of thinking, one gets the sense that philosophical utterance has an inherent tendency to make itself an exception to whatever it is claiming. It is as though we, who abjure above all the logical contradiction, habitually and complacently preoccupy ourselves with the difficulties that occur somewhere short of the terminus of thought. Rosen always seems to be reasoning from the terminus, where the self-referential implications of a position are irrepressible, and self-contradictions are conspicuous.

He begins from two recognized problems of coherence in Plato's *Republic*. The first is an inconsistency within the text itself. If the political arrangement of the Republic is just and actualizable as such, then it is doubtful that the two highest classes, the philosophers and the guardians, would be happy in it. Socrates says that the just city is a possible achievement, yet he does not demonstrate the essential consequence that the just life is also the happiest. The second problem is not internal to the account in the *Republic* but is a paradox generated by the fact that the Platonic dialogues are examples of mimetic poetry. Poetry is explicitly condemned by Plato; it leads away from knowledge because it is twice removed from the reality of the Ideas and because it is associated with the rule of pleasure. Yet in certain respects, Plato makes philosophy subordinate to poetry. Philosophy is spoken of in poetic figures in the *Republic;* even the account of the Good is essentially poetic.

What do all of these problems of coherence, if considered together, betoken? Rosen parlays them into one overarching question for the *Republic:* What is the point of having an internally incoherent poem that is inherently obnoxious to the leaders of the city that it celebrates? The point, on Rosen's analysis, is to show that all consistently and rigorously applied political programs must finally result in tyranny.

Rosen gives an intricate illustration using freedom of speech. Why should freedom of speech enjoy political approbation? The postmodern philosophical answer invokes the absence of absolute standards. Since there are no eternal paradigms for human discourse to approximate, there is no definitive standard by which any particular discourse is deserving of suppression. But the self-referentiality of this conclusion is inescapable. If there are no standards, then there can be no injustice. Consequently, suppression of speech cannot itself be unjust. Moreover, there could be no rational defense against anyone who claims to be in possession of a particular standard for the regulation of speech. Thus, a truly consistent adherence even to a paradigm of freedom results in tyranny. In practice, the freedom that is actually defended contains some exclusions—of censorship, for example. But then a standard is indeed presupposed, and its complete articulation would share the obnoxiousness of Plato's Republic.

The place to which Plato's paradoxes direct us is where Rosen is skillfully leading us. We ought not to think our political principles through to the end. In extremis, all such principles reduce to self-contradictory error. That is the point of Plato's political satire called the *Republic*.

This volume's purpose is to call attention to the use of historical traditions by this influential group of philosophical thinkers; to suggest that their association be viewed as a significant movement; and to offer what appears to be a viable direction for prospective philosophy. The epigraph of this introduction, "What's past is prologue," is borne as an inscription on one of the pair of statues in front of the National Archives in Washington, D.C. The statue bearing this inscription is a personification of The Past: an old man holding a closed book. The other is a statue of The Future: a caped and hooded woman who carries an open book. The inscription on her statue is, "Study the past."

We invoke all of this as allegory and submit that the present project contributes to its meaning. Arthur C. Danto comments that it is the mark of living in the postmodern period that we face the future without a narrative of the present. But the essays in this volume will show that history, memory, and tradition are at last being reclaimed and resurrected. Introspection and retrospection seem to be reaching for an alliance that will eventually define "post-postmodernity." Perhaps it is only that the end-of-the-millennium Zeitgeist is upon us. In any case, a narrative of the present is finally being forged.

Part I

Philosophy

and

Cultural

Memory

George Allan

Traditions

and

Transitions

This is a time, it would seem, when whirl is king. The vast complexity of the world overwhelms us not because the complexity is so ponderous but because it changes so rapidly. Now this, now that: baffling us by its unprecedented surprises, confusing our purposes by constantly undermining our assumptions and scattering our efforts into a thousand unconnected gestures. We are no longer sure who we are or why. Or so it often seems, and the more so the more we find ourselves struggling with the fundamentals of our lives, with matters of birth and development and death, of the meaning of our dreams and the significance of our deeds.

I

The traditional role of a cultural tradition is to provide us with the resources we need to stave off the rule of whirl. It provides us with a way of taking things so that they do not surprise or overwhelm. It tells us what to expect and why, even when what is to be expected is some overwhelming surprise, some fundamental challenge to our hopes, our purposes, our havings and our doings. Our tradition wraps us in a world that discloses itself for us in ways we can comprehend and with which we can therefore cope.

We never simply experience things; we always experience them *as* something. We take the distant patch of dark as trees, the whispered words as a friend's advice, the lump as cancerous, the war as a vindication of our national destiny. This structure is triune: a given; something else able to serve as a sign of it; an interpreter who takes the sign as meaning that given. The philosopher C. S. Peirce calls this structure Thirdness and says it is the necessary condition for every intelligible experience. Sheer givenness, which he calls Secondness, is a possible mode of experience, the bare "there" of an intruding otherness, such as my being unexpectedly hit on the head from behind. Unless I am too stunned to do so, my immediate response is to take the intrusion as a sign of something else: as an object falling on me or thrust on me, as a tree branch I had overlooked, as a club swung to knock me out, as an annoying accident or a threatening enemy.

My initial interpretation will prove to be right or mistaken depending on how it fits with how I take the experiences that follow it, just as it was formed because of its fit with the way I had taken things up to now. I will be more likely to think myself attacked if I am worried about such an eventuality because I take myself to be where I have no right to be or because I take yesterday's burglary of my neighbor's house as implying that my house is next. But the intruder could turn out to be merely a wayward tree branch. Unless, of course, I were to take the branch as a bad omen or its odd location as an indication of a trap laid for me just up ahead.

We are never free of interpretation because we inhabit a world that is a complex of interpretations. Our world tells us what things are likely to mean, how to take them so that we are aware of their location and their function with respect to ourselves, so that we can understand them adequately and therefore use or enjoy them appropriately. Everything in our world is prefigured, anticipated; the tools we need to grasp what is going on are ready at hand. Our responses to things are typically habitual, unthinking, taken for granted. And even when such responses will not do, when invention is required, here too the necessary intuitions, concepts, values for creating a novel response are provided in advance, constituents of possible interpretations readily available for our use.

Where this world is wide and old, its complex of interpretations shared by many people over an extended period, we call it a tradition. And where the interpretations have no boundary but claim to exhaust all possibilities, where the world is taken as dependent on no wider elder world, then we call it a cultural tradition. Or rather, the world of traditions out of which others live is what we call their culture. We call our own world of traditions, truth.

The anthropologist Clifford Geertz points out that a repertoire of cultural interpretations is necessary to complete our biologically given response mechanisms. Human instincts are relatively few. Most of our natural, preformed responses are unfocused: protean, unspecialized, incomplete. Culture supplies the habits by which the biologically vague is tailored into a specific pattern of responses, a characteristic way of understanding and dealing with things. I take that object as a branch because my cultural world has trees among its objective realities and a lore of beliefs about how branches develop and decay, how best to cope with them, under what sort of conditions and for what kinds of reasons they fall on a person's head. The extent of my biological responsiveness to intrusion is withdrawal. More is required for my response to be reasonable and appropriate. Bare otherness must be made into a branch and the branch into an omen or an accident for my response to be more than a disconnected impulse, for it to become an action embedded in a pattern of actions that are effective, that make sense to me and can be explained to others. What we do depends on how we see things, and how we see things depends on what our cultural traditions are.

Frameworks of interpretation are necessary for being human. Without them we are disoriented. Without them there is no way for us to focus our response to things so as to render them meaningful. Not knowing the what and why of the things around us, we do not know what to feel, whether to be afraid or comforted, bemused or filled with dread. We do not know what to expect of things. We do not know how they work and how we might best come to terms with them. We do not know whether they are worth our time, whether they are trivial or important. But if this is so, then we also do not know who we are, what to expect of ourselves, whether we are able or authorized or willing to relate to such things. What is not within our world is unintelligible, opaque, absurd. And if we are ourselves excluded from that world, we become unintelligible to ourselves, our character puzzling, our life absurd. Without a tradition wrapped around us, our humanity falls away and we perish.

Traditions are not straitjackets, however. We are not automata whose every move has been programmed, puppets dancing on strings controlled by our ancestors or by the officials, governmental or religious, who are their intermediaries. A hammer does not make me build a house nor tell me how, although it sets some of the parameters to my design and construction activities. I may locate the studs anywhere I choose, but they must be attached to shoe and plate by nails instead of bolts or pegs or screws. And to drive the nails true, I will need to swing the hammer in a certain way, using it in the manner it was designed for, submitting myself to its functional constraints to achieve what otherwise would be impossible for me or would require a different, perhaps less efficient or less convenient, approach.

Traditions provide what Michael Oakeshott calls a "platform" of "understandings" and "practices." An understanding is a schematic idea, a general concept for helping to organize experience intelligibly. My everyday notion of a tree is vague, having to do with a rough trunk-and-canopy shape, a greenish color range, an expected environment of mountainside or curbside, a use for shade or lumber or climbing. I bring this notion into play when trying to make sense of an experience for which it seems appropriate and which it turns out to fit, even though no specific thing I have ever identified as a tree replicates my idea exactly. That ancient gnarled oak, this filigreed Japanese maple, those sapling birches: all are trees for me because their specific differences seem to me expressions of the same general characteristics. Cultural understandings provide the thematic notions by which specific things are identified, categorized, named, and organized. But I need not believe in Aristotelian natural kinds or Wittgensteinian family resemblances to think this way. Any such theory of universals would be, after all, itself an interpretation, within an abstract and highly specialized system of categorization, of my taken-for-granted schematic notions regarding how the world works.

Practices, like understandings, are schemata: but for action instead of thought. They are general ways of responding to a situation, of accomplishing an end. Climbing a tree is a practice, and so is cutting one down. I can clamber onto the lower limb of an oak or shinny up a birch; I can fell the tree by reiterated swings of my ax or by subjecting it to the bite of a chain saw, and either action can be done gracefully or awkwardly, with the confidence of a skilled woodsman or the hesitations of a novice. My concrete actions actualize in some specific way the generic practices available to me, as constrained by the forms those practices vaguely delineate and as, in turn, empowered by them. Knowing how to climb trees gets me high up into their canopy, from which I can do what until then was impossible. I am now able to survey the far horizon, to stand as though on the shoulders of giants to enjoy the view or to look for enemies or to seek a familiar landmark by which to orient my journey.

Some of our understandings and practices are explicitly learned and critically refined: my understanding of road signs and my driving know-how, my talent for reading philosophy texts and my grasp of the ideas they contain. Other planks of this platform, including the most important ones, are implicit and unthematized, habits of the heart or mind or muscles that serve me without having to be thought about. One evidence that what has been explicitly taught has been fully learned is for it to have become implicit. I have finally learned the new word-processing software when my fingers press appropriate keys on the computer without my having to think about where the specific key is and what finger is best to press it with. I type without thinking about the mechanics of typing; that knowledge has gotten into my muscles and I am thereby freed to attend to what the words are that I might wish typed. And my know-how of the words frees me to focus on the ideas I might wish them to express.

The most fundamental of these habits, these unreflective ways of taking things and interacting with them, constitute my cultural horizon, the tradition that comprises the traditions I take as composing truth. A cultural platform is all of the ways of thinking and seeing and acting that are so obvious, so useful, so successful, that I take them to be a part of the way things are: natural givens, brute facticities. Indeed, I normally do not take them to be anything at all: they are that in terms of which I take all other things to be what they are. A cultural tradition is the always-in-use and hence never-criticized framework of the world. This is how a tradition wraps us within itself—by providing all the conceptual and practical means by which we live our lives.

We make ourselves by how we use what is provided for us. For if cultural practices and understandings must be actualized in some specific way in each situation in which we find ourselves, and if the specific ways are many, even where the generic way is singular, then the choices by which we incarnate our culture are individuating. I am an adjective of my cultural notions, an adverb of its practices. I drive my car cautiously, philosophize in a Platonic manner, worship in accord with an ancient liturgy, and doubt the value of attempting any radical reform of county politics. Insofar as my concretizing choices are consistent, insofar as I develop habits for how I will realize the cultural repertoire at my disposal, ways of thinking and doing will emerge that are characteristic of me and hence definitional. My character is a matter of dispositions; I am how I am likely to behave. What is unique about me, my essential self, the ground of my identity as this person and not another, are the habits I have created by having repeated choices for how best to put the tools of my culture to use in giving shape to the experiences that constitute my days and years.

We are conservatives with respect to our self-identity if we are strict constructionists in the way we take our own individualizing habits, worrying that small departures from established patterns of behavior or belief might undercut our integrity. We revere the familiar places, persons, and routines that give shape and importance to our world. We think that we can bind ourselves securely to these realities only by careful repetition or reverence. In contrast, we are liberals with respect to our self-identity if we do not focus on the specifics of our realizations of tradition but on tradition's more abstract features. We define ourselves more in terms of processes than results. If we are fair in our dealings with others and take responsibility for our decisions, then it matters little what the results actually are. Wherever we happen to live, whomever we chance to know, whatever the appropriate modes of interaction required by the situation, we remain throughout the selfsame person. We are our competence to adapt to the changes swirling around us.

The conservative self requires stability. It has little tolerance for change and so is most threatened by the intrusion into its world of new ideas or practices. It fears pluralism because it cannot encompass it. But the liberal self is as thin as the conservative self is narrow. It cannot deal effectively with commitment, with the recalcitrance of those who value familiar truths more than agreement. And in its quest for consensus it is always in danger of abandoning any meaningful sort of character, thereby losing its individuality for the sake of an abstract conformity. Thus, whether we are conservative or liberal selves, we are at risk when our interpretation of our cultural platform of understandings and practices seems unable to accommodate the rapid transitions engulfing us.

One crucial safety valve available to combat the collapse of our self-identity is recognizing that we do not always have to be in character to have a character. Anyone is bound to act out of character from time to time. I do something in an unexpected manner, departing from a pattern of responses that others have come to assume of me. He's not himself today, they say, when I grumble and glower instead of smiling pleasantly at their good morning salutation. That's not like him at all, they whisper, when I castigate a Platonic idea as foolish and irrelevant. Were I to persist in such departures from my normal ways, my identity as a self would be called into question: perhaps he's undergoing a mid-life crisis, doubting the value of who he has been and will become. This departure will be temporary if I eventually return to my old beliefs and practices. It will be permanent if I become thereafter a different sort of person, a new man, a maturer self. If the change is radical enough, I may symbolize it by taking on a new name such as often happens to people when they successfully negotiate the rite of passage from adolescence into adulthood or convert to a new religion or commit themselves to a new political movement. No longer Jamie but James, not Saul but henceforth Paul, no more the despised servant but now the respected comrade.

Yet all of these variations within character, and even those that transform our character from conservative to liberal or liberal to conservative, may well be acceptable expressions of our encompassing cultural tradition. It is okay to be out of character occasionally, to play the fool at times, even to alter social roles on Sadie Hawkins Day or at Carnival or on Beltane eve. In our culture there is an available practice for growing up or changing our allegiances; there is an acceptable understanding about the way in which our beliefs can change under the press of changing circumstance. Where there is no such practice or understanding, however, benign deviation becomes malign deviance. To violate the acceptable social patterns is to put myself outside of society, to be alienated from it, to be considered obscene, insane, criminal, traitorous. My freedom is to be whom I choose within a kind of personhood that is never itself in question. I can be liberal or conservative, but only as those terms are meaningfully defined by my tradition. There are things that Americans simply do not do; there are beliefs and practices that threaten the very fabric of a society and so cannot under any circumstances be tolerated.

So who we are can be understood only by taking into account the interpretive schemata provided by our society. We are individuals by thinking with culturally given concepts and actualizing culturally provided practices in a uniquely characteristic way. We are not merely echoes of our culture, yet without its stabilizing interpretive resources our nature would be incomplete and our lives purposeless and brief. We would lack the capacity to become selves, to be persons with aims we seek to realize and achievements for which we take responsibility. We live our cultural traditions uniquely, but it is those traditions we live and without which we could not live. This is the vertical dimension of selfhood. Just as we cannot account for the tides by attending only to the movement of the waves and the lay of the land, so we cannot make sense of ourselves without reference to vertical transcendence, to the cultural moon that gives shape to our ways of acting and thinking.

The vertical dimension of self-hood

II

Selfhood has a horizontal, interpersonal dimension as well. We not only create our selves by how we actualize tradition but also reveal ourselves to others by doing so. Oakeshott calls this "self-disclosure" in contrast to "self-enactment." In taking some wooded enclosure as a sacred place and so approaching it reverently, I define myself as a person of appropriate piety. When I turn to you and invite you to enter the enclosure with me, I reveal that piety to you as well. Take me as a believer, my words and gestures say; take me as someone who knows the proper way to approach divinity. Join me in this obeisance; share in my adoration and prayer. By invoking for you my way of taking things, I invite you to inhabit my personal world, to see things from my perspective, so that you will then respond accordingly.

The horizontal dimension of self-hood

Your response might be mimetic, following my lead with regard to the attitudes, understandings, and practices that govern a mortal's relationship to the gods. Or you might reject my interpretation as misplaced or silly. Perhaps you doubt that this is really one of the sacred places, or you may doubt that there are such things as places where the divine and the earthly are in constant touch, or it may be the reality of gods as such that you call into question. Yet any of those responses presumes your recognition of my frame of reference. You take me as a believer because that is how I present myself to you. You come into my world, drawn there by my disclosure of it as important to who I am. You take me for who I say I am. You expect, in virtue of that taking, that I will be constantly seeing the presence of the gods in bubbling brooks and finding sermons in stones, that I will have certain kinds of attitudes toward objects and events that flow from such perceptions, that my views will be of a certain supernaturalist sort and my actions will encompass certain ritualistic patterns on specified occasions. Your response in turn discloses who you are: fellow worshiper or atheist, desiring to be taught the ways of this new god or wishing to convince me that the world is devoid of divinity. Whatever our specific differences, we share this one intimacy: I have bared my soul to you and you to me. We have disclosed to one another who we take ourselves to be, invoking an ambience for our interactions, a world in which our worlds are linked and so intercourse between them is made possible.

For people to interact, they need to share a common platform of under-standings and practices. As we have seen, they need not realize those generic patterns in the same way. Indeed, they could not, were they to try, for even absolute fidelity to another involves an interpretation of that other's inter-pretations, a new concretizing based on an old one but agreeing with it only generically. Nor need they even work from the same patterns. Yet their repertoire of possibilities, their platform for making sense of what each other thinks and does, must overlap. Your atheism defines an attitude that rejects my piety, but nonetheless understands it. Were there no tradition in your culture of religious belief and worship, no cultic places appropriate for believers to seek out when needing the succor of transcendent realities, then my pieties would be incomprehensible to you. You would not laugh at me for starting to speak in hushed tones or for taking off my shoes; you would, rather, think me mad. Or confident that I could not be mad, you would simply be baffled, unable to respond to me at all, dumbfounded, cut off from me as though suddenly finding yourself in the presence of an alien being.

Traditions make human interaction possible, for they define the horizon of what counts as human and hence prefigure for us the range of possible explanations for what we are encountering when we are in the presence of others. We take those others as human beings and so anticipate their be-havior as instancing any of the vast range of possibilities available to, definitional of, such beings. In seeing how they respond to us, or in observ-ing their responses to things and people other than ourselves, we discover which practices from the human repertoire are theirs, which understandings they embrace. So we take them to be humans of this culture or that, and our responses are geared to what that further specificity requires. The particular person we then address discloses her particularity in the special ways by which she has concretized the tradition she inhabits.

And so our interactions grow less formulaic and uncomfortable as the process of mutual disclosure articulates the full complex of relevant takings. Two persons from very different cultures have a long journey ahead of them if they are to come to the sort of intimate knowledge and habitual coordina-tion needed to be close friends. Two persons from the same community can effect a complex exchange of commodities or services without having to give the matter any thought since both are at home in the same world of economic practices and need no more knowledge of their counterparts than the assurance that each understands how barter or bargaining works.

This thicket of mutual interpretations always threatens to entangle us in error. Every interpretation is in need of interpretation, but there is always more than one way to interpret anything, including an interpretation. You have to take how I took you in order to respond to me, and then I have to take what I think was how you took my taking in order to respond to your response. I took you as a believer; you are concerned to make it clear that you do not share my beliefs; I indicate that I appreciate our differences and that I respect your sensitivity to my religious convictions. But suppose you meant to patronize me when you acknowledged my beliefs. In taking your gestures and words as meaning respect rather than disdain, I mistook your purpose, misread your intentions, gave a wrong interpretation to the self-interpretation you meant to disclose to me. You will think me rather stupid to have missed the point; I will wonder why your initial respect seemed so suddenly to go sour. We are all too often veiled rather than revealed by our disclosures.

Such misunderstandings are temporary misreadings and can usually be resolved by further disclosure: explicating in words what was meant by a gesture, or vice versa; explaining things in a more detailed fashion or by reference to a wider context. The tools for accurate understanding and appropriate action are readily available to us. We simply need to be more sensitive or thorough in their use. But if you cannot make sense of my ways at all, if my traditions are strange beyond your ken of them, then your mistake can be corrected only by expanding your platform of intelligible understandings and practices to include mine. You will have to learn how to see the world through my eyes to be able to make sense of what I say and do. You mistook my intent not because it was ambiguous, although it may have been that as well, but because you did not know how to take it rightly. Overcoming your ignorance will thus require more than pointing out the alternative interpretation I intended; it will mean widening your world to include my alternative among your repertoire of possibilities. You may still disagree with me, and you may on any given occasion still mistake my meaning. But it will no longer be because what I do is incomprehensible, but rather because it was merely on that occasion not adequately comprehended.

Familiarity breeds acceptance, or at least the latter is impossible without the former. Hence, as the diversity of our group increases, so does the need for increased empathy. A practice needs to arise for how to go about expanding our repertoire of practices. We must learn to be alert to the external signs of cultural difference, to become aware of how our gestures and tone of voice, our politics and even our clichés, can mean something radically different to strangers. We should develop a way to ask politely about another's world. We should pride ourselves in being multilingual, or at least in knowing the proper protocol for greeting strangers, exchanging pleasantries, conducting business.

The line between acceptable diversity and unacceptable deviance is obviously contextual. Since the elements of a social platform are vague, what is acceptable shades off by imperceptible degrees into what is unacceptable; the platform has no sharp edges. A culture may tend toward the cosmopolitan, substantially enlarging the scope of acceptable realizations of a practice or understanding. This is most likely to occur at either of two moments. Permissiveness flourishes in the heyday of a culture, when its members are confident about the truth of their world, its foundation in natural necessity or divine purpose. New versions of the old ways are evidence of the culture's universality, the ubiquity of its founding insights into the meaning of things and the destiny of its people. Permissiveness also flourishes, however, when a culture is in disarray, when the old unifying truths have fallen into disrepute and the resulting multiplicity of beliefs and practices are running amok. The old ways are emptied of their specific content in an attempt to hide the de facto chaos, to offer a fig leaf of abstract unity that might mask the embarrassment of societal fragmentation.

The scope of acceptable versions of a culture's defining platform of understandings and practices is parochial when it is in the making, when it is emerging as a viable tradition against competing traditions, a definitive "this" in contrast to an ambient otherness. A cosmopolitan culture constricts its platform, becomes once more parochial, when the society is seriously threatened but not yet in disarray. What is created by human artifice can be sustained only by repetition. The more at risk our collective achievements and hopes for achievement, therefore, the more rigid our repetition of them needs to be. At such times, the mimesis of the past by the present can tolerate no novelty, no unpredictable element that might result in greater harm rather than improvement. Where there is no margin for error, obedience is the only acceptable test of our loyalty.

The mark of a cosmopolitan tradition is the relative superficiality of relationships, the anonymity of mobile, rootless persons for whom acquaintance is the unavoidable substitute for friendship. This minimalist form of intimacy has its virtues, but the unity it provides is as thin as it is broad and hence is exceedingly fragile. When threatened, the tendency of a cosmopolitan tradition is either to fragment into several intense parochial traditions or to force the pluralism of its constituents into a single framework. The virtues of a maximalist form of intimacy have their vices as well, for the unity it provides is as narrow as it is deep, and hence is also exceedingly fragile. The tendency of a parochial tradition is to generate an internal factionalism that it cannot encompass, and so either to reassert its authority by repressing dissent or in its weakened condition to be caught up into the pluralistic culture of some neighboring hegemonic power. Uniformity or factionalism, tyranny or balkanization, these seem to be the only viable alternatives.

It is at just such polarized moments, when conformity is the regnant virtue, that a creative, fresh response is most needed. New kinds of persons need to arise, people with a different sense of themselves and hence of their abilities and responsibilities—conservatives in a time of vapid conformities, liberals in an age of fanatical conformities. Not absolutely new personalities are required, to be sure, for selfhood cannot be ex nihilo. But there is a need for new expressions of what it has traditionally meant to be a person, a parent, a friend, a citizen. Our old ways are threatened precisely because they are no longer effective in providing us a world that satisfies the human need for security, fulfillment, and worth. A new approach can adapt our tradition to present needs, effect a smooth transition from accustomed habits to ones better suited to the realities of the day. The tragedy is that people think they must choose between a liberal or conservative character, between license or uniformity, anarchy or repression, when in fact the latter by themselves only afford a circuitous way to reach what the former by themselves achieve immediately: the collapse of our world.

We require the parochial interpretive framework of a cultural tradition in order to be distinctive selves in relation to other selves. But the complexity of contemporary life threatens such clannish traditions. It pressures us to take a more comprehensive, tolerant, cosmopolitan stance. Yet in doing so, it increases our vulnerability to loss of meaning, to confusion about who we are and what we should do, what our role is in society and what our society's role is in history and in the natural or divine scheme of things. Either narrowing our horizons in order to protect our values, or else subordinating our differences for the sake of some one envisioned whole, either alternative provides us scant security against the relentless changes swirling around us. Narrowness breeds fanaticism, a romantic yearning for a past that perished with the emergence of the global village. Cosmopolitanism breeds totalitarianism, a utopian hope for a future that can come only at the expense of individuality and dignity.

III

Any viable solution to this dilemma must begin by recognizing that it is a genuine dilemma. We are impaled on one horn if we insist on the importance of roots, if we say that we must feel ourselves part of a tradition the value of which rests on its power to give meaning and direction to our lives. For the power of tradition resides in its antiquity, its historical massiveness, the authority it derives from continuities that stretch back to human origins and beyond. But such traditions are parochial. They exclude those who do not share that history, whose ancestors were of another faith or clan or region. Belonging to a tradition is not an act of will. We cannot choose to be something that is given only by virtue of inherited qualities, whether that inheritance be biological or cultural. There is something happenstantial, gratuitous, accidental about a tradition when seen from the outside. But to those who live it from within, these unique characteristics, these ungeneralizable particularities, are its truth. What is so important about some barren mountain in the Sinai or some cornfield south of Gettysburg? So what if ancient relatives whose names I do not know were driven from their land by Cromwell or snatched from western Africa into New World slavery? And yet a chosen people, a manifest destiny, a righteous hatred, a racial pride are each entwined essentially with such contingencies. Traditions are inherently this-not-that.

We are impaled on the other horn of the dilemma if we insist on the significance of being human. For if what is essential about us is our humanity, we share this quality with all other human beings. Even if we argue that what is essential is our need for roots, if exclusionary traditions are what is most important to each of us, this need to be different is no more than an ironic expression of how we are all alike. Our variety binds us in a more fundamental unity. We should therefore celebrate our differences and in doing so commit ourselves to whatever makes for a community that is able to encompass them. So what if no utopia has ever been realized before? It is nonetheless the ideal implicit in what has so far been realized. But if the utopian ideal is comprehensible, then it is possible. And what is possible can be actual if we make it so. We have discovered that we are all inhabitants of the same planet; it is our task to create a planetary community appropriate to that fact. Traditions are inherently one, a universal this.

Robert Bellah and associates in *Habits of the Heart* argued that we Americans are in danger of losing both the parochial and cosmopolitan versions of our founding tradition. The parochial version is biblical, its understandings couched in terms of God's saving acts in history and the special role assigned to Americans that they should create in the New World a new kind of nation. The United States was to be a nation dedicated to justice and benevolence, one in which God's faithful children are recognized as all of equal worth, living within a commonwealth of mutual caring and shared opportunity. The operative interpretation of these beliefs was Puritan. God's chosen people were those able to enter into covenant with the divine; they were those whose faith had purified them of sin and sloth and whose rational capacities had made possible a compact with God. God's covenant was with them as individuals—but individuals gathered into a community for the sake of carrying out a special collective mission: to be God's new Israel, a light to the world, a righteous city set high on a hill as an example for the rest of the world to follow. Here for the Puritans was a life-centering understanding, a story about the meaning of their history, their place within purposes as old as time and as surefooted as necessity. It gave them an indication of what they should be responsible to and for. Theirs was manifestly a destiny calling for their cooperative effort for the sake of ends of infinite significance. Once we were no people, but now we are God's people, called into this American wilderness to begin the work of realizing the Kingdom of God on earth.

The cosmopolitan version of our founding tradition—Bellah calls it civic republicanism—secularizes the religious content while retaining its structures. Membership in the American commonwealth is open to anyone with purity of heart sufficient to acknowledge the rights of others as equal to one's own and with rational will sufficient to accept the responsibilities of citizenship in a democracy. United by these procedural importances, Americans were then free to fashion whatever specific content of beliefs and practices they preferred. This tolerance of diversity rested on respect for a law that guaranteed its continuance. Constitutional republican democracy, so understood, was a model for others to emulate as well as a magnet drawing others to it. First among equals, this land of emigrants would lead the nations of the world into a new international order where empire, poverty, and privilege would make way for peace, prosperity, and equal opportunity.

Bellah argues that this tradition, in both its religious and secular expressions, is slipping out of American consciousness. It no longer commands a central place in our platform of understandings and practices. We Americans do not talk about God's mission for our nation any more; we do not believe America's democratic ideals are the last best hope of humankind. Consequently, our willingness to sacrifice personal comforts for the sake of a higher good falters, our sense of responsibility as citizens to secure the common good fades away. In its place, self-interest runs rampant, our sole motivation for action a desire to increase our power and possessions, and to express ourselves through these material goods in whatever manner we see fit.

It goes without saying that unfettered individualism of this sort is a recipe for anarchy or tyranny—the rule of whirl in either of its senseless guises. Without a tradition to provide the cultural meanings that explain and exhibit our selves as individualized expressions of a greater whole, a mere desire for self-gratification and survival is all that remains. We have seen how both parochial and cosmopolitan readings of a tradition, and both conservative and liberal interpretations of self-identity within each such reading, have difficulty coming to terms with persistent, accelerating change. The authors of *Habits of the Heart* have mapped these difficulties onto the American terrain, and they have indicated that our problem is not whether the parochial or the cosmopolitan version of tradition is most crucial, but that we are in danger of losing both versions.

Bellah's solution is to recover the fullness of the American tradition, to bring both biblical and civic republican understandings back into our public discourse, thereby breathing new life into our societal practices. But this seems a futile gesture. Our Puritan heritage is exclusionary: it privileges those whose ancestors were English, Protestant, and Roundhead, who came to the New World voluntarily and for the sake of their religious beliefs, for whom both blood and faith find meaning in an eschatological notion of being chosen. And the secular, more cosmopolitan version of this heritage has been equally exclusionary. Initially, it was a civic order open to everyone on an equal basis, insofar as they were white, male, propertied, and Congregational; subsequently, it has grown more inclusive, but to this day it is poisoned by the suspicion that its claims to inclusiveness cover up and justify entrenched privilege of one kind or another. God's new Israel; the *novus ordo seclorum*—the words ring hollow because of the abuse they permit and, indeed, encourage.

And yet they remain our ideals. They point, however feebly, to the horizon of our world, to the assumptions that we have taken for granted even amid our shrill disputes and violent altercations concerning religious doctrines and political ideologies, public pieties and party politics. We despise our traditions because they never practice what they preach or because they have practiced their preachments all too fervently. But such criticisms exemplify what they condemn, for it is by appealing to ideals implicit in what is going on that our condemnations make any sense or will have any lasting effect.

Martin Luther King, Jr., for instance, used the Judeo-Christian tradition to attack segregation in the United States. Southern whites were for the most part good and pious Christians, confessing their sins and asking Jesus to forgive them while they sat in church pews no black could ever occupy, carried out the work of the Lord through occupations designed to perpetuate a colored underclass, and raised God-fearing families in homes financed by the benefits of that system. Northern whites practiced a more indirect, less self-conscious, but equally effective form of segregation. For these conditions to change, it was not enough to marshal countervailing power, to meet force with force, to repeal unjust laws and bring blacks into positions of political authority. All of those things were needed, most definitely, but King also saw the importance of using the piety of the oppressors against themselves. His words were thick with scriptural allusion, his arguments always set against the backdrop of the Christian worldview in which his opponents as well as his followers believed. Love thy enemies, suffer all the little children to come unto me, seek first a kingdom that knows no invidious differences among the faithful who are its citizens. Both the moral vision, the dream of a just America, and the prophetic warning that the nation must choose either repentance or God's punishment were intelligible to segregationist and integrationist alike because they articulated a world to which both groups belonged. What King wanted was for Americans to live up to their ideals, to say genuinely and to do concretely what the tradition they inhabit presumed of them.

What appeals such as King's call for is a self-conscious, self-critical return to the platform of vague understandings and practices that provides the cultural repertoire by means of which people make sense of themselves and their relationships with others. This platform's planks are schematic ways of taking things; we have given them one or another specific content, made them actual characterizations of our selves and our communities. In condemning that specific content as wrong, we need not be opposed to its underlying schematic practice or understanding. Our complaint is with how it has been concretely interpreted. We contend that it is a wrong reading of the schemata, a distorted version, an inadequate, partial, or superficial way of actualizing what our tradition permits. It is not that the Christian tradition is wrong, but that segregationist religion is a twisted instance of what that tradition calls on us to do and think.

When I act out of character, some specific thing I did or said was incongruent with my accustomed way of behaving and thus violated the definition of who I am. I should be ashamed of myself; rather, I should be ashamed to myself, for it is my self that I have denied by what I did or said. My character is a norm that stands in judgment of my deeds, an enduring essence it is my task to perpetuate. To repudiate my character would be to say that who I am and what I stand for has no significance. Therefore, I should repudiate that deed, expel it from the circle of things that exemplify who I am, make myself whole again. I should reaffirm the schemata of continuities that trace my self-identity by interpreting my errant interpretation of them as a mistake. The reason for the mistake might have to do with ignorance or willfulness or momentary passion. My shame, accordingly, will take the form of thinking myself stupid or sinful or undisciplined; my wholeness, my integrity, must be reclaimed by means of some appropriate inquiry, repentance, or resolve. The schematic understandings and practices composing my self-identity are an ideal, a regulative principle tracing the boundaries of what it is permissible for me to be and a constitutive principle carved into the givenness of things as the individual I have become.

Our conduct, as selves disclosing who we are to others and adapting to their disclosure of themselves to us, creates communities that share the same ideals, even though they realize them differently. This shared world of ours, this community to which we all belong, acts out of character whenever our individual pursuits generate conflicts for which an effective resolving practice is not already provided. To repudiate the ideals we share would be to put our society into question and hence ourselves as well. It would be to claim, for instance, that America is inherently racist or that people are by nature driven by the desire to exploit others for their own advantage.

But we are not forced to such pessimistic conclusions, for we can repudiate our specific practices as out of character with our American heritage. We can be ashamed of what we have done in the name of faith, calling it a distortion of God's will for us. We can be ashamed of how we have degraded Jefferson's ideals, turning his egalitarian dream into an arena where greed and selfishness abound. That this nation under God could have a new birth of freedom, could be once more a city on a hill, a lure and a model for peoples everywhere, is a regulative ideal sketching general practices and understandings consonant with our origins, tracing the boundary of what it is permissible for us to do in these changing times. That this nation, conceived in liberty and dedicated to a proposition about universal and inalienable human rights, could help fashion a global community as a new order suited to the ages yet to come is a constitutive principle consonant with our sense of having a manifest destiny, some significant and positive role to play in human history.

We are more comfortable with individual than with societal shame. We are ready to help others recover their dignity, reconcile themselves to their limitations, regain their sense of purpose. We are not so sure that this recovery can happen to families or voluntary associations, much less to societies or civilizations. But the structure is the same for both kinds of reality because communities are made up of individuals who are interpretations wrought out in flesh and bone of the interpretations of wider, deeper, more enduring scope we call a culture. In appealing to the ideals of a person's self-identity, we appeal to the ideals of the community of which that self is an individuated expression. And inversely, in appealing to the community's ideals we address the self-identity of its citizens.

So our ideals are not empty as long as there is any sense left to life. Our traditions are a resource to which we can turn, to which indeed we must turn, to keep from succumbing to the despair of a truthless world. Their resourcefulness, however, is not merely recidivist. We are not reduced to pleading for a return to the good old days when people believed the old truths, whether cosmopolitan or parochial, liberal or conservative, and were seriously committed to the way of life those truths commanded. Such pious antiquarian platitudes have no authority in a time of rapid transitions that clearly call for new truths and new commitments. The resourcefulness of our traditions lies in their ideality, in the schemata for truth and commitment they provide. We cannot return to the old ways, but through returning to the kind of way the old ways were we may be able to recover the ancient meanings they embodied, meanings from which convincing new beliefs and enabling practices can be fashioned.

This is difficult to do in terms of our self-identity. Can we be conservatives whose practice encompasses pluralism rather than fearing it, whose insistence on stability is a commitment to a social order in which destabilizing inequities have been overcome? Can we be liberals whose commitment to tolerance celebrates the importance of differences, whose procedural rationalism has room for stubbornly irrational values? Of course we can, and one way or the other, systematically or willy-nilly, we shall. This is always how individual selves are made: by giving concrete shape to possibilities made available by their tradition within the exigencies of present experience. The problem is to do this well, to fashion selves liberal enough to adapt to the important transitional factors in experience, conservative enough to resist the trivial ones. Our answers will vary; their value will lie in the integrity of the selves that result.

Using the ideals of a tradition to effect the societal transformations demanded by changing times is a more baffling task because cultural assumptions and their institutionalized habits elude our resolve to alter them. The ideals that constitute the horizon of our intelligible world cannot be explicitly evoked. A speech or monograph giving a fresh interpretation to those ideals is only one idiosyncratic voice murmuring in a crowd too busy with its routine pursuits to pay attention. A new policy or institutional structure fashioned as a creative interpretation of those ideals is only another layer of bureaucracy needing to be integrated into the daily routines of governance. It is harder to change a world than to change a person.

This is what led the philosopher Martin Heidegger, in his later years, to celebrate the flux of history, to talk of the power that makes and unmakes worlds. We live within a cultural tradition that has arisen to give a sense to our times; there is no reason to its origin, says Heidegger, or any destiny that it serves. There have been predecessors to our tradition; there will be successors as well. Each has its own integrity, its own way of being a world, its own disclosure of Being. But each is only a plaything of the Heraclitean child-king who rules without why. We are lived by our traditions, and the beginning of wisdom is the recognition that when those traditions perish the meaning of our lives perishes with them. The only sense to things is the play of worlds, the meaningless sequence of historical meanings that marks the kingdom where whirl alone is king.

Postmodernism in general, from Derrida and Lyotard to Kuhn and Rorty, echoes this absolute historicism, this unrelenting relativism. It is an obvious but nihilistic response to the crumbling of what was once thought to be unassailable truth. I have been attempting in this essay to indicate an alternative reading of our situation, to suggest that truths of word and deed cannot be understood solely in terms of their specific expressions. To do so is precisely to see them as an unconnected sequence of cultural worlds. I have argued that worlds are interpretations and that interpretations are hierarchial, any given one of them a more specific reading of some more general counterpart. When an established frame of reference begins to lose its authority, when the center can no longer hold and things come apart, our recourse is to the vague, ambient principles that undergird what we have put in question.

What I have not until now said explicitly is this: that such a hierarchy of platforms is foundational. For any frame of reference rests on a more general framework that is its foundation. Relative to any platform of understandings and practices, whether personal, cultural, or natural, there are the plurality of more specific interpretations by means of which the platform is concretely realized and there is the single more inclusive principle that supplies its context and its ground. Reframing my world, our world, or the world of worlds without end does not require us to invent first a new foundation, as though we were gods able to create ex nihilo, or, as Heidegger would have it, as though we were the playthings of such a god. For even if what appears to us to be the very foundation of things were to be put in question by some intrusive and incomprehensible brute facticity, that very questioning would reveal to us the basis of that foundation and we would discover in its ineffable elusiveness the resources for laying a new foundation of human practice and belief and for erecting on it a world worth our dwelling in.

In this way, we are borne up by tradition and provided with an inexhaustible resource for preserving, deepening, and widening the integrity of our individual selves and the importance of our shared culture even in the midst of the most terrifying transitions. It is we, not whirl, who is king.

Works cited

Bellah, Robert N. et al. *Habits of the Heart*. Berkeley: University of California Press, 1985.

Caputo, John D. *Radical Hermeneutics*. Bloomington: Indiana University Press, 1987.

Geertz, Clifford. *The Interpretation of Cultures*. New York: Basic Books, 1973.

Oakeshott, Michael. *On Human Conduct*. Oxford: Clarendon Press, 1975.

Peirce, Charles Sanders. *Collected Papers*. Especially vols. 5–6. Cambridge, Mass.: Belknap Press, 1960 [1934].

Donald Phillip Verene

Two Sources

of Philosophical

Memory: Vico

Versus Hegel

1   Elio Gianturco, the great expert on Roman law and translator of Vico's *De nostri temporis studiorum ratione,* began the introduction to his translation by saying: "We live in a Cartesian world, a world of scientific research, technology, and gadgets, which invade and condition our lives."[1] Cartesianism is not only a way of thought; it is a way of life. As part of this legacy of Cartesianism, we have forgotten memory. By memory, I mean what is often called "cultural memory." But more, I mean that power possessed, Hesiod says, by the Helicon Muses, who govern the arts of humanity, and which their mother, who is called Memory, imparted to them—the power to sing of what was, is, and is to come.[2]

2   I wish to suggest that memory is not an art of thinking the past, but the art of grasping the providential order of things; it is connected to what in Greek is known as *phronesis* and in Latin, *prudentia.* I wish to claim, with Vico, that "memory is the same as imagination" ("la memoria è la stessa che la fantasia")[3] and with Hegel that true philosophy is a "mythology of reason" (a "Mythologie der *Vernunft*").[4] To put my aim in a syllogism:

> Imagination is memory.
> Philosophy is imagination.
>
> ───────────────────────
>
> Philosophy is memory.

The middle term that joins philosophy to memory is imagination, or what Vico called *fantasia.* Mnemosyne, or Memory, not being one of the Muses, Hegel called *die absolute Muse.*[5]

3   Cicero quotes Heraclides of Pontus, a pupil of Plato, who reports that Pythagoras was asked by Leon, the tyrant of Phlius, to explain what philosophy is.[6] Pythagoras recalled that when the great games are held at Olympia some go as slaves to fame, to compete; others as slaves to money, to buy and sell. But there is one kind who goes to watch and see what is happening and

how. In life, there are those whose only pursuit is to contemplate the universe. They are spectators or lovers of wisdom.

4   In the preface to the *Phänomenologie des Geistes*,[7] Hegel says, "what I have set myself to do" is to bring philosophy to the point where it "can lay aside the name of 'love of knowing' and be *actual knowing*" (12/3). To do this, Hegel must make natural consciousness "walk on its head" (25/15). He must affirm "the True is the whole" (21/11). The True "is the process of its own becoming, the circle that presupposes its end as its goal, having its end also as its beginning; and only by being worked out to its end, is it actual" (20/10). Hegel reminds the reader that "the wealth of previous existence is still present to consciousness in memory" (16/7). At Hegel's hands, the theater of the great games has become the theater of memory, and the spectator is no longer at a distance but has become the elusive "we" of Hegel's phenomenology, who is both observer and yet within the circular movement of Hegel's thought.[8]

5   The product of memory is self-knowledge, which memory offers in two senses. It provides us with the autobiography of humanity and the autobiography of the individual to the extent that the individual is a microcosm of the life of humanity. Such autobiography, once understood, provides us with a practical wisdom because memory shows that all which has been in the past is in the present and will be in the future. Autobiographical knowledge as I wish to understand it is also *phronesis*. The ancient spectator of the world at the hands of Vico and Hegel becomes the spectator of history. The spectating of the spectator becomes the key to the real. Or as Hegel puts it, "everything turns on grasping and expressing the True, not only as *Substance,* but equally as *Subject*" (20/10). The *Scienza nuova* and *Phänomenologie* are texts through which the book of history can be read, and as such they contain what is necessary to guide action. They are books of wisdom that contain knowledge of both virtue and the real.

6   I wish to raise two questions: (1) What is the nature of the wisdom that these two major works contain—Vico's *Scienza nuova* (1730) and Hegel's *Phänomenologie des Geistes* (1807)? (2) What is the difference between them?

7   In pursuing these questions, I recall Vico's second axiom, that familiarity is the enemy of philosophy, "that whenever men can form no idea of distant and unknown things, they judge them by what is familiar and at hand" (122). This can lead, Vico says, to the conceit of scholars (*boria de' dotti*) "who will have it that what they know is as old as the world" (127). Hegel has his own version of this axiom—the dangers of requiring familiarity. Hegel says "the commonest way in which we deceive either ourselves

or others about understanding is by assuming something as familiar, and accepting it on that account," and he adds: "such knowing never gets anywhere, and it knows not why" (28–29/18).

8   It is said that Vico never looks at history and smiles. History, or what Vico calls the world of nations or the world of "civil things" (*cose civili*), outlives every form of social order that is established. Every nation lives a life; it is born and it dies. No polity masters history. A "nation" etymologically is a birth. Vico plays on this: *nascere*, "to be born," *nazione*, "nation." The life of every nation is a *corso* that runs from its birth to its zenith to its end. Vico describes this cycle: "Men first feel necessity, then look for utility, next attend to comfort, still later amuse themselves with pleasure, thence grow dissolute in luxury, and finally go mad and waste their substance" (241).[9]

9   Vico holds that humanity has three *principi,* three beginnings: religion, marriage, and burial. Religion establishes the cause of all things; through marriage is established the lineages or causes of families, which are the basis of the social world; burial establishes or causes the families to be of one place. Once born, each nation in the *corso* of its life passes through three stages—the *age of gods* (that in which all thought and social order are based on gods), the *age of heroes* (that in which the gods recede and are replaced by heroes, whose deeds embody human virtues), and the *age of humans* (in which the gods and heroes are lost in a world of logic, method, flattery, and reflection, a Cartesian world like Vico's and our own). Vico says that anyone who would attempt to make a speech or live a life by geometrical method engages in a kind of rational madness.[10]

10   For Vico, a nation is a circle. It is born through the barbarism of sense (*la barbarie del senso*), and when it reaches its stage of the barbarity of reflection (*la barbarie della riflessione*)—which Vico says is even more barbarous than that of sense, which he says is an honest state of crudity—the nation returns to its origins to await a rebirth in a *ricorso* (1106). What Vico says of a myth can be said of a *corso*: it is a severe and true story (814). As a nation develops from its birth, Vico holds that our understanding of the principles of humanity must follow the cycle of their life. Thus Vico says: "Doctrines must take their beginning from that of the matters of which they treat" (314).

11   To think from the origin is always to think in a circle. It is to think from where one is, back to the beginning, and then back to the point of departure again. This is the natural sense of narrative understanding that follows the thing to be understood in its own natural course and organizes its apprehension of the thing in terms of its birth, zenith, and anticipated end. Narration is the natural form of memory.[11] To remember in the sense of an

act of self-knowledge is to narrate the inner form of a thing. There can be no "vacuous actuality"[12] in a metaphysics built on the narration of the real.

12   In the *Physics*, Aristotle says that circular motion is the measure of all motion. He says: "This also explains the common saying that human affairs form a circle, and that there is a circle in all other things that have a natural movement and coming into being and passing away. This is because all other things are discriminated by time, and end and begin as though conforming to a cycle; for even time itself is thought to be a circle" (223b25–30). As mentioned, Hegel says the *Phenomenology* is a circle; he further says, in the *Logic,* that his system of science is a "circle of circles." At the end of the *Logic,* he says that each of the sciences in his system is joined like links in a chain (*Kette*).[13] In Vico's account, our experience of history is one of *corsi e ricorsi*. In Hegel's account, our experience of the thought of thought is a circle of circles, *ein Kreis von Kreisen*. To the circle that is in all things, Hegel adds his conception of dialectic as the logic of its motion. By the internal dialectic of Hegel's speculative sentence (*spekulativer Satz*) all else is measured (51/38).

13   In ordinary speech, the speech of the circle is neither that of prescription nor description; it neither issues a command nor states a fact. The suggestion is closest to circular speech. A suggestion that is truly suggestive has both a prescriptive element that accounts for its force and a descriptive element that accounts for its relevance to the context in which it is. The suggestion is circular in its internal motion. Made with its highest rhetorical force, the suggestion brings forth a possibility of a given situation and draws forth from the inner form of that situation a meaning that indicates a direction to be taken.

14   A suggestion that is fundamental to the resolution of a problematic situation brings the conditions that create the problem back on themselves so as to point beyond these conditions to a new stance—a new course of action, a new way of thinking. This is the internal movement of Hegel's speculative sentence. Starting from the subject as if it were a permanent ground, consciousness moves to the predicate; but once at the predicate, consciousness moves back to the subject, looking for its connection with the predicate (48–53/36–41). When it has experienced this inner movement of language, thinking can no longer "roam at will" (50/37).

15   When consciousness has experienced this circular sense of subject and predicate inherent in the copula, it has entered the form of speculative thinking. Hegel's language in the *Phenomenology* is a speech of speculative sentences that is neither normative—that is, its purpose is not to set up an ideal; nor is it factual—it does not assert truths of an object independent from the subject. To Vico's notion of the narration of the birth, middle, and end, the speech of the *corso,* Hegel adds the dialectic of the speculative

sentence in which the inner logic of the circle is captured. In Hegel's dialectic the means by which the narrative moves from moment to moment is revealed.

16   The dialectical narration mirrors how the thing narrated gets beyond itself in the cycle of its own life course. Every stage in Hegel's *Phenomenology* is a drama in which consciousness, caught within the oppositions or tensions of that form of life, plays its roles out to their ends. At the end of each stage, consciousness can see beyond the specific endpoint to a new stance. In this new stance, consciousness immediately encounters new oppositions, and it has no peace. It has no peace at least until it reaches the end point of its own tale, what Hegel calls *absolutes Wissen*. Then it can tell its own tale to itself.

17   Hegel says four times, in the final paragraph of the *Phenomenology*, that absolute knowledge is "recollection," or *Erinnerung* (563–64/492–93).[14] The form of the True that is the whole, in the *Phenomenology*, is narrative. Aristotle says in *On Generation and Corruption* that "it follows that the coming-to-be of anything, if it is absolutely necessary, must be cyclical— i.e., must return upon itself" (338a4–5). Hegel is clear that the account of the experience of consciousness is necessary. Vico's tale of the world of nations is also necessary, with its basis in the art of the Muses to say what was, is, and is to come.[15] Hegel says that "it is in this nature of what is to be in its being its own *Begriff* [*in seinem Sein sein Begriff zu sein*], that *logical necessity* in general consists" (47/34). He says in this alone consists "das Spekulative."

18   Both Hegel and Vico are against reflection as the basis of philosophy. Reflective knowing, which Hegel associates with the Understanding (*Verstand*), yields only a table-of-contents mentality. It presents experience like a skeleton with tickets stuck all over it (43/31). Reflection leaves the life of its object untouched. As mentioned, Vico calls the barbarism of his third age of human thought, where the deeds of the heroes and the divinity of the gods are lost, the barbarism of reflection. The barbarism of reflection comes about through the attraction to "intelligibility" or abstraction as a guide to life and thought. Reflection, in Vico's terms, is the infatuation with "intelligible universals" (*universali intelligibili*) (34, 209, 934–35). Both Vico and Hegel claim the truth and necessity of their order of thought because of its adherence to the circle.

19   Aristotle says in the *Posterior Analytics*: "There results for those who say that demonstration is circular not only what has just been described, but also that they say nothing other than that this is the case if this is the case— and it is easy to prove everything in this way" (72b33–35). In the *New*

Science and *Phenomenology* we confront demonstration by complete speech. We begin with what we know, and we end in our beginning.

20   These texts are not reasonings from first principles that are held to be true and that purport to demonstrate by deductive necessity the truth of their specifics. They are instead speeches that locate and expand on *archai*. Each is based on a grasp of *topics* (*topoi*).[16] They demonstrate by eloquence, that is, they say all that there is to say on a subject. Eloquence is the principle of completeness in rhetoric. Vico's master *topos,* from which he draws forth all other commonplaces on which he bases his speech, is his image of ideal eternal history (*storia ideale eterna*) (239–45, 294, 349, 393). "Ideal eternal history" is not included in Vico's axioms, but is used by him to explain them. It is to look at history and see in a moment that there is eternal pattern—to see providence in the events.

21   Vico's *storia ideale eterna* is the cycle of the three ages of *dèi, eroi,* and *uomini* (gods, heroes, and humans), which he claims to take from the Egyptians (52). All of the elements of this history are in the engraving or *dipintura,* which he commissioned as the frontispiece for the second *New Science* and which he compares to the famous Tablet of Cebes (1).[17] It is a complete picture of the science, the complete speech done as a graphic. The objects depicted function as *topoi* from which Vico can draw forth all that there is to say. They are the set of hieroglyphics from which he begins his complete speech and which in turn hold it together. They give him access to what he calls the "common mental language" or "mental dictionary," in which resides the *sensus communis* or communal sense of humanity (35, 145, 445).

22   In the *Topics,* Aristotle says: "For just as in a person with a trained memory, a memory of things themselves is immediately caused by the mere mention of their 'places' [*topoi*], so these habits too will make a man readier in reasoning, because he has his premises classified before his mind's eye, each under his number" (163b26–30). Hegel's *topoi* are what he calls his *Galerie von Bildern* (563/492), which is the *Phenomenology* itself. In this *Galerie* are, among others, the *verkherte Welt* (inverted-perverted world), the *Herr und Knecht* (the so-called Master and "Slave"), the *unglückliches Bewusstsein* (the unhappy consciousness of the bad infinity), the phrenological skull (the *caput mortuum,* which Hegel wishes "to beat in"), the *geistige Tierreich* (the spiritual menagerie, or sideshow, of empty but busy individuals), the *schöne Seele* (beautiful soul), and the Calvary of the Absolute itself. These are what initially impress the reader and are the keys that bring the reader back into the work once read. Hegel's *Galerie* is like Vico's *dipintura,* which Vico says will "serve the reader to conceive the idea of this work

before reading it, and to recall it most easily to memory, with such aid as the imagination may afford, after he has read it" (1).

23   The necessity that both Vico and Hegel claim of their respective portrayals of humanity is the sense of necessity attached to the poem or the myth, not that of logical deduction. The sense of order that is first grasped by humanity in the poem or myth is what later allows us to grasp *modus ponens* as the basis of necessary connection in logic. It is a scandal to logic (a scandal to which attention is only infrequently called) that the starting points of logical demonstration are not arrived at by logic, and it is a further scandal that the laws of thought, which are the heart of any proof, are themselves not in any way subject to proof.

24   In Vico's view we first grasp mentally the sense of necessary connection through our powers of *fantasia*, or imagination, that is, through our ability to formulate a truth in terms of what Vico calls an imaginative universal (*universale fantastico*).[18] The first humans, Vico says, thought in terms of "imaginative genera (images for the most part of animate substances, of gods or heroes, formed by their imagination [*fantasia*]) to which they reduced all the species or all the particulars appertaining to each genus" (34; cf. 209, 403).

25   Vico solves the ancient quarrel with the poets that takes shape in the tenth book of the *Republic* by recasting poetry as a kind of original wisdom, what he terms *sapienza poetica*, that precedes philosophy. He transforms the ancient claim stated by Aristotle in the *Poetics*, that poetry is more philosophical than history because poetic statements have the nature of universals (1451b5–7), by making history originally poetic and grounded in the notion of the imaginative universal. Hegel says that poetry is the *Lehrerin der Menschheit*—the teacher of humanity. There can be no philosophy without it. Hegel says "the philosophy of spirit is an aesthetic philosophy. One can in no way become ingenious [*geistreich*], one cannot even argue about history ingeniously [*geistreich*] without aesthetic sense."[19] In the logical demonstration, only intellectual connection between ideas is needed. In the poem, all must fit: sound, idea, order of words, etc. Every part, every syllable, is necessary to the whole.

26   The French historian of the eighteenth century, Paul Hazard, says: "If Italy had listened to Giambattista Vico, and if, as at the time of the Renaissance, she had served as a guide to Europe, would not our intellectual destiny have been different? Our eighteenth-century ancestors would not have believed that all that was clear was true; but on the contrary that 'clarity is the vice of human reason rather than its virtue', because a clear idea is a finished idea. They would not have believed that reason was our first faculty, but on the contrary that imagination was."[20] Hegel speaks of our "literal-minded philosophers." He says: "The philosopher must possess just as much aesthetic power as the poet. Men without aesthetic sense are our literal-minded philosophers [*unsere Buchstabenphilosophen*]."[21]

27   Our literal-minded philosophers always miss the connection between poetry and metaphysics. Vico says: "If one does not begin from—'a god who to all men is Jove,'—one cannot have any idea either of science or virtue. . . . For the metaphysics of the philosophers must agree with the metaphysic of the poets, on this most important point."[22] Modern philosophers, who have never studied poetry, always believe that *supposition* is sufficient for a beginning point in thought. Like Descartes, one supposes something and then attempts to show it is literally the case. Or, one tests a claim by supposing something opposite and then reasoning toward a refutation. This is the process that Hegel calls *das Räsonnieren* (48/35). It is the metaphor, the poetic act, not the intellectual supposition, that always gives us the true beginning. In Vico, Jove is the apprehension of a beginning of beginnings, the master imaginative universal that names the divine and divides god from world, knower from known. Jove is the first name, and, as Vico says, every nation had its Jove (193). Poetry is always the teacher of humanity, and metaphysics must begin where thought begins (374–84).

28   To make remarks such as the foregoing invites the fear that philosophy has been turned from a form of knowledge into a form of poetry. Hazard says that everything Vico touched turned to gold. One might say that everything the literal-minded philosopher touches turns to logic. Socrates says in the *Phaedo* (and I agree), to be a misologist in philosophy is not a good thing. It is equivalent to being a misanthrope in society (89D). Both are against humanity. But the search for the method of right reasoning, when divorced from the power of memory, leaves us in society with T. S. Eliot's "The Hollow Men," those who have never studied poetry. And it leaves us in philosophy as "a pair of ragged claws/Scuttling across the floors of silent seas."[23]

29   To identify philosophy with argument and demonstration, generated through supposition, is to scuttle from argument to counterargument, from antinomy to antinomy. Then, ingenious thinking, divorced from memory and imagination, becomes an end itself. Logic goes about the world without a keeper. Hegel says that we learn one thing from history, namely, that we learn nothing from history. His point is readily applied to the philosopher imbedded in argument. For every argument it is never beyond human wit to create the counterargument, for every theory, the countertheory. Here is philosophy as Hegel's bad infinity, his *Schlecht-Unendliche*. The philosopher scuttles from one move to the next, from one case to the next, never knowing how he got there. Like a stage in Hegel's phenomenology, he is always

forgetting, and starting again from the beginning ("aber vergisst es nur ebenso immer wieder und fängt die Bewegung von vorne an") (86/109).

30   In both Vico's and Hegel's view, the poets are the teachers of humanity. With both, the poets are also there to receive their philosophies. The great rediscoverer of Vico in our time was James Joyce, who built his last work, *Finnegans Wake*, using the *New Science* as a grid. While writing it in the installments of *Work in Progress*, Joyce recommended Vico's *La Scienza nuova* to friends who could not understand what he was writing.[24] *Finnegans Wake* begins with Vico's Latin name: "a commodius vicus of recirculation."[25] Joyce speaks later of "the producer (Mr John Baptister Vickar)."[26] Joyce adopts Vico's three ages into his four, in such combinations as "eggburst, eggblend, eggburial and hatch-as-hatch can."[27] He speaks of "our wholemole millwheeling vicociclometer"[28] and of "IDEAREAL HISTORY."[29] Joyce's main character, the modern man H. C. E., Humphrey Chimpden Earwicker, may himself be Mr. Earwicker, Mr. Ear-Vico. *Finnegans Wake* is Vico's wake.

31   What Joyce has done, from a Vichian reading, is not so much use Vico's sense of history as use Vico's sense of memory and imagination. Joyce said he was fascinated with Vico's notion that "Imagination is memory."[30] Joyce attempts to write in the barbarism of the modern world the language of poetic memory, Vico's imaginative universals or, as Joyce puts it in the schoolday section, "IMAGINABLE ITINERARY THROUGH THE PARTICULAR UNIVERSAL."[31] The Vico road runs round and round throughout Joyce's works, but it comes home in *Finnegans Wake*.

32   If Brian Johnston is right in his study *The Ibsen Cycle*, Hegel's *Phenomenology* is the basis of Ibsen's famous twelve-play cycle that goes from *Pillars of Society* to *When We Dead Awaken*, which appeared between 1877 and 1899.[32] According to Johnston, there is a close parallel between the cycle of twelve plays and the stages of Hegel's *Phenomenology*, beginning with the forms of pseudo or preethical individuality in the last section of "Reason" and running through the stages of the chapter on "Spirit," with *A Doll's House* corresponding, for example, to the first stage of spirit, Hegel's discussion of man and woman and the family, and *Hedda Gabler* corresponding to the element of the final two stages of spirit, from *Die Verstellung* (duplicity) through conscience, the beautiful soul, and evil and its forgiveness. The last four plays of the cycle, according to Johnston, beginning with *The Master Builder*, correspond to aspects of the movement from religion to absolute knowledge.[33]

33   What holds Hegel and Ibsen together, in Johnston's view, is recollection. "Hegel's *Phenomenology*," Johnston states, "supplied Ibsen with the dialectic and with a wealth of recollected spiritual forms to which, I believe, Ibsen added his own not meager cultural experience."[34] Johnston holds that

Ibsen can best be understood "if we see his art recollecting and recreating the entire cultural expression of European history: its events, literature, arts, philosophies, and religions."[35] In a letter to John Grieg in 1866, Ibsen wrote: "It is strange how history repeats itself in different forms like variations on a musical theme."[36]

34   Ibsen ends his cycle in a way having some resonance with Hegel's quotation from Schiller at the end of the *Phenomenology* concerning the constant flow of God's creating, and especially his statement about the Calvary of spirit. The last line in *When We Dead Awaken* is spoken by the nun to the main characters, the sculptor and his mistress, who are seen indistinctly, being buried in drifting snow while ascending a mountaintop, and his wife Maja, who is joyfully saying, "I am free!" There is the sound of thunder and the nun exclaims, "Pax vobiscum!"—Christ's greeting to the disciples on the first Easter morning—"Peace be with you."[37] Hegel's images of the "Calvary of absolute spirit" and Ibsen's "Pax vobiscum" are not the same, but they both play on parts of the great Judeo-Christian image of renewal and the cycle.

35   The notion of *poiein,* the verb upon which Plato plays in the tenth book of the *Republic,* to make generally and to make poetry (596E), is crucial to memory. The quarrel with the poets and the philosophers is over who owns memory. The rhapsodes such as Ion recall the wisdom of Homer and Hesiod—the wisdom of the *eikon* or image—and the philosophers, who are the purveyors of a new kind of wisdom, connect memory to a new kind of object, the *eidos* or form. Both the philosopher and the reciter of poetry are masters of a linguistic art based in memory. The agenda of the tradition of the association of philosophy with rational form is set in this ancient quarrel. In it, poetry is separated from philosophy and from the ancient task of self-knowledge.

36   But this is not true of Plato's philosophy itself, in which there is a constant movement between the myth and metaphor and the discursive conversation of opposites and definitions. In my view, there is a kind of truth that depends on memory, and I would put this kind of truth itself ahead of whether it is seen as philosophy or poetry in modern terms. The crucial question is whether what is said claims to have necessity attached to it. This separates philosophy from theory, supposition, a statement of facts, a strategy, a puzzle, a discussion of borderline cases, a search for examples. It attaches to philosophy the necessity within the cycle of the Muses' power to say what was, is, and is to come. The aim of philosophy is to be a *vera narratio.*

37   Another way to say this is that philosophy is not science in the contemporary sense. The ideal of philosophy is that of a complete memory.

Science is always the work of the present—to witness exactly the form and the content of what is there. Vico and Hegel, however, claim their work to be "science." Vico's title, *La Scienza nuova,* is inspired by Bacon's *Novum Organum* and by Galileo's *Dialoghi delle Nuove Scienze.* Hegel calls his *Phänomenologie des Geistes* the first part of a "System of Science" (*System der Wissenschaft*), and he specifically titles it the "science of the experience of consciousness" (*Wissenschaft der Erfahrung des Bewusstseins*).

38   Vico and Hegel, each in his own time, steal the club of Hercules of the sciences. Vico steals it from the origins of the sciences that lead up to Descartes and seventeenth-century natural philosophy. Hegel steals it from the eighteenth-century Encyclopedists, the rising scientific study of custom and the study of the organic natural world. Vico's *scienza* and Hegel's *Wissenschaft* are both sciences of the inner form of experience—what Vico calls knowledge *per caussas* ("through causes," "from within") and what Hegel calls the transformation of substance into subject, the inner life of the real self, spirit. Both have a concept of consciousness on which their concept of science rests, and both define consciousness in terms of the certain.

39   Vico, in his famous principle *verum ipsum factum* or *verum et factum convertuntur* of his *De antiquissima Italorum sapientia,* distinguishes between science (*scientia*) in which the true (*verum*) is convertible with the made (*factum*) and consciousness (*conscientia*) or conscience, the activity in which something is witnessed as definitely so.[38] *Certum* is the product of the power of consciousness to be definite about something which consciousness does not itself make.[39] But science is had only when true and made are indeed convertible. Vico's example in the *De antiquissima* is mathematics, in which the truth of such reasoning depends on our having made it. Natural science is not *scientia* but *conscientia* because its object is not "made"; we can have no knowledge of it *per caussas.* Vico says that experiment is so crucial in natural science because it simulates the conversion of true and made. In relation to nature, God is the master knower who makes by knowing and knows by making.

40   *Certum* is not convertible with *verum.* In Vico's and in Hegel's view, consciousness cannot produce science, but there can be a science of consciousness. Vico's *Scienza nuova* depends on his philosophical-philological method, in which the *certi* of the civil world (institutions, laws, languages, deeds, customs) (7) are made into a story or autobiography of humanity, a story of self-knowledge in which the whole of the human world is seen as a conversion of the true and the made through philosophical principles. The theme of the certain in Hegel's *Phenomenology* runs from the *sinnliche Gewissheit* of the opening chapter right up to religion and absolute knowing in the third major stage of Spirit: "Der *seiner selbst gewisse* Geist." The quest for certainty is present at each stage. At each stage, consciousness searches for the precisely correct witnessing of the object that it only very slowly comes to realize may be its alter ego. Hegel's *Wissenschaft* encompasses all the separate quests of consciousness for the certain in experience.

41   *Verum, scientia, certum, conscientia—Wahre, Wissenschaft, Gewissheit, Bewusstsein* are the terms of Vico's and Hegel's philosophies. Both are also philosophies of the made, what is done in consciousness—what Vico calls *factum* and Hegel *Erfahrung*. Vico's science is based in meditation and narration—Hegel's in dialectic and narration. How are these works of *phronesis, prudentia*? And how do these works differ from each other?

42   The great Renaissance Florentine historian and statesman Francesco Guicciardini, in his *Ricordi,* says: "All that which has been in the past and is at present will be again in the future. But both the names and the surfaces of things change, so that he who does not have a good eye will not recognize them. Nor will he know how to grasp a norm of conduct or make a judgment by means of this observation."[40] Here is the wisdom of the Muses connected with the mind of the historian and statesman. The good eye, the *buon occhio* that is required for good action, requires the ability to see the cycle in all things.

43   Vico's *New Science* moves the classical doctrine of prudence, as the study of the lives and actions of great historical figures, onto the study of the whole of history. This study, in Vico's terms, is the apprehension of providence in history. In Vico's view *prudentia* depends on *providentia.* The perception of the providential order of history, which is the perception of history as cycle, is what Vico offers to the alternatives, as he puts them, of the blind fortune or chance (*cieca fortuna* or *caso*) of Epicurus and the deaf necessity (*sorda necessità*) of Descartes and the Stoics.[41] The true is the whole, and only the wisdom that comes from the grasp of the whole can issue in true prudence.

44   Hegel's *Phenomenology* is also a book of practical wisdom because only when we have taken the "highway of despair" (67/49) and entered into the cycle of each illusion of consciousness, each attempt by consciousness to fulfill its quest for certainty, are we in a position to see in any future situation the dialectic of it. When we have the full science of the experience of consciousness before us, we have the power, the wisdom, to think through the situation back to its origin, then to its own midpoint, and finally to project its course to its natural end. The key to the thought of the cycle is analogy. Any present situation has a life that it will live out and, by knowing all forms of the cycle, those that we have understood by analogy with the particular cycles of events in history we can now form by analogy as the "likely story," the narration of the course of events we currently hold before

us. Having followed each illusion of consciousness through to its end in the *Phenomenology,* we know that any situation we encounter has its own dialectic that relates to those dialectics we have learned as readers of Hegel's work.

45   In Vico's terms, each particular event has its own inner form or inner writing that can be read, like the inner writing of history in general, by employing the axioms of his science, which show the ways to bring the true (*il vero*) into contact with the certain (*il certo*). Vico's model, as he formulates it in his work on jurisprudence, *Il diritto universale* (and which he carries over into the *New Science*), is that *certum est pars veri,* that the certain is part of the true.[42] Any specific case embodies the law that applies to it. Thus, once we know the principles of human events generally, of the civil world, we can reason by analogy from the nature of a past case so formed to the meaning of a present case or situation that calls for action. In this way, we can say with the *Digest* of Roman law that jurisprudence is philosophy.[43]

46   Practical wisdom is part of both Vico's and Hegel's books of wisdom. But how do they differ? From Hegel's standpoint, there is no explicit conception of barbarism. Because there is no conception of barbarism in Hegel there is no real idea of a beginning nor of an end to his system. Hegel does not have a concept of the first man, nor of the last man, who is holding out against history. Vico might say, with the quotation from Ovid's *Tristia* with which Rousseau begins his *First Discourse:* "Here I am the barbarian because no one understands me."[44] Ovid, the master of Latin, exiled to Tomis, each day finds himself among people with uncut hair, who go about in skins, speaking in barbaric tongues he must himself try to learn. Vico, like Rousseau, knows he lives in a barbaric age. His philosophy is powerless to change the course of history. Vico's is the speech of a man in exile, a man not of his own time, who speaks in terms of origin. The speech against barbarism, which is against the barbarism of reflection, attempts to revive what is there at the origin—a speech that goes back to the first barbarism, the robust and honest barbarism of sense.

47   When the speech of the gods and heroes is gone, they are gone. Rousseau says: finally, men "chased the gods out in order to live in the temples themselves."[45] Vico says: finally, men "go mad and waste their substance." Stephen in *Ulysses* says: "History is a nightmare from which I am trying to awake."[46] Joyce also was a man speaking in an age of barbarism in the world of modern man, of H. C. E. Vico was thought mad (*pazzo*). As Finetti reports, before Vico wrote the *New Science* he was taken as learned, but after the *New Science* was published, he was thought quite mad. Capasso, Vico's great *tormentatore,* ran to a physician, having seen the *New Science,* claiming to have suffered a stroke that had taken all reason from him.[47] In his autobiography, Vico says of himself that among the caitiff semilearned, he was called a fool, and the more courteous said he had odd ideas.[48] Vico's own ideal was *sapienza che parla,* wisdom speaking—the ancient definition of eloquence, the complete speech—to say all that there is to say on a subject, in the manner of Cicero or the mighty enthymeme of Demosthenes.

48   Last men are always in some way first men. Last men like Vico and Rousseau are such because they have a strong conception of the origin of the beginning of humanity. They are the ones who have the special knowledge of the beginning. Hegel has no explicit theory of barbarism. Perhaps any philosopher speaks in the face of barbaric conditions. Indeed, if Vico's concept of the third age of his *corso* is correct, the beginning of any third age is marked by the disappearance of *fantasia* as the dominant mode of thought and the arrival of philosophy. Philosophy does not exist, nor can it exist apart from a barbaric period of history, that is, a barbarism that is not the barbarism of sense, of the beginning, of myth.

49   Hegel sees philosophy as "its own time apprehended in thoughts."[49] Despite his early endorsement of poetry, Hegel is in the end the voice of the Prussian state. Hegel is not a modern Ovid in Tomis. His philosophy almost begins with the gods, with the myth, with his interest in Greece.[50] But even the *Phenomenology* has no such beginning point. The *Phenomenology* begins in the experience of here and now as the objects of sense. It does not begin in the myth, in the here and now felt and expressed as gods.[51] Something is presupposed in order that the first stage of the *Phenomenology* can be what it is, but we do not know what. Hegel has spoken of a mythology of reason but he has not followed his own advice and begun with the poets. Poetry is the teacher of mankind, but it does not actually appear in his philosophy as the beginning of consciousness, despite his lectures on aesthetics and on religion.

50   Hegel's wisdom, like Vico's, is the wisdom of the circle, yet in Hegel's case there is but one circle, or a circle of circles. There is no *ricorso* in Hegel, only the total *corso* of humanity. In this sense, Hegel, with the one great drama of history, is the Christian; and Vico, with his cycles, is the pagan. Hegel's *Aufhebung* is in the end not to be found in Vico. For all of Hegel's insistence on the "labor of the negative" *Arbeit des Negativen* (20/10) and the need "to stare the negative in the face" (30/19), the negative is always surmounted. For Vico, the *ricorso* is no *Aufhebung.* Because history is eternal *corsi e ricorsi,* providence or the divine truth that is there to be learned in history is never learned, and things must begin all over again, with only some vestiges of the previous *corso* to be found in the new world of the *ricorso.* Hegel's cycle, like Ibsen's cycle, is a single totality.

51   It was Croce's ambition to see Vico as the Italian Hegel, a wish that he carried so far as to write a fictitious "Unknown Page from the Last Months of

Hegel's Life,"[52] in which an Italian visitor introduces Vico's work to Hegel, who reads it and informs the Italian visitor that it is in agreement with his own. Croce in his own great work on Vico's philosophy declared it to be deficient in only one respect—that Vico formulated the notion of an imaginative universal and thus failed to realize the true sense of the *Begriff*. Vico was reborn in our time as a part of the tradition of Hegelian idealism.

52   Vico was chained to this rock for decades, and he was not freed until the importance of his magnificent discovery of *fantasia* as the first faculty was realized. Hegel has in our own time become different, and it is Vico that can allow us to release Hegel himself from the fetters of Hegelianism. Vico and Hegel point the way back toward the recovery of a kind of speaking that makes wisdom its goal. Vico and Hegel are willing to reaffirm in their own enterprises the ancient connection between philosophy and wisdom—to make the act of philosophy conform to the etymology of the word that denotes it.

53   In conclusion, I wish to return to the syllogism I formulated at the beginning. I take the first premise—*imagination is memory*—from Vico's claim that "memory is the same as imagination." I take the second premise—*philosophy is imagination*—from Hegel's claim that "the philosophy of spirit is an aesthetic philosophy," the aim of which should be a mythology in the service of ideas or a "mythology of reason." My conclusion—*philosophy is memory*—joining its two terms through the middle term of "imagination," is meant to emphasize how *eikasia,* image-making or imagination, is always *principium sapientiae. Sapientia,* that wisdom, good sense, discernment, prudence—what the ancients thought of as proficiency in philosophy—begins and is founded in the image. Love of wisdom, which takes the True to be the whole and thus delivers a speech on the whole, depends above all on its powers of memory and imagination to guide its reasonings and its words.

54   The three terms of my syllogism correspond to Vico's definition of memory. Vico claims: "Memory [*memoria*] thus has three different aspects: memory [*memoria*] when it remembers things, imagination [*fantasia*] when it alters or imitates them, and ingenuity [*ingegno*] when it gives them a new turn or puts them into proper arrangement and relationship. For these reasons the theological poets called Memory the 'mother of the Muses'" (819; cf. 699). In my syllogism, I intend "imagination," the middle term, to correspond to *fantasia,* the "making imagination" or the power to convert *factum* and *verum.* I intend "memory" to contain the double meaning assigned to it by Vico in this passage, namely, *memoria* as the power of remembering what originates in sense (*senso*), and *memoria* as the source of the power of the Muses to order the present and future in relation to the past, to order time as a cycle. This second sense of *memoria* is a way of under-

standing, what is often called "recollection" (*reminiscentia*), or in Hegel's term, *Erinnerung;* it is *memoria* employing all three of its aspects to make a total order.

55   I intend "philosophy" to correspond to *ingegno* (*ingenium*). Within Vico's threefold memory, *ingenium* is the aspect that constitutes the directly philosophic moment. In the *De antiquissima,* he says: "*ingenium* is the faculty that connects disparate and diverse things." He claims that for the Latins *ingenium* and *natura* (nature) were one and the same. This power of connection, of proportion and symmetry, is the basis of man's nature as maker. As physical nature generates things, so human nature generates things: "as God is nature's artificer, so man is the god of artifacts." Vico understands *ingenium* not simply as the power to apply geometry and arithmetic to fashion things, as *ingegneri* do. He connects *ingenium* with his conception of *scientia:* "because human knowledge is nothing but making things [in the mind] correspond to themselves [in the world] in beautiful proportion, which only those endowed with *ingenium* can do."[53]

56   This corresponds to the two places in the *Scienza nuova* where Vico makes reference to the conversion of the true and the made. He says that there is "a truth beyond all question: that the world of civil society has certainly been made by men, and that its principles are therefore to be found within the modifications of our own human mind" (331). Vico repeats this point concerning modifications of the human mind and adds that "history cannot be more certain than when he who makes the things is the same one who narrates them [*che chi fa le cose esso stesso le narri*]" (349). "History" in this passage refers to Vico's conception of "ideal eternal history" (*storia ideale eterna*). The construction of ideal eternal history depends on *ingenium* as the power to connect "disparate and diverse things."

57   In this same passage, Vico says that "he who meditates this Science narrates to himself this ideal eternal history so far as he himself makes it for himself by that proof 'it had, has, and will have to be' [*in quella pruova "dovette, deve, dovrà"*]" (349). Thus, Vico's science depends on this "ingenious" art of memory, in which all the diversities of the world of nations are connected together in the cycle of ideal eternal history, which Vico takes back to the art of the Muses. Philosophy in its specific sense is the ingenuity of giving things a new turn and seeing the proper arrangement and relationships between things. But when this activity is extended across the whole of the world of civil things, philosophy becomes the same as the larger, threefold sense of memory—recollection.

58   Behind Vico's threefold memory is Aristotle's view of memory in *De memoria et reminiscentia,* which is, in fact, an appendix to the *De anima.* The key to Vico's conception of memory is his identification of memory and

imagination. Aristotle says: "if asked, of which among the parts of the soul memory is a function, we reply: manifestly of that part to which imagination also appertains; and all objects of which there is imagination are in themselves objects of memory" (450a21–24). Vico, like Aristotle, holds that "without an image thinking is impossible" (450a1).

59   Vico says that the first humans "who were almost all body and almost no reflection, must have been all vivid sensation [*vivido senso*] in perceiving particulars, strong imagination [*forte fantasia*] in apprehending and enlarging them, sharp wit [*acuto ingegno*] in referring them to their imaginative genera [*generi fantastici*], and robust memory [*robusta memoria*] in retaining them" (819). In this pattern of the origin of memory in sense, Vico differs in an important way with Aristotle because, unlike Aristotle, Vico claims that children have exceptionally strong memories and thus exceptionally vivid imagination (211). Vico also claims that the first humans, being "the children of the nations, they must have had marvelously strong memories" (819). Aristotle, however, claims that "both very young and very old persons are defective in memory" (450b6).

60   Vico takes his equation of memory with imagination not from Aristotle but from the fact that imagination (*fantasia*), he claims, is called *memoria* in Latin. As evidence, he cites a line in Terence's *Andria* (625) that associates *credibile* and *memorabile!* In the *De antiquissima,* Vico says that the Latins understood *memoria* both as a faculty that stores sense perceptions and as *reminiscentia* when it recalls perceptions, "but memory also signified the faculty that fashions images (which the Greeks call *phantasia* and the Italians call *immaginativa*)."[54] Vico may have in mind Cicero's line: "memory is the firm perception in the soul of things and words [*Memoria est firma animi rerum ac verborum ad inventionem perceptio*]."[55] The object of memory is not the sensation pure and simple but the sensation formed as image.

61   Vico says imagination is also taken for ingenuity (*ingegno*). He claims that in the "returned barbarian times *fantasia* was used for *ingegno,* and an 'ingenious man' [*uomo d'ingegno*] was called a 'fantastic man' [*uomo fantastico*]" (699). Vico's evidence is that Cola di Rienzo was so described by his biographer (699, 819).[56] Thus, Vico uses imagination as the middle term to connect *ingegno* with *memoria.* Aristotle's description of what is required for recollection over simple memory involves something like what Vico attributes to *ingegno.*

62   Recollection is a deliberate hunting through the contents of memory to find what we desire to recollect. This requires a power like *ingenium* to connect what is disparate and diverse. Aristotle says: "Whenever, therefore, we are recollecting, we are experiencing one of the antecedent movements until finally we experience the one after which customarily comes that

which we seek. This explains why we hunt up the series, having started in thought from the present or some other, and from something either similar, or contrary, to what we see, or else from that which is contiguous with it" (451b16–19). The process of recollection is not simply a process of recovery but a process of finding connections in order to recover something in a particular way.

63   Aristotle says, however, that to recollect "one must get hold of a starting-point. This explains why it is that persons are supposed to recollect sometimes by starting from 'places' [*topoi*]. The cause is that they pass swiftly from one point to another, e.g., from milk to white, from white to mist, and thence to moist, from which one remembers Autumn if this be the season he is trying to recollect" (452b13–18).

64   In Vico's conception of recollection as the formation of the world of nations into the narration of ideal eternal history, the places required are the sensory topics (*topica sensibile*) of the first humans "by which they brought together those properties or qualities or relations of individuals and species which were, so to speak, concrete, and from these created their poetic genera [*generi poetici*]" (495). These starting points correspond to the common sense (*senso comune*) of the human race, from which issues what Vico calls the "mental dictionary" (*dizionario mentale*) (141–45). Recollection as the basis of a science of the human world does not simply seek possible starting points, or *topoi*, but seeks those *topoi* that will allow us to begin to associate and recall all the disparate and diverse elements of the human world.[57]

65   Where Vico's threefold memory departs finally from Aristotle's conception of memory is in the relation of memory to the present and to the future. Aristotle says: "Now to remember what is future is not possible . . . nor is there memory of what is present, but only sense-perception. For by the latter we do not know what is future or past, but what is present only. But memory relates to what is past" (449b10–14). Although this might be said to be true of memory per se—Vico's *memoria* "when it remembers things"—it is not true of his threefold memory when it is identified with the speech of the whole of history, the relation of the ideal eternal history.

66   The power of memory in this sense is to mirror the providential order in history, to say what "providence has wrought in history" (342). This is to be able to relate with the Muses what is, was, and is to come as a cycle. Vico's *memoria* is also a prudence because it is an art that, once practiced on history as a whole, can be practiced on any particular event—to find its starting point and develop its course in language and thought until its end is expressed through attention to how it seems to be on a course similar to past courses, to which we know the outcome.

67   Cicero calls prudence one of the four virtues, the others being

justice, fortitude, and temperance. He says: "Prudence is the knowledge of what is good, what is bad and what is neither good nor bad. Its parts are memory, intelligence, foresight [*memoria, intelligentia, providentia*]. Memory is the faculty by which the mind recalls what has happened. Intelligence is the faculty by which it ascertains what is. Foresight is the faculty by which it is seen that something is going to occur before it occurs" (*De invent.* II. 53).

68   Although this is Stoic in tone, and Vico, in opposition to the Stoic's concern with controlling the imagination, would put *phantasia* in the place of *intelligentia*, it has a resonance with Vico's view. Vico says: "Wisdom among the gentiles began with the Muse defined by Homer in a golden passage of the *Odyssey* [8.36] as 'knowledge of good and evil', and later called divination" (365; cf. 391, 508). The key to prudence, which requires foresight (originally understood as divination), is memory.

69   Our power to understand and express the nature of the event as a cycle allows us the knowledge necessary to consider our own course of action in relation to it and its probable outcome. Having looked deeply into history itself, we can look deeply into any of its events, including those now in the making. Our sense of the cycle in the event gives us a much-needed understanding of our situation in regard to its reality and outcome. Because of our philosophical *buon occhio* on the event, we have the possibility of acting accordingly. The good eye gives us the needed distance and the sense of how its end will be connected to its beginning.

70   Philosophy, in its quest for understanding the providential structure of history, acquires the basis for prudence at the same time. The poets as the teachers of humanity never saw as separate their knowledge of the conduct of the world and their knowledge of the conduct of human affairs. So philosophy, in following the absolute Muse, reestablishes this association of these two senses of wisdom. Nothing less is the goal of the love of wisdom, pursued as the science of wisdom, a science claimed by both Vico and Hegel.

Notes

1   Elio Gianturco, translator's introduction, Giambattista Vico, *On the Study Methods of Our Time*, with a translation of "The Academies and the Relation between Philosophy and Eloquence," trans. Donald Phillip Verene (Ithaca, N.Y.: Cornell University Press, 1990), p. xxi.

2   Hesiod, *Theogony* 36–39.

3   Giambattista Vico, *La Scienza nuova seconda, Opere di G. B. Vico*, 8 vols. in 11 (Bari: Laterza, 1911–41), 4:819; *The New Science of Giambattista Vico*, trans. Thomas Goddard Bergin and Max Harold Fisch (Ithaca, N.Y.: Cornell University Press, 1986), p. 819. All references to Vico's *New Science* are to Nicolini's paragraph enumeration common to the Italian and English editions. I have occasionally modified the translation.

4   G. W. F. Hegel, "Das älteste System programm des deutschen Idealismus," *Werke*, 20 vols. (Frankfurt am Main: Suhrkamp, 1971–79), 1:236.

5   G. W. F. Hegel, "Über Mythologie, Volkgeist und Kunst," fragment of a Jena lecture manuscript in the Staatsbibliothek Preussischer Kulturbesitz, Berlin. This is translated in my *Hegel's Recollection: A Study of Images in the Phenomenology of Spirit* (Albany: State University of New York Press, 1985), 36–37.

6   Cicero, *Tusc.* 5.3.7ff. See also the discussion in H. B. Gottschalk, *Heraclides of Pontus* (Oxford: Clarendon Press, 1980), 23–36. The interpretation that men can love wisdom, but only God is wise, derives from the reports of this conversation by Iamblichus and Diogenes Laertius (see Gottschalk, *Heraclides*, p. 24). Hegel's view that wisdom is attainable by philosophers appears to derive more from Cicero's account (see n.7, below).

7   G. W. F. Hegel, *Phänomenologie des Geistes* (Hamburg: Meiner, 1952); *Phenomenology of Spirit*, trans. A. V. Miller (Oxford: Clarendon Press, 1977). Hereinafter cited by page of German edition, followed by page of English translation. I have occasionally modified the translation.

8   The dialectics of the "we" (*wir, für uns*) have been worked out in David M. Parry, *Hegel's Phenomenology of the "We"* (New York: Peter Lang, 1988).

9   Cf. Jean-Jacques Rousseau, *Discours sur les sciences et les arts* and *Discours sur l'origine de l'inégalité*, ed. Jacques Roger (Paris: Garnier-Flammarion, 1971), 205–18; *The First and Second Discourses*, ed. Roger D. Masters (New York: St. Martin's Press, 1964), 141–57. Rousseau begins part 2 of the *Second Discourse* with a cycle similar to Vico's.

10 Giambattista Vico, *De antiquissima Italorum sapientia ex linguae latinae originibus eruenda, Opere di G. B. Vico*, 1: chap. 7, sec. 5; *On the Most Ancient Wisdom of the Italians Unearthed from the Origins of the Latin Language*, trans. L. M. Palmer (Ithaca, N.Y.: Cornell University Press, 1988), chap. 7, sec. 5.

11 See my "Imaginative Universals and Narrative Truth," *New Vico Studies* 6 (1988): 1–19, and Alasdair MacIntyre, "Imaginative Universals and Historical Falsification: A Rejoinder to Professor Verene," *New Vico Studies* 6 (1988): 21–30.

12 A. N. Whitehead, *Process and Reality: An Essay in Cosmology* (New York: Harper and Row, 1960), viii, 43, 253.

13 G. W. F. Hegel, *Wissenschaft der Logik*, ed. Georg Lasson, 2 vols. (Hamburg: Meiner, 1971), 2: 504; *Hegel's Science of Logic*, trans. A. V. Miller (London: Allen and Unwin, 1969), 842. See also my discussion in *Hegel's Recollection*, chap. 10.

14 See my discussion of Hegel's use of *Erinnerung* in *Hegel's Recollection*, chap. 1.

15 See my "The New Art of Narration: Vico and the Muses," *New Vico Studies* 1 (1983): 21–38.

16 For the rhetorical structure of Hegel's *Phenomenology*, see John H. Smith, *The Spirit and Its Letter: Traces of Rhetoric in Hegel's Philosophy of Bildung* (Ithaca, N.Y.: Cornell University Press, 1988), chap. 4.

17 See *Cebes' Tablet: Facsimiles of the Greek Text, and of Selected Latin, French, English, Spanish, Italian, German, Dutch, and Polish Translations*, intro. Sandra Sider (New York: Renaissance Society of America, 1979).

18 See my *Vico's Science of Imagination* (Ithaca, N.Y.: Cornell University Press, 1981), esp. chap. 3. See also Mary B. Hesse, "Vico's Heroic Metaphor," in R. S. Woolhouse, ed., *Metaphysics and Philosophy of Science in the Seventeenth and Eighteenth Centuries* (Dordrecht: Kluwer, 1988), 185–212. I agree with Hesse's point that to my interpretation of Vico's imaginative universals should be added that they have a normative function.

19 Hegel, "Systemprogramm," 235.

20   Paul Hazard, *La pensée européenne au XVIIIᵉ siècle de Montesquieu à Lessing* (Paris: Librairie Arthine Fayard, 1963), 43. My translation.

21   Hegel, "Systemprogramm," 235.

22   *Scienza nuova seconda,* 1212. This is one of Vico's additions to the *Scienza nuova seconda,* which does not appear in the English translation. See my "Giambattista Vico's 'Reprehension of the Metaphysics of René Descartes, Benedict Spinoza, and John Locke': An Addition to the *New Science* (Translation and Commentary)," *New Vico Studies* 8 (1990): 2–18.

23   T. S. Eliot, "The Love Song of J. Alfred Prufrock," in *Selected Poems* (London: Faber and Faber, 1954), 14.

24   Richard Ellmann, *James Joyce,* rev. ed. (New York: Oxford University Press, 1982), 564. See my "Vico as Reader of Joyce," in Donald Phillip Verene, ed., *Vico and Joyce* (Albany: State University of New York Press, 1987), 221–31.

25   James Joyce, *Finnegans Wake* (London: Faber and Faber, 1939), 3.

26   Ibid., 255.

27   Ibid., 614.

28   Ibid.

29   Ibid., 262.

30   Joyce told his friend Frank Budgen: "Imagination is memory" (Ellmann, ed., *James Joyce,* 661 n.). Joyce converts the terms of Vico's proposition, which is the word order I have used in my syllogism.

31   *Finnegans Wake,* 260.

32   Brian Johnston, *The Ibsen Cycle: The Design of the Plays from* Pillars of Society *to* When We Dead Awaken (Boston: Twayne, 1975), pt. 1. See also Brian Johnston, *Text and Supertext in Ibsen's Drama* (University Park: Pennsylvania State University Press, 1989). There is, incidentally, a connection between Joyce and Ibsen, Joyce having begun his career at eighteen with publication of a review of *When We Dead Awaken,* for which he received a letter of appreciation from Ibsen.

   Johnston's correlation of Ibsen's cycle with Hegel's *Phenomenology* is open to question. Michael Meyer, in the first volume of his multivolume biography, says of Ibsen's university years: "It has, similarly, been asserted that Ibsen probably studied Hegel at this time, because Hegelian philosophy was now sweeping Europe and the professor of philosophy at the University, M. J. Monrad (the author of the kind editorial note about *Catiline*), was a disciple of Hegel; but we have no evidence that Ibsen ever read a line of Hegel . . ." (*Henrik Ibsen: The Making of a Dramatist 1828–1864* [London: Rupert Hart-Davis, 1967], 81–82). Meyer, however, holds that there may have been an influence from Kierkegaard (198–99). In a letter of April 30, 1873, to Georg Brandes, however, Ibsen speaks highly of Hegel as fundamental for writing on any philosophical ideas; by contrast, he finds little of value in Mill and English philosophy generally (*Ibsen: Letters and Speeches,* ed. Evert Sprinchorn [New York: Hill and Wang, 1964], 137).

33   Johnston, *Ibsen Cycle,* 36–37.

34   Ibid., 63.

35   Ibid., 63–64.

36   Ibid., 165.

37   Henrik Ibsen, *The Complete Major Prose Plays,* trans. and ed. Rolf Fjelde (New York: Farrar, Straus and Giroux, 1978), 1092.

38   *De antiquissima,* chap. 1.

39   Ibid., chap. 8, sec. 3.

40   Francesco Guicciardini, *Ricordi* (Milan: Rizzoli, 1977), 131. My translation.

41   Letter to Abate Esperti in Rome (1726), in Mario Fubini, ed., *Autobiografia, Seguita da una scelta di lettere, orazioni e rime* (Turin: Einaudi, 1970), 110. Cf. *La Scienza nuova seconda*, 5.

42   *De universi iuris uno principio et fine uno, Opere di G. B. Vico*, 2: pt. 1, 10–11. See also Guido Fassò, "The Problem of Law and the Historical Origin of the *New Science*," in Giorgio Tagliacozzo and Donald Phillip Verene, eds., *Giambattista Vico's Science of Humanity* (Baltimore: Johns Hopkins University Press, 1976), 3–14.

43   For a full account of how Vico's *New Science* is grounded in his conception of "a jurisprudence of the human race," see my *The New Art of Autobiography: An Essay on the "Life of Giambattista Vico Written by Himself"* (Oxford: Clarendon Press, 1991), chap. 4.

44   "Barbarus hic ego sum quia non intelligor illis" (*Tristia* [V.10.37]); on Ovid's general conditions of life in exile, see V.7. *Discors sur les sciences et les arts*, 2; *First and Second Discourses*, 31.

45   Ibid., 52, 54.

46   James Joyce, *Ulysses* (London: Bodley Head, 1960), 42.

47   See my discussion of Finetti's and Capasso's remarks in *The New Art of Autobiography*, chap. 1.

48   *Autobiografia*, 86–87; *The Autobiography of Giambattista Vico*, trans. Max Harold Fisch and Thomas Goddard Bergin (Ithaca, N.Y.: Cornell University Press, 1983), 199–200.

49   "So ist auch die Philosophie *ihre Zeit in Gedanken erfasst*," *Philosophie des Rechts, Werke*, 7: 26.

50   E.g., "Eleusis," *Werke*, 1: 230–33.

51   This is essentially Ernst Cassirer's criticism of the beginning point of Hegel's *Phenomenology*. See Cassirer, *Philosophie der symbolischen Formen*, vol. 2, *Das mythische Denken* (1923) (Darmstadt: Wissenschaftliche Buchgesellschaft, 1969), ix–xi; *The Philosophy of Symbolic Forms*, vol. 2, *Mythical Thought*, trans. Ralph Manheim (New Haven, Conn.: Yale University Press, 1955), xv–xvii.

52   Benedetto Croce, "An Unknown Page from the Last Months of Hegel's Life," trans. James W. Hillesheim and Ernesto Caserta, *The Personalist* 45 (1964): 344–45, 351.

53   *De antiquissima*, chap. 7, sec. 4.

54   Ibid., chap. 7, sec. 3.

55   Cicero, *De inventione* I.7. Cf. Quintilian, "Memoriae duplex virtus: facile percipere et fideliter continere" (*Institutio oratoria* I.3). See Fausto Nicolini, *Commento storico alla seconda Scienza Nuova*, 2 vols. (1943) (Rome: Edizioni di Storia e Letteratura, 1978), 1: 306.

56   Nicolini (*Commento*, 1: 306) points out that Cola di Rienzo was not described by his anonymous biographer in the way Vico reports. Instead of being called a *uomo fantastico* in the sense of a *uomo d'ingegno*, it is reported that Arcimbaldo, on hearing the grandiose plans of Cola, exclaimed ironically—"lo fantastico," thinking that what he had heard was fantastically extravagant. In relation to the above-mentioned use by Vico of *memorabile* in Terence's *Andria*, Nicolini (2: 28–29) thinks Vico is stretching his case. He points out that in *Heautontimorumenos* II.3.73 (*The Self-Tormentor*), Terence uses *memorabile* in the usual sense of something worth remembering. Vico often adjusts his evidence to his point.

57   Indispensable for the study of the history of *topoi* (but which does not take the subject as far as Vico's time) is Frances A. Yates, *The Art of Memory* (Chicago: University of Chicago Press, 1966).

Part II

Philosophical

Imagination

and the

History of

Philosophy

Alasdair MacIntyre

Are Philosophical Problems Insoluble? The Relevance of System and History

Nobody ever became rich by being a professional academic philosopher. But we academic philosophers are all supported, directly and indirectly, by the labor and earnings of others—this much was true long ago even of the unprofessional Socrates, who scorned to take fees for teaching—and from time to time the question naturally enough arises: why should quite so much in the way of private and public resources be devoted to supporting the inquiries of philosophers and the teaching of philosophy? When we are thus invited to justify ourselves and our activities, there is something of a tendency to stammer and stutter. Philosophy after all is not technologically useful; it does not supply us with ever more adequate agreed empirical results, as chemistry does; much of it is arid and dry, lacking the charms of literature and the arts. "What good then can philosophy be?" it will be asked.

How we respond to this question will depend in key part upon how we understand the relationship between ourselves and those who pose it. If we think of ourselves as philosophers by profession and those who question us as lay nonphilosophical and unphilosophical persons, ourselves as insiders and them as outsiders, then the problem will be that of how to construct a justification of philosophy in nonphilosophical terms, terms available to those external to what is conceived as a specialized and professionalized activity. To justify philosophy to nonphilosophers will be like justifying engineering to nonengineers or golf to nongolfers. And there are those among our colleagues who have supposed that this is what needs to be done. What they sometimes say is that an education in philosophy is useful. It provides excellent training in lucid writing, in analytical skills, and in problem-solving. This is true; but this was how the teaching of Latin in secondary schools used to be justified, and Latin then disappeared from the secondary school curriculum.

Yet what is wrong with this appeal to the external utility of philosophy is not only that it is likely to be ineffective. In asking, "What good can philosophy be?" those who are asking for a justification have themselves posed a specifically philosophical question in a way which suggests that the distinction between insiders and outsiders is deeply misleading. Philosophical assumptions, theses, arguments, and questions are already present, in one way or another, in the idioms, actions, beliefs, forms of cooperation, and conversation that constitute everyday life. What the academic philosopher does is to make explicit and to pursue with some persistence questions that are posed to and answered by everyone. So a first stage in the justification of academic philosophy has to proceed by bringing those who have not yet recognized this to understand that their choice and ours is not between doing philosophy or not doing philosophy, but between doing it badly and doing it well. And a second stage will be that of showing how the inquiries of professional academic philosophers not only achieve the relevant kind of excellence, but, in addition, provide the resources to enable those who are not professional academic philosophers, in their own nonprofessional way and at whatever level they need or desire to do so, also to achieve the relevant kind of excellence. But can this be shown?

This is the hard question, and part of what makes it hard is a salient and continuing feature of academic philosophy, of which those outside academia are often very well aware, the large inability of professional academic philosophers to arrive at agreed solutions to their own central problems and the corresponding apparent lack of substantive progress within philosophy. Let me begin from an example.

A central fact of our culture is the extent and fundamental character of moral disagreement. Such disagreement arises, in part, from the multiplicity of considerations that are generally recognized as relevant in deciding what it is right to do in particular situations and, in part, from the seemingly incommensurable standards that are invoked in assigning weight to particular claims. So appeals to the rights of one particular group will compete not only with appeals to the rights of other groups, but also with claims based on utility. What some people *deserve* will be weighed against what other people *need,* and rival sets of needs will compete with one another for generally scarce resources. Some among us appeal to exceptionless moral rules, taken to have authority independently of circumstance and consequence; others are sometimes or often prepared to rewrite their rules in the light of circumstances and consequences. Hence, it is unsurprising that to some people at least, the moral life appears as pervasively problematic, a source of recurring dilemmas, while others avoid dilemmas by invoking some particular highly determinate moral scheme, but only at the cost of equally recurrent contention both with those who uphold some rival and incompatible scheme, and with those who oscillate between one position and another. So it is with disputes about abortion. So it is over issues of distributive justice and the morality of war. So it is on occasions when the claims of truthfulness compete with those of responsibility for the well-being of others or of oneself or of the state.

It is therefore unsurprising that distinctively philosophical questions about morality are often enough nowadays explicitly posed by ordinary plain persons who have discovered that they need to learn, if they aspire to be rational, how to argue their way through these apparently problematic situations. And one such central question is: are these situations genuinely or only apparently problematic? Are irreducible, perhaps irreducibly tragic, moral dilemmas an ineliminable feature of the moral life, or is belief in such dilemmas itself an illusion to be dispelled by adequate analysis? Is there perhaps for every human being in every moral situation something to be done that it is unambiguously best and right to do, even if it is sometimes difficult to discern what it is? It is at this point that a recognition that she or he is asking questions with a philosophical dimension may lead an ordinary plain person to turn to professional academic philosophy for assistance. And at first sight a great deal of assistance is available.

Since 1962, more than a hundred articles in philosophical journals, chapters of books, or whole books have been published either directly on the subject of moral dilemmas or on some closely related topic. The problem therefore is not that the lay person will have difficulty in finding philosophical advice. It is that the range and variety and fundamental character of the disagreements in recent and current philosophical literature about moral dilemmas, about whether or not they are real or only apparent, and if real what their character is, and if only apparent, why they are taken to be real, and how they are to be resolved, not merely match the range of disagreements already present in everyday moral debate, but extend and sharpen those disagreements. Nor are there in this large and growing literature any signs of converging agreement on the substantive issues, signs of what a lay person would take to be progress. Thus, to the external observer irresolvable disagreement may appear, in this case as in others, to be the permanent and irremediable condition of academic philosophy. But if so, then the kind of justification of academic philosophy on which I have embarked must seem doomed to failure. For what, it will be asked by the plain person, is the point of rendering explicit what is philosophically implicit in everyday discourse, if the outcome is only to replace one set of seemingly insoluble problems by another set of even more intractable problems?

At this point, a defender of academic philosophy may well reply that *some* progress has in fact been made on these questions in the philosophical literature, even if no agreement on the substantive issues has been arrived at. Some arguments have been discredited, some concepts have been clarified. Ruth Barcan Marcus, for example, has successfully answered the accusation that the very statement of a moral dilemma involves fatal inconsistency, inasmuch as it seems to provide grounds for holding of one and the same person at one and the same time that it is and is not the case that he or she ought to do such and such and therefore cannot describe a possible state of affairs. And Marcus did so by providing a conception of consistency that avoids this charge. Again, Bas C. van Fraassen has provided a novel interpretation of and new rules for deontic logic, which in another way rescue the statement of moral dilemmas from charges of inconsistency.

Yet although these are both clearly examples of philosophical progress, the plain person will be apt to observe that their effect has been not to eliminate or reduce the range of philosophical disagreements, but to sustain and even increase them by rendering certain positions in contention less vulnerable to refutation by their rivals than they previously were. So that what is accounted progress from the standpoint of professional academic philosophy turns out to be quite consistent with what will be accounted lack of progress by the everyday person looking to philosophy for help.

There is, however, another conclusion that emerges from this particular set of philosophical discussions which may not at first appear hopeful to that plain person, but which in the longer run is highly significant for his or her quest. It has been suggested both by Bernard Williams and by van Fraassen that one can appeal against certain theses that deny the possibility of genuine moral dilemmas to what Williams calls "the facts" about moral dilemmas and van Fraassen "the kind of fact of moral life on which ethical theories founder." But what emerges from recent discussions is that there are no such facts about dilemmas independent of and antecedent to all theories. Whether we take it to be a fact that genuine moral dilemmas do occur turns out to depend on how and from what theoretical standpoint we characterize the relevant types of situation.

Consider three very different kinds of moral theory and the different ways in which they will classify and describe one and the same type of moral situation, first taking it to be an instance of a genuine dilemma—that is, of a situation in which two mandatory moral rules prescribe incompatible conduct and there is no rational way of adjudicating between their claims, so that some important rule has to be disobeyed, a second, by contrast, taking that same situation to be an example of a hard case, that is, one in which the relevant mandatory rule unconditionally prescribes an action the performance of which involves a very high cost to the agent or to others or to both in suffering, a cost that however provides no good reason for either disobeying or revising that particular rule, and a third taking this very same situation to exemplify that type of occasion which provides sufficient grounds for revising one or more of our moral rules, as they have hitherto been understood, so that all appearance of a dilemma is removed, and the revision of the rule has taken into account the suffering otherwise involved.

So, for example, from the standpoint of the first type of theory, someone faced with the choice between telling a lie on a matter of some import and being unable otherwise to prevent an innocent person from suffering significant harm will be understood to be in a genuine dilemma in which the good of truth-telling is judged incommensurable with that of preventing harm to innocent people. Yet in that same situation adherents of the second type of theory will judge this a hard case, but one that provides no ground whatsoever for disobeying that exceptionless categorical precept which prohibits all lying. And those who espouse the third type of theory will see neither a dilemma nor a hard case here; they will instead argue that such circumstances justify a revision of the rule which prohibits lying in general, in order to add one more type of exception to a rule formulated in more and more complex ways to accommodate more and more types of situations.

Characteristically and generally, utilitarians will provide examples of this third type of standpoint; Thomists and Kantians in somewhat different ways, are examples of the second; and a variety of recent moral philosophers, such as Stuart Hampshire and Bernard Williams, who take there to be a number of independent sources of incommensurable values, the first. These rival standpoints are, it is clear, not merely those of the adherents of rival sets of moral standards. Their fundamental disagreements extend to the question of how the facts on which their standards are to be brought to bear are to be characterized and classified. Hence, each of these theoretical standpoints has internal to itself its own systematic way of understanding the relevant facts, and no neutral appeal to the facts as they are in themselves, independent of all theorizing, is available. We are thus confronted by three incompatible types of large-scale theory whose adherents have been unable so far to settle their disagreements.

Clearly, something further has emerged from the literature about moral dilemmas, but once again it is something that may appear to make the issues which divide the contending parties less rather than more resolvable. Is this perhaps confirmation that permanent, wide-ranging disagreement is an ineliminable condition of philosophy? A first step in answering this question is to ask what those things are about which in general philosophers do find it possible to secure agreement and correspondingly what it is about their enquiries that engenders and perpetuates conflict and disagreement. Philosophers often *are* able to agree about the structures of the concepts and theories that they study and even more often about the relationships of entailment, implication, and presupposition that hold among statements playing key parts in the elucidation of such concepts and the statement of such theories. Generally, that is, they agree about what follows from what, about what else one is committed to asserting if one asserts some particular statement. And they often, although not always, agree in their diagnoses of incoherence.

The sources of their disagreements are threefold. First, they do not agree on where to begin, either in the initial definition of the philosophical project or on what concepts should be taken to be primary and central in those constructions of philosophical theory that are their intended end product. And, of course, where one begins determines in key part where one ends. Even those philosophers who agree that we ought to begin by criticizing our best predecessors are not of one mind as to who those predecessors are.

Secondly, they do not agree on what weight to assign to different types of consideration, something that divides not only philosophers of vastly different perspectives, such as Heideggerians and Wittgensteinians, but even philosophers whose methods and insights are largely the same. For example, among the theorists of the semantics of possible worlds, David Lewis, Alvin Plantinga, and Robert Adams arrive at some strikingly different conclusions. This is, I take it, because, although philosophers may agree on what further commitments are involved in adopting this or that thesis, or relying on this or that argument, they do not share any overall set of standards by which to evaluate the intellectual costs attached to or the intellectual benefits to be derived from such commitments.

A third type of disagreement among philosophers concerns what they are *against*. A good deal of philosophy is by intention polemical, and some feminist philosophers have suggested that this adversarial character is the result of male domination of the discipline. But I note that they themselves have all too often advanced this thesis in a characteristically adversarial way. (I am happy to concede to such feminists that the too often unnecessarily disagreeable character of philosophical polemics may well arise from typically male vanity and petulance.) What is true is that much central philosophical theorizing has been informed by hostility to some chosen adversarial figure. Think of the very different ways in which Descartes has been used as a whipping boy by Maritain, by Ryle, and by Rorty, or of the way in which Hegel functioned for Russell, Husserl for Derrida, or the earlier for the later Wittgenstein. Whom and what one chooses to be *against* thus has one key part in determining both the direction of one's philosophy and some of the ways in which one will consequently differ from other philosophers.

Given this range of sources of disagreement, the interminability of philosophical conflicts and disagreements is not surprising. But philosophers may at this point be inclined to comment that persistent and apparently ineliminable disagreement is not peculiar to philosophy; it is also a feature of other disciplines. Psychologists have been unable to resolve the conflicts between behaviorists, psychoanalysts, and cognitive theorists, and internal to each of these parties there are also continuing disputes. Economists are able from their professional ranks to provide corporations and governments with equally expert advisers of widely disparate and incompatible points of view. And similar ranges of disagreement are to be found in literary studies, in sociology, and elsewhere. But this appeal to the conflict-ridden character of other disciplines may make the prima facie case against philosophy stronger rather than weaker.

For what are the sources of these conflicts in other disciplines? They arise, I suggest, at just those points within those other disciplines at which specifically philosophical issues become inescapable. The issues that divide psychoanalysts and behaviorists are inseparable from, even if not restricted to, issues in the philosophy of mind; the issues that divide Keynesians and monetarists are inseparable from, even if not restricted to, issues in the philosophy of social science. And so it is also in literary theory and sociology. The appeal to the condition of other disciplines may therefore turn out only to reinforce belief in the distinctively unsettlable character of specifically philosophical quarrels. So how then is the philosopher to respond? I have identified three main sources of philosophical disagreement in assumptions about what philosophy's starting point should be, about what kind of weight should be attached to different kinds of consideration, and about what types of error we especially need to avoid and to refute. Notice now that characteristically and generally there is a systematic connection not only among what positions are taken up in each of these three latter areas, but also among those positions and what is accounted a conclusive solution to a particular problem or an adequate treatment of a particular issue. And notice also that to insist on the explicit statement and articulation of these systematic connections would be to transform the appearance of the philosophical landscape. Where, previously, stances on particular issues and theses about particular problems had seemed to have been adopted and formulated in a piecemeal, issue-by-issue, and problem-by-problem way, so that each disagreement was apparently framed, in large part at least, in terms specific to each problem situation, it would now become clear that very many of these, at least, are the expression in particularized, small-scale terms of a much smaller number of large-scale, systematic disagreements. To understand this does not make the small-scale, more detailed disagreements any the less important; but it significantly alters our conception both of how they are to be characterized and of how questions concerning their resolution ought to be formulated.

Initially, of course, it may well seem that little or nothing is to be gained by adopting this type of systematic perspective. After all, the history of philosophy is in large part a history of philosophical systems engaged in conflict with one another, Aristotelians criticizing Platonists, Scotists attempting the refutation of Thomists, Cartesians deploring all of the above, empiricists savaging Cartesians, and so on. Thus, it may appear that we have merely added to the catalog of types of philosophical disagreement, rather than having made a first move toward an understanding of how such disagreement can be rationally resolved. But this would be a mistake, as I shall try to show by defending three theses.

The first of these is that adequately determinate solutions to philosophical problems and resolutions of philosophical issues are to be had only from philosophical inquiry within and from the standpoint of some system. Only the constraints afforded by systems supply the requisite kind and degree of determinateness. Secondly, conflicts among philosophical systems, contrary to appearances, are in fact rationally resolvable, but the character of these resolutions has still to be widely understood. And thirdly, the identification of the systematic character of philosophical disagreement enables us to formulate a sufficient rational justification for the activities of the academic philosopher to the layperson outside academic philosophy, even before such a resolution has been achieved and even in spite of the fact that such a resolution may well not be achieved within the lifetimes of the relevant set of laypersons and the relevant set of academic philosophers.

I turn first then to ask what difference it makes to pose philosophical questions from within the context and perspective afforded by the construction of a system rather than by posing such questions as though askable and answerable one by one, in minimal, separable units, the type of unit provided by that distinctive genre of piecemeal philosophy, the contemporary journal article, so that we make explicit not only to the characterization of what whole the characterization of each subordinate part or aspect of each topic or issue is to contribute, and in the light of what overall canons of method an answer to a philosophical question is to be deemed adequate and adequately well-grounded, but also to the standards set by what philosophical predecessors we are to be held accountable. In so doing, we make available a strong set of criteria, conformity to which characteristically provides conclusiveness, or at least relative conclusiveness in evaluating alternative formulations of philosophical issues and alternative solutions to philosophical questions. Consider in this light the questions posed about moral dilemmas.

I noticed earlier that what characterization a particular philosopher gives of that type of situation about which, characteristically, disagreement arises in answering the question of whether it does or does not confront us with a moral dilemma will depend on what large-scale theoretical standpoint such a philosopher either invokes explicitly or tacitly presupposes. And in a similar way, the answers to other questions about aspects and details of the problems treated under the rubric 'moral dilemmas'—problems, for example, about the logical status and structure of the rules that do or do not generate such dilemmas, or about the reactions appropriate to certain types of action that infringe on what is normally taken to be required of us, whether regret, remorse, or guilt—also turn out to differ with the type of theoretical standpoint invoked or presupposed.

It is then in fact the case, whether recognized or not, that in these controversies what systematically confront one another are rival, large-scale theoretical standpoints, such as those of utilitarianism, Kantianism, and Thomism, including as one more such standpoint the antitheoretical moral theory of such as Bernard Williams. Abstract the issues of detail from the contexts provided by such theoretical standpoints, and detach the various points of view expressed on those issues of detail from the premises and presuppositions afforded by such standpoints, and the outcome will be a set of necessarily interminable disagreements among positions whose truth or falsity is underdetermined by the only kinds of reasoning then apparently admissible, as indeed the literature shows that it is. It is not of course, as I also noted earlier, that a good deal of worthwhile clarification has not been achieved through the discussion of those disagreements; but the point and purpose of such clarification only emerges in those larger systematic contexts. So the move to or toward doing philosophy systematically issues in the replacement of a multiplicity of interminable disagreements by the emergence of a number of solutions, each taken to be conclusive, or at least relatively so, from within its own theoretical perspective. But what then of the charge that it is just the level of disagreement which has changed, but not the fact of its intractability? Now everything turns on whether or not the claims of one large-scale theoretical standpoint can or cannot be vindicated against its rivals.

In order to answer this question, let us for the moment put it on one side, and consider further some characteristics of philosophical systems. Such systems often enough arise out of an attempt to exhibit to some particular prephilosophical audience why they are finding some particular type of difficulty or problem of their own peculiarly intractable or some particular type of fundamental disagreement obstinately unresolvable, by providing a systematic philosophical setting within which those problems and disagreements can be reformulated in a way that makes them amenable, or at least more amenable, to rational solution. Philosophical systems, that is to say, are initially responses to prephilosophical questions.

An example is provided by Aristotle's ethics and politics—ethics and politics understood as having a systematic metaphysical dimension. What was it outside philosophy to which Aristotle in formulating his ethical and political views was responding? A variety of competing types of political constitution, oligarchic and democratic, rival adherents of which sometimes engaged in civil war; a variety of competing diagnoses of past Greek political failures invoked to support rival policies; a variety of well-established opinions held by poets, dramatists, and statesmen about what the human good is, what the virtues are, and how particular virtues are to be understood. To whom was Aristotle speaking? Primarily and immediately to young men who would by the time they were thirty share in the rule of some *polis* and who were confronted not only with this range of rival and competing opinions, but with disagreements about what kind of education would best enable them to act well, disagreements most notably between a range of sophistic views, Plato's philosophical antipolitics, Isocrates's defense of a rhetorical training informed by revived Periclean ideals, a defense which disdained philosophy as unpractical, and Aristotle's own theory and practice.

Aristotle also had, of course, a secondary audience: the ruling elites of the *polis* from whom these students were drawn and to whose ranks they would return. And we, belated members of a tertiary audience, need to understand how it was in virtue of his addressing these particular primary and secondary audiences, confronting this particular range of problems and issues, of *aporiai,* that Aristotle had to understand his relationship to these audiences. First, it was crucial to the kind of conversation in which he was engaging that his accounts of constitutions, of established rival opinions and of the *aporiai,* the problem and issues, arising from them should be recognizably accurate. And secondly, he had to enable his audience to recognize its own initial incompetence, including an incompetence to understand the nature of that incompetence, in confronting those *aporiai.* That is, the young and immature, the inexperienced and undisciplined, had to be induced to subject themselves to an education into a set of moral and intellectual virtues, the point and purpose of which they would be able to appreciate only once they had acquired them. So, according to Aristotle, in coming to understand the human good, the truths about that good which are finally to be attained through arduous inquiry must themselves already be presupposed in the earliest phases of that inquiry, by the way in which inquiry has to be organized at its outset. This type of circularity involved in initiating and carrying through philosophical inquiry, which Aristotle makes so plain to us, I take to be an ineliminable feature of systematic philosophy. Our *telos,* our end, theoretical or practical, is already in our beginnings.

That this is so has two important consequences. First, systematic philosophy cannot commend itself to members of its prephilosophical audience by arguing that what they are going to learn from it will serve their preexisting preferences and purposes, at least as they initially understood them. For almost the first thing they will have to learn is that until they have put those preexisting preferences and purposes in question, they will be debarred from genuine participation in the philosophical enterprise. So it turns out once again that the case against justifying philosophy by appealing to its external utility, as utility is prephilosophically understood, is from the standpoint of systematic philosophy illegitimate. What philosophy does and can speak to in our prephilosophical condition are those incoherences and unintelligibilities of which we become aware in the course of making explicit those philosophical assumptions that already informed our prephilosophical discourse and beliefs. Yet in learning from philosophy how to address these difficulties, we have to act in ways that presuppose what we have yet to learn. It is common enough not to recognize this point, sometimes because all circularity in philosophical inquiry is thought to be vacuous or vicious. And circularity in rigorous demonstrative argument is, of course, vacuous and vicious; but in dialectical inquiries of the kind from which systematic philosophy begins, one sometimes already has to presuppose, without recognizing it, what one is going to put in question, in order to be able to put it in question rationally. This is notoriously how Aristotle proceeded in *Metaphysics K* in defending the principle of noncontradiction, but he also proceeds in this way elsewhere, although sometimes less obviously. And we find the same type of fully defensible circularity in as different a philosopher as Descartes. That circularity has often enough been remarked, but characteristically in order to impugn Descartes. Descartes, it is rightly said, derives his fundamental criterion of clarity and distinctness from the *Cogito.* And, it is then equally rightly remarked, that he relies upon these criteria in determining the truth of the *Cogito.* And this clear and distinct circularity with respect to clarity and distinctness is then adduced by some critics as a ground for rejecting the structure of Descartes's argument. But what such critics once again fail to distinguish are the standards appropriate to demonstrative arguments and the standards appropriate to those dialectical arguments by means of which demonstratively structured systems of thought are brought into being. What the historical narratives of the *Discourse* and the *Meditations* recount is a story of how progress in dialectical inquiry had brought Descartes to a point at which he could from within what had now become Cartesianism—the "I" who had once been the historical René Descartes had been rendered into the timeless "*I*" internal to the *Cogito*—reject both history and dialectic. Like the Wittgenstein of the *Tractatus,* he threw away the ladder by which he had mounted. And in this, of course, he was quite unlike Aristotle. But so far as the circularity by which he had reached his goal is concerned, Cartesian circularity is no more objectionable than Aristotelian.

This, then, is how systematic philosophy begins. It deserves to be called systematic only when as large a range as possible of the problems, incoherences, and partial unintelligibilities of prephilosophical discourse, action, and inquiry are made the subject matter of an inquiry in which the questions to be answered are of the form: How are all of these to be understood in the light of the best unified and integrated conception of rationally adequate inquiry possessed so far? Every well-developed conception of rational adequacy is a conception internal to some particular philosophical system; indeed, from one point of view a particular philosophical system just is a well-developed, unified, and integrated conception of rational adequacy. But at the same time, rational adequacy is what we all aspire to in our prephilosophical arguments, assertions, debates, and inquiries. Yet it is at this point that another serious objection has been advanced. For it has been thought that if philosophical systems are informed by circularities of the type that I have identified, then they will be inherently defective in providing ideal conceptions of rational adequacy.

Each philosophical system will from the outset in developing its ostensibly rational accounts of this or that area of discourse, action, or inquiry tacitly presuppose or explicitly invoke just that conception of the *telos* of inquiry which in turn it will support by appeal to the findings derived from those accounts. So Aristotle's account of the ultimate human good supports his account of the virtues and is in turn supported by them. So his account of practical deliberation in choice supports his account of the good and is in turn supported by it. And so it is also with thinkers other than Aristotle. But then it seems that each such system will have internal to it its own conception of rational justification, and that therefore there will be no point at which the conception can itself be put in question. This has the consequence that two or more rival philosophical systems, with substantively different conceptions of what rational justification is, Aristotelianism, say, on the one hand, and Cartesianism on the other, will each provide for appeal only to its own standards of rational evaluation, and so the adherents of each will be confirmed in their belief in the superiority of their own system, but in a way that makes the encounter between such rival systems rationally barren. We shall end up with too many rationalities, too many conceptions of rational adequacy, each self-confirming and none able to provide genuinely good reasons for preferring it to its rival.

That this is indeed the case has been a powerfully influential view. In one form it underpinned a good deal of the logical positivist objection to metaphysics. But it has also been in a different way an influence on Heideggerian and post-Heideggerian evaluations of past philosophy. In the logical positivist version, the rejection of past philosophical systems depended on the alleged undecidability of the claims of rival metaphysical theses. In the Heideggerian and post-Heideggerian versions, the rejection depends on the ascription to past metaphysical systems of a claim to a kind of grounding that they cannot in fact have. The positivists impugned the credentials of past philosophical systems because their adherents were not able to appeal to some criterion that could be established independent of and prior to the particular claims of any systematic philosophical theory; the Heideggerians have impugned the credentials of past philosophical systems by ascribing to them just such an appeal, albeit an entirely illegitimate one, to something external to and independent of their systematic theories, which could provide those theories, and discourse and action issuing from them, with grounding.

Both positivists and Heideggerians are mistaken. Philosophical systems do not need, in order to provide themselves with rational justification, to appeal to some external, theory-independent standard of justification; and they did not in fact do so. But in what, then, does their own national justification consist? In the way in which and to the extent to which within each system provision has been made, explicitly or implicitly, for the possibility that by putting itself to the question in its own terms it will break down and exhibit a variety of forms of internal incoherence and resourcelessness, so that that system will fail by its own internal standards of rational justification. It is one of the marks of the rise of a major philosophical system, that its initial large-scale statement always engenders a new set of problems internal to that particular system. The internal problematic of each system provides its adherents with a set of tasks; their progress in or failure to make progress in dealing with those tasks provides initially a more important measure of intellectual success or failure than do the tasks of responding to external critics. And the merits of a system depend on and are relative to its problem-engendering character. What makes it possible for the adherents of a philosophical system to claim that it has been rationally vindicated is just that about it in respect of which it is also open to the possibility of rational defeat. Hence, it is one of the essential virtues for a major philosophical system that it will be stated in a way that renders it maximally vulnerable to refutation from its own point of view. This is a standard judged by which Plato, Aristotle, Descartes, Hume, Spinoza, and Kant excel; if we were to apply it to such postmodernist thinkers as Lyotard, Rorty, and Fish, they would fare very badly.

The radical criticism and rejection of a major philosophical system is then something that is able to and proceeds from its own point of view. But to say this is not to say that such criticism and rejection can be achieved only through the work of adherents of that particular philosophical system. Philosophical imagination enables us to inhabit temporarily a diversity of systems other than our own, and thus to participate both in the criticism of rival systems and of our own as though we were external critics; and the development of a philosophical imagination is a central part of a philosophical education.

Philosophical systems, then, can be rationally defeated—self-defeated. But, it may be retorted, this does not fully respond to the objection. For it might still seem that, although within each such system the activity of rational criticism of that system can go on, each system cannot but be isolated from criticism from the standpoint of its rivals. But this too is a mistake. For the claims of any developed, would-be comprehensive system depend in key part upon its ability to provide within itself, in its own terms and in a way that accords with its own standards, a representation of the relevant theses and arguments of its rivals. So there is a Kantian account of Plato and a Hegelian account of Aristotle and equally an Aristotelian account of Kant and Hegel, provided by modern Thomists. We have therefore moved to the point at which it is possible to understand how two theses often thought to be incompatible can both be true.

The first is that there are indeed no standards or criteria of rational evaluation in any area, no matter how fundamental, that are theory-independent and inquiry-independent, neutral between rival theoretical standpoints, whether philosophical, natural scientific, moral, or whatever, and available therefore to intelligent persons of any point of view. The second is that it is nonetheless possible on occasion to decide rationally between the claims of two rival competing schemes of thought and/or practice in a way that is equally rationally compelling to the adherents of both the rival standpoints. And this is possible because some particular scheme of thought and/or practice can be rationally defeated both by its own standards *and* by the standards of one of those competing rivals. When, in addition, that particular rationally victorious rival possesses the resources to provide an illuminating identification and explanation of just those limitations and inadequacies, the recognition of which as irremediable in the light of that system's own standards had led to the acknowledgment of its having failed by its own standards, something which that self-defeated system did not itself possess the resources to provide, then that particular rival will have satisfied the conditions jointly necessary for its rational superiority to have been established in the strongest terms possible.

In this respect there is no difference between philosophical systems and large-scale bodies of scientific theory—and sometimes, of course, although not always, such bodies of scientific theory themselves are, or are constituent parts of, philosophical systems. Galilean and later Newtonian physics rationally defeated Aristotelian physics not by appealing to some philosophically and scientifically neutral, theory-independent criterion, for there is none such, but because not only did Aristotelian physics, as it had developed into late medieval impetus theory, fail by its own standards in a way in which Galilean and Newtonian physics did not fail by their own standards, but also Galilean and more especially Newtonian physics were able to explain, and to explain precisely, just why and how Aristotelian physics, if developed to a certain point, had to fail in the way that it did.

It follows from all this that the history of philosophy can be written as a history of rational progress, provided that three conditions are satisfied. The first is that that history should be conceived primarily not as a history of problems or as a history of texts, but as a history of systems, of their rising, flourishing, and declining, within which problems and texts find their place. A second condition, implicit in the first, is that systems themselves should be understood as historical: there is no such thing as Aristotelianism or Cartesianism, but only Aristotelianism at each successive stage of its development, only Cartesianism in its first formulations, in its mature formulations, and in its uses by Descartes's successors. To inhabit a philosophical system is to be a participant in a history, a history in and through which some particular conception of rational adequacy in theory and in practice is formulated, developed, tested, revised, and perhaps finally defeated, but perhaps instead one that survives its encounters with both internal and external critiques, so that it remains a contender in philosophical debate.

A third condition, implicit in the first two, is that such a history should be written from the standpoint of some one particular system. For if it is to be justified as history, it must itself meet standards of rational adequacy, both theoretical and practical, and the particular set of such standards to which the historian will have to appeal will be standards developed within some particular system. No system, of course, will be able to provide a standpoint from which an adequate history can be written that is not itself conceptually rich enough to provide from within itself representations of those other systems that have been or still are the major contenders in philosophical debate. And indeed it will have to be rich enough also to provide adequate representations of their representations of it. So no Aristotelianism will be qualified to provide a standpoint for writing the history of philosophy that lacks the resources to furnish adequate and accurate representations not only of Cartesianism and Kantianism and Hegelianism, but also of Cartesian and Kantian and Hegelian representations of Aristotelianism.

One further characteristic, not only of such a history, but of the history of the various philosophical systems that provide it with its subject matter must now be noted. I have suggested that philosophical systems are elaborations of ideals of rational adequacy, both theoretical and practical, but of the rational adequacy of *what?* The answer is: those multifarious beliefs, arguments, assertions, and practices, persistent features of which forced on everyday plain persons a recognition of their need to raise philosophical questions about those beliefs, arguments, assertions, and practices. But this relationship between the initial self-questioning of the prephilosophical plain person and the answers delivered by those speaking from the standpoint of some philosophical system is not something that occurs at the inception of systematic theorizing, but thereafter disappears. It is only because and insofar as there are a more or less continuous set of dialectical interchanges between those philosophers who are engaged in articulating some particular system and those plain prephilosophical persons who are engaged in posing questions about the rational adequacy of their beliefs and practices, questions that arise out of their everyday discourse and interaction as well as from scientific and theological inquiries, aesthetic and legal and political activities, and so on, that philosophical systems continue to have an identifiable subject matter.

It is at this point that yet one more version of a difficulty which in different forms has arisen again and again in this chapter can be relevantly advanced. Even if plain persons do come to understand, it may be said, that philosophical systems articulate ideals of rational adequacy which provide answers to some of their own central questions, they cannot but notice that rival philosophical systems persist, and that the disagreements and conflicts among major systems have not yet been resolved. So the justification of philosophy still has to confront continuing large-scale disagreement among philosophers. But these disagreements must now surely appear in a new light.

For if there are recognizable within our culture philosophical systems that articulate rival and conflicting conceptions and ideals of rational adequacy, it is now clear that this must be because disagreement on these fundamental matters is deep-rooted and pervasive in our culture. It is these disagreements, so often concealed behind the platitudes of official rhetoric, that philosophy enables the plain person to identify and to understand, so enabling her or him to engage with these disagreements more rationally and less confusedly than would otherwise be the case. When understood thus, the continuing disagreements of philosophy no longer stand in the way of a rational justification of philosophy.

So it is that in satisfying the conditions for the successful development of a philosophical system or systems of any depth and sophistication, the conditions are simultaneously satisfied for answering the question of how and in what terms the philosophical enterprise is to be justified to those not professionally engaged in it. It is because and insofar as a particular system articulates ideals of rational adequacy, which in successive formulations provide more and more satisfactory answers to the continuing questions of some particular prephilosophical public, that it both flourishes as a philosophy and can be seen to discharge its responsibilities in the world at large, even if it is in continuing conflict with other such systems. Hence, there is a social dimension to the history of philosophy, one generally omitted or very largely so from the history of philosophy when studied as an academic discipline. And this is an omission that deforms the history of philosophy. For philosophy does not generate its own most fundamental questions, even when it is a philosopher who, as Socrates did, initially guides others into posing questions that they might well not otherwise have asked, so revealing the extent to which those others had already been concerned with and perhaps entangled by distinctively philosophical issues.

Insofar as there are those among them who continue to reformulate and reiterate those questions, so constituting a continuing public for some particular developing philosophical system, a public of everyday plain people for whom the standards by which they judge the rational adequacy or inadequacy of their own reflective discourse and inquiry are standards furnished at different stages by that system, the relationship of academic, professionalized philosophy needs no further justification. For insofar as some plain people in a social group discharge their part as a public in bringing their own questions about the rationality of what they judge and do to philosophy, to that same degree philosophers are able to discharge their part in eliciting, revising, and sustaining the standards of rationality required by a variety of types of human activity, and indeed by human activity as such. And in this lies the only justification of philosophy.

Yet if this is so, the rational justification of philosophy is not something that can be carried through for anyone whatsoever at any time or place. Only when philosophy is in a particular condition, and that social group to the members of which philosophy is to be justified is in a corresponding condition, is the enterprise of justifying philosophy a possible one. There have, of course, been a variety of times and places when the necessary kind of symbiosis between the life of systematic philosophy and the life of the corresponding social group or groups has been achieved. So it was at certain times in ancient Greek city-states and in Islamic medieval caliphates and in medieval Christian universities both in their agreements and in their conflicts; so it was in a number of periods in Chinese and Japanese history. In each such case, a justification of philosophy was possible in terms of the highly specific character of some particular philosophical system or systems and the nature of the sustained interchanges between those engaged in explicitly philosophical inquiry and other key members of the relevant social groups.

It follows, of course, that, in times and places where either or both of these two conditions go unsatisfied, it will not be possible to provide any rationally compelling public justification of philosophy. If and when philosophy is no longer a largely systematic activity, but is instead, at least for the most part, conducted piecemeal, and if and when social and cultural life is such that there is a widespread inability or reluctance—for whatever reason—to press questions to the point at which their inescapably philosophical character becomes evident, then the claims of philosophy on scarce academic and educational resources, in competition with other claimants, will become difficult to vindicate. Those of us who are committed to philosophy should pray not to live in such a time.

J. B. Schneewind

Modern

Moral Philosophy:

Philosophers who ask, "Why should anyone be moral?" are often chided for supposing that being moral is simply a means to something else. Once it is admitted that being moral is valuable, perhaps supremely valuable, in itself,

From Beginning

to End?

the question's crassness becomes evident, and we stop asking it. We might treat the question, "Why should anyone study the history of philosophy?" in the same dismissive way. Asking how it pays to study that history is like asking why one should read masterpieces. The question assumes that the activity must be good for something beyond itself. Surely, the assumption is philistine and should be dismissed.

There is something right about these responses, but since people keep asking both questions something else may be at issue. In the case of morals, the questioner may be asking about the place of morality within the whole economy of the active life, or what it is about morality that gives it unquestionable claim on our rational adherence. These questions deserve answers, not dismissals, and the answers help us understand our own involvement in morality. Similarly, good reasons may exist for asking why the history of philosophy is worth study, and the answers may help us understand what we are doing when we engage in philosophy. The desire to know how our forebears thought about these things needs no justification; but the work to which it leads may have philosophically important results that go beyond satisfying this deeply human desire to sustain the connection to our past.

I think this is indeed the case, but since I can find no single satisfactory account of what it is to do philosophy, I can give no single explanation of how historical study fits into that activity. Some who engage in historical inquiry claim they do so only because their predecessors often turn out to have had good ideas about solving perennial philosophical problems. For them, it is merely accidental that history is useful to philosophy as we do it today. Others see philosophical views as arising and developing within enduring separate traditions of inquiry, and they believe that it is only within such traditions that rational inquiry can be carried on. For them, since deeply rooted disagreements can only be understood as involving whole traditions, history is indispensable. I am inclined to think that those who rummage in the past merely to salvage usable bits and pieces from the junk heaps underestimate the degree to which the problems that engage them are historically conditioned, and that those who see all philosophical inquiry as enmeshed in traditions are trapped by a totalizing demand for comprehensive systems, which is itself philosophically questionable. But as a historian, I have no desire to outlaw these approaches. Each of them has generated valuable investigations. Those of us whose primary interest is in finding out how people thought about these things in the past can take what they have to offer and see how helpful it is in our inquiries.

In studying the history of philosophy, I think it is more helpful to suppose that different aspects or areas of current work bear different relations to their pasts than it is to assume that there must be some single relation between past and present for any two values of those variables. The best way to learn about the instrumental value and the philosophical role of the history of philosophy is through case studies, and it is such a study that I shall present here. I shall discuss some aspects of the history of ethics; useful results of the kind that I think emerge from *this* piece of history may or may not be found to result from studying the history of other parts of philosophy.

The project from which this study emerged began as an effort to find out what questions about morality Kant himself thought his ethical theory answered. While working on the topic, I came to think that in uncovering this aspect of the development of Kant's ethics I was learning something about the origins of modern moral philosophy itself and of the morality implicated in it. I begin with a stripped-down account of why Kantianism is so central.[1]

I

At the heart of Kant's ethical theory is the proposition that normal adults are capable of being fully self-governing in moral matters, which are matters of supreme practical importance. Kant speaks of this capacity as displaying our "autonomy"; and autonomy, as he understands it, has two components. The first is that no authority external to ourselves is needed to constitute or inform us of the demands of morality. All of us are equally able to know without tutelage what we ought to do because moral requirements are those we impose on ourselves. The second component is that in moral matters we can effectively control ourselves, even though we do not always do so. The obligations we impose on ourselves override all other constraints or requirements on action and frequently run counter to our desires. We nonetheless find in our knowledge of what morality requires a sufficient reason to act as we ought. No external sources of motivation, no threats of punishment or promises of reward are needed for our self-legislation to have the potential for guiding our conduct.

Other eighteenth-century philosophers besides Kant argued for the equal ability of normal adults to be fully self-governing in moral matters, although none of them tried to explain it in terms of self-legislation. Richard Price and Thomas Reid would have agreed with Kant about the supremacy of morality and about our ability to know what morality calls for and to be moved by that knowledge. But they would have strongly rejected Kant's claim that we create moral requirements by imposing them on ourselves.

Kantianism and intuitionism were two of the main determinants of nine-teenth-century debate in moral philosophy. The third was utilitarianism. It is not so clear that Bentham's version of that view allowed him to assert the full and equal moral competence of all normal adults. But the later Benthamites felt a need to work out a way in which allegiance to the utilitarian principle could be fitted together with the assertion of such competence. John Stuart Mill's theory that the rules of commonsense morality are really summaries of the experience of the human race about the typical beneficial and harmful consequences of action was an effort to show how ordinary people could know what it is right to do without having to carry out immense calculations prior to action. And his associationist explanation of how we build an immediate attachment to morality into our desires was meant to show why external rewards and punishments are not, as Bentham seemed to suggest, necessary for moral knowledge to be efficacious. The utilitarian acceptance, however difficult and perhaps tenuous,[2] of the belief in equal moral compe-tence that Kant and Reid shared made it the general background assumption of the work we do and the courses we teach in what we call ethics or moral philosophy.

It is also central, I think, to modern morality itself. If we do not believe that everyone alike is "essentially" or by nature a fully competent moral agent, we believe that we ought to educate everyone to be so. We are uneasy about the idea of moral experts. We remain so despite the widespread desire for carefully focused moral advice reflected in the rapid growth of the studies known vaguely as "applied ethics." Much of what the "ethicist" does is to put specialized knowledge of some field of technical practice, such as medicine or engineering, at the service of specific moral inquiries. The *moral* compe-tence of those involved in and affected by the moral decisions is presup-posed, since a substantial amount of agreement from them is required for the alternatives or policies proposed by the ethicist to be acceptable. Ours is a society in which the idea of a moral authority is at best marginal.

It would be absurd to say that modern moral philosophy is the sole source or cause of our belief that in moral matters everyone's views have to be considered equally. But in the course of its development, modern moral philosophy produced the major ways in which this belief came to be articulated and defended. The study of its history is therefore the study of the emergence of one central aspect of our self-understanding.

II

Our belief in the full and equal moral competence of normal adults would have surprised a good many seventeenth-century philosophers. We do not usually appreciate the distance that separates all of us on this matter from what was widely believed during that period and well into the eighteenth century. It is worth being reminded. What I take to be the standard early view was expressed with unusual clarity by an important political theorist of the early seventeenth century, Johannes Althusius. His major work, *Politica methodice digesta atque exemplis sacris et profanis illustrata,* was first published in 1603. In the course of discussing "the knowledge imprinted within us by God, which is called conscience," Althusius cites Saint Paul's central pronouncement from Romans 2:14–15, asserting that the Gentiles, though lacking the law, do by nature what the law requires because the law is written in their hearts, and because their consciences disturb and accuse them when they act wickedly. Commenting, Althusius says:

> There are different degrees of this knowledge and inclination. For law is not inscribed equally on the hearts of all. The knowledge of it is communicated more abundantly to some and more sparingly to others, according to the will and judgment of God. . . . Nor does God urge and excite all persons to obedience of this law in the same manner and to an equal degree. Some men exert themselves more strongly, others less so, in their desire for it.[3]

A more admiring view of ordinary people's ability to see for themselves how to live was not to be found among the privileged few who professed to be aiming at the life of a Stoic or Epicurean sage, or of an equable Skeptic. "Good, in good truth," says the Stoic Du Vair, "is not so placed that all the world may see and perceive it."[4] The knowledge required of the sage was never thought to be something that everyone could acquire, nor was the continuous dosage with antithetical arguments needed to preserve the indifference of the accomplished Pyrrhonian skeptic. Whatever the originators of these ancient sects thought, their Renaissance and early modern inheritors did not think themselves to be delivering a path to the good that was equally available to everyone. They were writing for an elite.

We would expect to find a more generous attitude within more orthodox Christianity. But the passage from Althusius shows it was possible to admit that all men have consciences without admitting that all of them have equally capable consciences; and the Roman Catholic practice of casuistry, tied to confession[5] and continued by some Protestant groups well into the seventeenth century, presupposes that most consciences need to be directed.

In natural law theories, the foundations for this belief are clear. We can see this view in the work of Francisco Suarez (1615), the greatest of the Spanish neo-Thomist system builders. To be properly binding, Suarez says, laws must be adequately promulgated; and those of God's laws that are binding on all people alike are promulgated through the natural light of reason,[6] which in this case exercises itself through conscience.[7] The light of reason shows us three classes of truths. There are "primary and general principles of morality, such principles as 'one must do good, and shun evil.' . . ." Other principles, which Suarez describes as "more definite and specific. . . . are also self-evident," such as that justice must be observed and that God must be worshiped. And the third class contains inferences from principles of the first two groups. Some of these conclusions are fairly easily grasped and so are available to many people, for example, that adultery and theft are wrong. But "other conclusions require more reflection, of a sort not easily within the capacity of all, as is the case with the inferences that fornication is intrinsically evil, that usury is unjust, that lying can never be justified, and the like."[8] The law works more frequently, Suarez adds, through these hard-to-infer proximate principles than it does through the obvious, very general ones.[9] And while ignorance of the latter is not possible, ignorance of the former is. Moreover, ignorance respecting the precepts that require greater reflection can be invincible, "especially," Suarez says, "on the part of the multitude."[10] The preface to his great treatise makes it clear that the theologian is the ultimate source of knowledge on law because he is the one concerned with everything to do with God, and the moral law is simply one manifestation of God in our lives. The need for an educated clergy instructing the consciences of "the multitude" is thus evident.

Low views of the multitude were not confined to Jesuits with an interest in defending casuistry; they also are prominent among natural law theorists. Grotius does not say much about the matter, no doubt because it could be taken for granted. "For alike children, women, and men of dull intellect and bad education are not well able to appreciate the distinction between just and unjust."[11] Hobbes thinks the masses must be reminded by constant sermons of what they ought to do; he also thinks it seditious, within civil society, to teach that every private person is judge of good and evil.[12] Pufendorf leaves us in no doubt about the ordinary man's capacity for moral knowledge. The first principles of natural law can be understood by all, he says, at least after those principles have been properly explained. But most men, not knowing how they are to be demonstrated, usually learn and observe the law by imitation. Pufendorf finds no problem here: "As for the common throng," he says, "the authority of their superiors . . . should be enough to make them certain regarding [the law]."[13]

At times, Locke writes as if he agreed with his fellow theorists of natural law. The basic precepts of morality, he says in a late work, could not have been discovered by unaided human reason—witness the failure of the ancient philosophers to find them—and had to be taught us by a divine mediator. And even now that we know them, and think them perfectly reasonable (as in his view they are), we cannot teach them as purely rational precepts. Even if philosophy had "from undeniable principles given us ethics in a science like mathematics, in every part demonstrable," it would not avail.

> The greater part of mankind want leisure or capacity for demonstration; nor can carry a train of proofs, which in that way they must always depend upon for conviction. . . . And you may as soon hope to have all the day-laborers and tradesmen, the spinsters and dairy maids perfect mathematicians, as to have them perfect in ethics this way. Hearing plain commands is the sure and only course to bring them to obedience and practice. The greatest part cannot know, and therefore they must believe. . . . And were all the duties of human life clearly demonstrated, yet I conclude, when well considered, that method of teaching men their duties would be thought proper only for a few, who had much leisure, improved understandings, and were used to abstract reasonings. But the instruction of the people were best still to be left to the precepts and principles of the Gospel.[14]

Similar views are found in the rationalists—in Samuel Clarke and, earlier, in Malebranche and Spinoza, whose belief in "the stupidity of the masses, and their failure to think,"[15] underlies Spinoza's interpretation of our common moral vocabulary as showing only a deep confusion about necessity. And the widely influential predecessor of Kant, Christian Wolff, taught an ethic that made knowledge of the metaphysical constitution of the universe essential to right action. Admitting that most people could not acquire this knowledge "from their own reflections," he added that "it is not necessary that all men be discoverers." There are those among the learned, like himself, who will do the hard work, and then teach the others rules they can memorize and follow, and that will suffice.[16] In his view, it is obligatory for the more gifted to spread their learning; his own writing, he tells us, is intended to carry out this obligation.[17]

An episode from the life of Salomon Maimon will make clear one implication of this kind of view. The impoverished Maimon, invited as a needy scholar to the home of a wealthy merchant for dinner, was taken to the son's room after the meal. The son reports:

> as he told me that the purpose of his trip to Berlin was only to pursue knowledge, I showed him some mathematical books, from which he begged me to read him aloud some sentences. I did so; but never was I so shaken as then, when I saw tears flowing from his eyes, and heard him weep aloud. O, my son, he said to me, weeping, how happy you are, to have and to be able to use, when you are so young, the tools for the perfection of your soul. Lord of all the world! If achievement of perfection is the vocation of man [as Wolff taught], pardon me the heavy sin if I ask, why until now the means for living true to my vocation were kept from poor me. . . . [18]

Maimon did not know of the work of the British moralists, and he was unaware that Kant had already hit on a principle that he thought would enable anyone, even the simplest and least-educated, to know what morality requires.

III

The clearest view of seventeenth-century beliefs about normal moral motivation comes from a look at the prevailing understanding of the concept of obligation. It was generally agreed that somehow or other recognition that one has an obligation or feels obliged to do a certain act motivates one to do that act. It was also accepted that there must be a distinction between actions that we do at our own discretion, because we please, or because we want to, and actions we do whether we want to or not because we have to or because they are necessary. The latter constitute our obligations. A theory of obligation had to explain the motivational force of obligations and the kind of necessity involved in them.

Suarez offered one influential account. The necessity involved in obligation, he held, is the necessity of using the means needed to attain an end.[19] The laws of nature, in pointing out our obligations, show how we must all act in order to attain the good proper to humans generally, and the laws a sovereign lays down are aimed at securing the good proper to us as members of the commonwealth. But pointing out how a good may be attained is not the same as obligating someone to act. Giving someone such information is only advising or counseling him. A teacher or someone who is one's equal might give such instruction, but doing so does not obligate the hearer to act. Only a superior can obligate.[20] A superior obligates someone when the superior, possessing sufficient power to help or harm him, promulgates a rule pointing out acts that will achieve an appropriate good and demands compliance, under threat of penalties for disobedience.[21]

Suarez explains the motivational force of obligation in terms of the threat of penalties. I have already noted that he thinks many people are unable to understand the rationale for the laws that govern them. This means that they will not see the good that compliance brings about, and therefore that they cannot be moved by a desire to attain that good. In its place Suarez puts the motive of avoiding threatened punishment. We can know, he holds, that God will be displeased by disobedience, and so will punish it, even if we do not know anything in detail about the punishments.[22] Obligatory acts are necessary to attain the main end of our common life, but the compelling reason people have for carrying out their obligations is the necessity of avoiding a personal evil.

Suarez's analysis of obligation enables him to distinguish between advising someone and obligating someone, and to show how God's existence and concern for the world are indispensable to morality. It also enables him to avoid the charge that God's imposition of obligations on us is arbitrary. God commands only acts that in themselves are suitable for bringing about human felicity.[23] But acting from one's own recognition of that suitability itself is not acting as an obedient subject. And Suarez takes it as evident that intellectual creatures, in virtue of being created, have a superior whom they are to obey.[24] The concept of obligation as Suarez understands it thus carries the idea of our status as creatures who are meant to obey.

The elements of the Suarezian view are to be found in a wide range of seventeenth-century theories. Time does not permit me to trace the steps through which the picture altered, but I must mention the main development.[25]

Seventeenth-century philosophers accepted the view that what moves us to act when we are being reasonable is the belief that some good will be attained by our action.[26] The common theory of obligation results from the thought that the agent can see no good in obedience except the good of avoiding his own punishment. The natural law thinkers agree that what we are obligated to do under the laws of nature is a means to a good, and that in most cases the agent cannot see this. But the laws of nature are supposed to be rational guides of conduct. The only reason the agent can have to obey,

it seems, is the fear of punishment. Obedience not grounded on this consideration would be simply irrational. Spinoza—not himself a natural law
thinker—gives a very clear statement of a widely accepted view: "The real
object of law," he says, "is seldom obvious to more than a few; most men are
practically incapable of seeing it. . . . Thus in order to bind all men equally[,]
legislators have wisely introduced another motive for obedience . . . by
holding out the sort of reward [and] penalty . . . that appeals most strongly
to the hopes and fears of the masses. . . . [27] The common view of obligation
carries a definite sense of the need in human life for a strong superior power
to keep order, and this sense rests on a specific view of ordinary human
moral capacities. Dissatisfaction with the common view expressed different
political and moral estimates. There were religious thinkers, among them
the Cambridge Platonists, who held that this theory of obligation accorded
less dignity to human beings than God intended them to have, and that it left
no proper room for action out of love, which was after all central to Christianity. Admitting, however, that many people usually did not act lovingly,
they were unable to construct a theory of obligation that would show how all
of us equally can have obligations even if some of us do not need to be made
to comply by threats of punishment. The political implications of the Pufen-
dorfian theory of obligation, which look uncomfortably similar to those of its
predecessor, the Hobbesian view, motivated others to seek some alternative
view. Their common move was to abandon the legislative model of law and
to work with a different model. One way in which this thought was developed had crucial bearings on the psychology of obligation. Those who
appealed to self-evident moral laws were ultimately forced to make a drastic
revision of the common seventeenth-century moral psychology.

Although Samuel Clarke modeled moral law on the laws of mathematics,
he was not as clear about the shift in psychological theory required by this
move as was Richard Price. Price claimed that action can be rationally
motivated in two ways, not just one. It is reasonable to act in pursuit of some
good; it is equally rational to act at the behest of principles whose own
rationality the agent perceives. Only by accepting this psychology, Price
held, can we give an adequate account of the scope of the obligations we all
acknowledge. In asserting that "the perception of right and wrong does
excite to action, and is alone a sufficient *principle* of action,"[28] he is claiming
for us a sense of duty different in kind from any sense of what is good. There
is no need for a lawgiver for this sort of law, and no need of a law enforcer to
set up an effective reason for carrying out one's obligations.

In different ways, Reid and Kant developed views similar to Price's. Kant
in particular worked out the thought that we can be motivated by our
recognition of the constraints rationality imposes on action, without any

thought of good or ill to be derived from the action. And he went beyond Price and Reid in the clarity of his recognition that this way of construing human motivational capacities has its justification in the requirements of morality itself. We all acknowledge that there are some categorical obligations arising from our own rational agency, and we can see that unless we were free to act as those obligations require us to, this would be impossible. We must therefore conclude that we are free—are able—to act as morality requires. The picture of the moral self that Kant draws is one whose main lines are determined by the needs of a morality that does not permit us to see ourselves as ruled by another.

IV

On the remaining point about morality as we think of it now, its supremacy, it is not easy to elicit a consensus from seventeenth-century thinkers. But here the difficulty is not that earlier thinkers would directly disagree with what I have supposed to be our present general understanding. Rather, insofar as the question of the supremacy of morality arises in the seventeenth century, it does not have its modern meaning.

The natural law thinkers could indeed give the question a sense. "The laws of nature," one of them might say, "which constitute the moral laws as distinct from divine and human positive laws, are God's laws. Hence, they are supreme in the sense that they override any human laws. If your concern is with a conflict between morality and self-interest, since morality is the truest prudence, the only thing to say is that morality takes precedence over shortsighted self-interest. If you are asking whether there is some other sense in which the natural laws are supreme, we can only suppose that you mean to ask whether God himself could make exceptions to, or abrogate, the laws of nature, or whether he can grant dispensations from them. Perhaps you have in mind God's dispensation to Abraham exempting him from the fifth commandment, or some of the other episodes in the Bible. We are divided on this issue. Some—the voluntarists—believe that God could do away with the whole force of the law. Others hold that this is impossible, but that at least some of the inferred precepts of the natural law could be abrogated, or that God could grant dispensations from them. And there are those who hold that even this latitude is not permitted. I suppose the strictest of these latter thinkers might be said to hold that the moral law is supreme in something like your modern sense."[29] Suarez himself took a strong line, denying that God could abrogate the laws of nature, and therefore held them to be always in force. Grotius follows him; but Pufendorf as late as

1672 is eager to defend a voluntarist position. He takes the view that God, in fact, never will abrogate the laws of nature—but not that he cannot.[30]

The issue is yet more complex. One thing Kant meant by saying that the moral law is supreme—perhaps it is something we do not now wish to mean ourselves—was that compliance from the right motive entitles one to happiness. And since the entitlement is plainly not honored in the present, Kant notoriously if quite unoriginally argued that it must be cashable in a life to come. Now if this is what is meant by the supremacy of morals, then it was certainly challenged by all of those who in the seventeenth century took to heart the denunciations of Pelagianism by Saint Augustine and many later religious thinkers. The whole question of salvation by faith or by works, and of the extent of the human need for grace, is involved here. And though the reformed confessions insisted more absolutely than the Roman on the absolute need for grace to be given to each individual as such before that person could do anything meritorious, the Catholic church also held that without grace man can do nothing acceptable to God. Even if moral standards are the highest standards for our action, devoted obedience to them is either not possible without divine assistance or is not sufficient to entitle us to the highest kind of merit.

V

During the seventeenth century, then, and indeed for many thinkers of the eighteenth century, moral philosophy did not proceed on the assumptions about the capacities of moral agents that have dominated the subject since Kant, Reid, and the later utilitarians. What led to the changes was not—at least not in the earlier stages—a conscious aim of bringing them about. The changes began as a response to a specific view of the central problem for practical philosophy. This understanding of the problem, I suggest, was itself a major change from earlier views; and it has remained central to our own thinking about morality.

The accepted distinction between modern moral philosophy and its ancient predecessors is one given classical formulation by Henry Sidgwick more than a century ago. The ancients, he said, "argued, from first to last," about the good taken generically and about its relations to its different species, among which they counted the right. "Their speculations," he continued, "can scarcely be understood by us unless with a certain effort we throw the quasi-jural notions of modern ethics aside and ask (as they did) not 'What is Duty and what is its ground?' but 'Which of the objects that men think good is truly Good or the Highest Good?'"[31] Accepting this as far as it goes, I want to suggest that we need to deepen it. We need to try to see what is behind the shift from an inquiry about the highest good to an inquiry about duty, where the latter is conceived to take, as Sidgwick says, a "quasi-jural" form. And to do this, there is no better place to begin than the work of the founder of modern natural law, Hugo Grotius.[32]

Grotius's major work, *On the Law of War and Peace* (1625) is a treatise on international law, not on moral philosophy. His central subject is conflict. The very first paragraph of the treatise tells us that the topic is controversies, not only those that culminate in formal ways, but "such controversies, of any and every kind, as are likely to arise."[33] In that period of religious and commercial warfare, it is hardly surprising that Grotius built the problems of rivalry and strife into the heart of his theory. What is surprising is that Grotius did not try to show that warfare and its personal counterparts might be eliminated. Instead, he presented a view of the moral psychology of the individual according to which we should expect conflict to be ineradicable. His hope was that he also could show the psychological resources which would enable us to confine it within bearable limits. Grotius was not interested in the problems of individual decision-making or character-assessment as such. Moral philosophy entered his work as a continuation of politics by other means.

Grotius was educated as a humanist and knew the classical authors well. But in building a theory of how people are to live with one another, he simply ignored the way in which the ancients framed the questions of ethics. His dropping of the question of the highest good is memorable for its casual brevity. In the course of discussing the issue of the people's sovereignty, he remarked:

> Just as, in fact, there are many ways of living, one being better than another, and out of so many ways of living each is free to select that which he prefers, so also a people can select the form of government which it wishes; and the extent of its legal right in the matter is not to be measured by the superior excellence of this or that form of government, in regard to which different men hold different views, but by its free choice.[34]

Grotius here takes it for granted that there will be disagreement about ways of living, and he has no intention of entering into a debate. Our controversies with one another and their possible resolution are what engage him, and he simply assumes that these cannot be solved by discussing the individual good.

That the control of strife is for Grotius the central issue becomes plain when we look at his discussions of various laws of nature. The very first law he derives says that war is not against the law of nature. It is not so because it is in accordance with the innate tendency of each animal to try to preserve itself and its body intact. Our rational nature requires us to add that war is only just if it does not infringe on society or try to take away someone's rights. Thus, the first law provides a basis for the many ways in which conventions about limiting war can be arranged, but Grotius makes no effort to ban war. He is saying: men will fight, but the fighting can be contained within certain limits, and the point of the law of nature is to set those limits.

It is worth noticing how very different Grotius's understanding of natural law is in this respect from that found in the Thomist tradition. For Saint Thomas, as later for Richard Hooker, the universe is taken to be governed by an all-powerful and all-knowing deity who intends that the good of the whole be brought about in ways that assure the good of its parts taken separately. God includes in his care the inanimate as well as animate creation, the lower animals as well as man and other higher created beings. Hooker compresses the point into a memorable sentence: "For we see the whole world and each part thereof so compacted, that as long as each thing performeth only that work which is natural unto it, it thereby preserveth both other things and also itself."[35] God governs not by giving individual and special direction to each particular thing, but through laws. To explain his governance, the term "law" must be taken in a very broad sense. Saint Thomas tells us that law is to be defined as "an ordinance of reason for the common good, promulgated by him who has the care of the community."[36] Hooker follows him, defining law as "a directive rule unto goodness of operation"[37] and discussing without any sense of ambiguity laws that govern everything from stones to angels. The law, he says, directs things to their own perfection, but "another law there is, which toucheth them as they are sociable parts united into one body," bidding them serve the needs of other things, even at their own expense: "as we plainly see they do, when things natural in that regard forget their ordinary natural wont; that which is heavy mounting sometime upwards of its own accord . . . even as if it did hear itself commanded to let go the good it privately wisheth, and to relieve the present distress of nature in common."[38] Similarly, the angels care for both their own good and for what concerns them "as they are linked into a kind of corporation amongst themselves, and of society or fellowship with men."[39]

Grotius, by contrast, does not consider natural law to be giving us rational guidance to the perfection of our nature, nor does he see each person as a member of an essentially harmonious community with a part to play in bringing about a common good. He does think, with his predecessors, that "if the authorities issue any order that is contrary to the law of nature or to the commandments of God, the order should not be carried out."[40] But, typically, this claim is made in the context of answering whether it is permissible for those subordinate to a sovereign to wage war against him. It is not a conclusion drawn from a view about the proper natural order in the universe and its inviolability.

When Hobbes made avoiding the war of all against all the central problem for his version of natural law theory, he was showing his Grotian allegiance. The extreme to which he pushed the vision of individuals as inherently prone to conflict with one another, and the drastic remedy he proposed, made the subject inescapable for his successors. I do not mean to suggest that every modern moral philosopher saw social disharmony as the central question for his theory. Spinoza, for instance, clearly returned to the quest for the highest individual good, which Grotius and even more drastically Hobbes had rejected; and if Spinoza was largely ignored during the formative period of modern moral philosophy, there were other, more influential writers who approached morality through the problem of the highest good. Nor do I mean that everyone accepted the natural law view that conflict is ineradicable. What is true, however, is that the impact of Hobbes and even more of Pufendorf gave preeminence to the natural law understanding of morality as the solution to the question of how to sustain the sociability that we quarrelsome and unsociable creatures want and need. Even those who wished to deny that this was the central problem could not ignore it.

VI

The dominant practical problem for those who thought about politics and morality during the seventeenth century differed from the practical problems that occupied earlier theorists. The new problematic does not explain everything about the development of moral thought from that starting point to the assumptions that are common now, but it helps us understand a number of prominent features of that development's outcome—to see, that is, why modern moral philosophy came to be as it is. I will touch briefly on the points I have said are central to modern morality and its moral philosophy. I must, of course, take them separately, although they are actually intertwined.

Consider first the issue of the extent of the availability of awareness of what morality requires. Denial that such awareness is equally available to everyone is more likely to perpetuate than to confine conflict. If people are prone to controversy, then no matter what starts a quarrel—whether it concern who owns what or what religious beliefs or ceremonies are to be accepted[41]—appeal to moral norms will be useful for containing or settling it only if the norms are not seen as something that one party to the quarrel can use and the other cannot. In a society where people understand themselves as existing in potentially conflictual relations, the claim of a writer like Wolff to the authority to tell the masses how to behave must seem to be simply a covert rationale for domination. The belief that people are unalterably prone to conflict thus generates a pressure toward allowing that moral awareness must be open to everyone. And if it is to be so, the basic principle of morals must not only be simple enough for all to understand but easy enough for everyone to use. In showing how awareness of morality is generally available, Kantian and intuitional theories and the later forms of utilitarianism make sense as a response to the Grotian problematic.

The centrality of obligation, with its emphasis on what must be done regardless of its motivation, can be understood in a similar way. For the Grotian, the very existence of society will be threatened unless people respect certain minimal conditions in their interactions. A society organized around obligations and rights recognizes this truth. But a conception according to which obligations can exist only if there is some authority, human or otherwise, who can impose them is more likely to exacerbate than to settle conflict. Any understanding of God or of a secular authority may be open to challenge. And anyone may need to appeal to rights and duties to protect important interests. The obligations grounding such appeals cannot helpfully be derived from challengeable authorities perceived as partial to one party or another. In a Grotian society, obligation must be independent of sanction, as Grotius himself presciently held that it was.[42] The kind of reconstruction of the older, sanction-tied conception, which in fact occurred during the development of modern moral philosophy, represents an intelligible solution to one aspect of the problem that Grotius brought to the foreground.

Finally, the eventual acceptance of the supremacy of morality over other kinds of directive also fits into the pattern I have been sketching. This acceptance stands out most clearly, I think, if we contrast belief in the supremacy of moral norms with a very different view, articulated in radical form by Luther and Calvin but shared in essentials by Catholics. "God has ordained two governments," Luther says,

> the spiritual, which by the Holy Spirit under Christ makes Christians and pious people, and the secular, which restrains the unchristian and wicked so that they must needs keep the peace outwardly, even against their will. . . . these two kingdoms must be sharply distinguished, and both be permitted to remain; the one to produce piety, the other to bring about external peace and prevent evil deeds. . . .[43]

Modern moral philosophy eventually constructed a third realm, one where we are each governed by ourselves and where our conflicts can be adjudicated by something other than the magistrate's laws and God's commands. It is a social space that limits the authority of the magistrate as well as the demands of those who speak in the name of religion. It had to be the source of directives superior to those emanating from the other two kingdoms precisely because those directives were open to challenge in the Grotian world, and a conflict-settling body of norms had to be admitted somehow if society was to continue. What emerged as a solution to the problem was a domain of discourse in which the ruling vocabularies of justification and guidance are neither religious nor political nor prudential, but something else. They are what we now call moral.

VII

Since the work of Kant, Reid, and the post-Bentham utilitarians, moral philosophy has been concerned with the self for whose construction they supplied alternative means. Of course, the idea that the bearers of morality are fully competent moral agents conflicting as well as cooperating with one another has been frequently attacked. But that has been the idea requiring consideration by moral and political theorists, whether favorably, as in the mainstream of British and American thought, or unfavorably. I do not believe that either ancient or medieval moral thought revolved around anything like the same complex idea. Consequently, I believe that it makes sense to consider the period of the emergence, defense, and critique of this idea as constituting a distinctive epoch in Western thought about ethics.

If a new problematic and a new range of solutions to it can emerge as the focal point of discussion, they also can drop out of sight. Modern moral philosophy is the target of widespread opposition at present. Is there reason to suppose that we are coming to the end of the period whose beginning I have tried to point out? And what help can a historical grasp of modern moral philosophy give us in answering this question?

I shall begin with the second question. Effective criticism of the program of modern moral philosophy must obviously be directed at what is central or essential to it. How, then, are we to distinguish the superficial from that which matters? It is not helpful to suppose that there is an "essence" of moral philosophy, some unchanging question such as "how should one live?"[44] around which moral philosophy has always turned. That assumption obscures the kinds of differences between periods of philosophy that I have been trying to highlight. We can only determine what is and is not central by looking at history. But, from my view, what are we to look at the history of?

Of discussions, I reply, whose participants have seen themselves as linked in carrying on controversies or working out theoretical programs about issues on whose importance they agree. We see ourselves as carrying on a conversation in which Kant, Reid, and, say, Bentham were important participants, and they saw themselves as engaging the Grotians and their critics. This discussion is what constitutes modern moral philosophy, and its history must serve to show us what is superficial and what is essential in it. Without a good grasp of the history, we cannot tell whether a criticism of the enterprise is important or not.

To illustrate this claim, I shall touch briefly on a few of the recent challenges to modern moral philosophy. I do not mean to mount a comprehensive defense, but I hope my comments will round out and suggest the usefulness of the portrait of the form of moral philosophy that still engages us.

1. *The antifoundationalist criticism.* The objection is that modern moral philosophy, like its counterpart in epistemology, has been caught up in the age-old effort to find unshakable cognitive justification for some morality, and since we now see this endeavor to be futile, we must shift to something new if we propose to continue doing ethics.

No reference has been made to the search for cognitive foundations in my account of the emergence of modern moral theory because that quest, insofar as it existed, seems to come second to the effort to find some set of principles that are adequate for settling or delimiting conflict which reasonable people would have to hold in common. The standard term for the faculty that yields results everyone must accept was and is "reason"; but the importance of Hutcheson and Hume in the development of Western ethical thought should remind us that reason and cognitive foundations are not the only conceivable sources of shared moral awareness.

2. *The neglect of virtue objection.* Numerous writers, beginning with Elizabeth Anscombe in 1958,[45] have objected that modern moral philosophy is fundamentally flawed because it omits consideration of virtue and the virtues. I have argued elsewhere against this allegation.[46] But it is surely true that virtue in the Aristotelian sense as requiring something like the educated insight of the virtuous agent, incapable of being captured in rules, was granted a relatively minor place in the moral thought of the period. It is not hard to see why. If conflict between individuals, groups, or countries is the chief issue, an appeal to the inarticulate insight of a virtuous man is not going to be of much help. There will be those on both sides who claim to be virtuous; and the classical virtue theories available to seventeenth- and eighteenth-century philosophers had little or nothing to say about the kind of rational discussion that could take place between them. So it is easy to see why theorists of the early modern period might think that if morality were

wholly a matter of virtue, we would be constantly involved in shouting matches that would do nothing to settle the conflicts bound to arise.

3. *The communitarian or anti-individualist objection.* The objection is that modern moral philosophy assumes individuals who are prior to and not formed by the communities of which they are members, and that if this assumption were given up, the ties we have to one another would be seen to be more vital than the interests that separate us. The autonomous agent is only needed, so the objection goes, to counteract the falsifications of individualistic liberal psychology. In response, it must be agreed that much modern moral theory does suppose individuals who have a certain constitution regardless of their community. Like the social contract whose theory so often accompanies this kind of individualism, the abstract individual of moral philosophy is to be considered a theoretical device through which we may obtain some kind of understanding of the conflicts that in fact are so endemic to the societies in which we actually live. If the communitarian psychology or ontology of the individual is correct, it must be our communities that engender this conflict, and then either the problem remains to be solved, or the communitarian theory turns into a recommendation to change our societies so that they no longer create conflict-prone members. Aside from the feasibility of such a recommendation, there are grave questions about its desirability.

4. *Finally, the unified subject objection.* Modern moral philosophy and the liberalism with which it is often associated rest, it is said, on belief in the unified subject, a self that is separate from and able to control desires and actions. Once we show this belief to be the myth that it is, we eliminate the possibility of the kind of moral philosophy that has so far dominated modern thought.

It would take a lengthy discussion to deal adequately with this objection. Here, I can suggest only the rudiments of an answer.[47] In the case of Kant, the unified self is the free self and is indeed above and able to control desires and actions. Kant defended this view by claiming that it is the way in which we must conceive ourselves in order to understand our own moral commitments. The transcendental moral self is not a metaphysical given, prior to the moral order, but a necessary presupposition of that order. I have been suggesting throughout this essay, in fact, that the distinctive conflict-prone and morally competent individual of modern ethics was primarily constructed in response to social realities and to moral and political demands, not because of metaphysical or epistemological needs. Criticism of modern moral philosophy and the morality it has helped to create is superficial if it does not address, even if only to dismiss, the practical problems and normative pressures that led to the modern construal of the moral individual.

R. G. Collingwood long ago tried to teach us that we cannot understand past thinkers unless we know what questions they were trying to answer, and that we must not assume that their questions were the same as ours. He also held that we will not understand our own aims and achievements until we become aware of the historically specific presuppositions from which they arise. In the case of moral philosophy, it seems to me, Collingwood was right. But Collingwood offered philosophical reasons for holding that his view must be true for all philosophical issues.[48] I think we will be able to tell only by doing historical study of the issues one by one.[49]

Notes

1   I offer a fuller account in "Autonomy, Obligation and Virtue: An Overview of Kant's Moral Philosophy," in Paul Guyer, ed., *The Cambridge Companion to Kant* (Cambridge: Cambridge University Press, 1991).

2   Consider R. M. Hare's account in *Moral Thinking* (Oxford: Oxford University Press, 1981) of two levels of moral thinking, one for "proles" and one for "angels." The terminology as well as the doctrine betrays a certain unease about ordinary moral thinking.

3   *The Politics of Johannes Althusius,* trans. Frederick S. Carney (London: Eyre and Spottiswoode, 1964), 135–36.

4   Guillaume Du Vair, *The Moral Philosophy of the Stoics,* trans. Thomas James, ed. R. Kirk (New Brunswick, N.J.: Rutgers University Press, 1951) 54. Excerpts are to be found in J. B. Schneewind, ed., *Moral Philosophy from Montaigne to Kant,* 2 vols. (Cambridge: Cambridge University Press, 1990), 1: 202–14. Page references to this book, indicated as *MPMK,* are given where relevant.

5   See John Mahoney, *The Making of Moral Theology* (New York: Oxford University Press, 1987).

6   Francisco Suarez, *De Legibus ac Deo Legislatore (On Laws and God the Lawgiver),* trans. and ed. Gwladys Williams et al. (Oxford: Oxford University Press, 1944) II.vi.24; *MPMK,* 1:79.

7   Suarez, II.v.10; *MPMK* 1:75.

8   Suarez II.vii.5; *MPMK* 1:80; cf. II.viii.3, *MPMK* 1:82–83.

9   Suarez, II.vii.7; *MPMK* 1:81.

10   Suarez, II.viii.7; *MPMK* 1:84.

11   Hugo Grotius, *Law of War and Peace,* trans. Francis W. Kelsey (Oxford: The Clarendon Press, 1925) II.II.xxxi.1, 497.

12   Thomas Hobbes, *Leviathan,* ed. Richard Tuck (Cambridge: Cambridge University Press, 1991) II.29.

13   Samuel Pufendorf, *The Law of Nature and of Nations,* trans. C. H. Oldfather and W. A. Oldfather (New York: Oceana, 1964) II.iii.13, 204. For an earlier statement, see Pufendorf's *Elements of Natural Jurisprudence* (1660, 1672), trans. W. A. Oldfather (Oxford: The Clarendon Press, 1964) II.iv.1: "as human society coalesces and is preserved by the law of nature, so this is by no means the least fruit of societies already established, that, in them, through instruction from others and by its very exercise, even the duller may learn the law of nature" (240).

14   John Locke, *The Reasonableness of Christianity, Works* II.535; *MPMK* 1:194–96. There has

been a good deal of controversy about Locke's position on this point; in other writings he expressed different views.

15   B. de Spinoza, *A Treatise on Religion and Politics,* trans. A. G. Wernham (Oxford: Oxford University Press, 1958), 83; *MPMK* 1:243.

16   Christian Wolff, *Vernünftige Dedancken von der Menschen Tun und Lassen (Reasonable Thoughts About the Actions of Men)* (1720) 1733, sec. 150; *MPMK* 1:341.

17   Wolff, sec. 233; *MPMK* 1:343.

18   *Salomon Maimons Lebensgeschichte,* ed. Zwi Batscha (Frankfurt: Insel, 1984), 344–45, quoted from a memoir about Maimon published in 1801.

19   Suarez, I.iii–iv; in part in *MPMK* 1:70–73.

20   Suarez, I.xii.4; *MPMK* 1:74.

21   Suarez, II.vi.6; *MPMK* 1:76–77.

22   Suarez, II.ix.3.

23   Suarez, II.vii.7; *MPMK* 1:81.

24   Suarez, I.iii.3; *MPMK* 1:71.

25   For Pufendorf's views on obligation, see my "Pufendorf's Place in the History of Ethics," *Synthese* 72 (July 1987): esp. 143–48.

26   Locke began to break with the common view when in the second edition of the *Essay,* II.xxi.31ff., he argued that it is a present uneasiness that moves us rather than a desire for a future good. *MPMK* 1:186–89.

27   Spinoza, *Treatise on Religion and Politics,* trans. A. G. Wernham (Oxford: Oxford University Press, 1958), 240; *MPMK* 1:240.

28   Richard Price, *Review of the Principal Questions of Morals,* ed. D. D. Raphael 3d ed. (1787) (Oxford: Oxford University Press, 1948), chap. 8, 185; *MPMK* 2:600.

29   On this issue, see the complicated discussion in Suarez, II.xv.

30   On the tradition that lies behind Pufendorf's position, see Francis Oakley, *Omnipotence, Covenant, and Order* (Ithaca, N.Y.: Cornell University Press, 1984).

31   Henry Sidgwick, *The Methods of Ethics,* 7th ed (London, 1907), 106. The passage is in all editions, from the first (1874, p. 94) on. Sidgwick claims that there are two further differences between ancients and moderns. One is that the ancients assumed that rational individuals aim at their own good, while the moderns regard it as rational to have other aims (*Methods,* 91–92). The second is that the ancients thought there to be only one regulative faculty that is the faculty of Reason, and the moderns think there are two— "Universal Reason and Egoistic Reason, or Conscience and Self-love" (*Outlines of the History of Ethics* [London, 1896], 198).

32   In what follows here and in the next section, I elaborate on points on which I have touched briefly in the introduction to *MPMK* and in "The Misfortunes of Virtue," *Ethics* 101 (October 1991).

33   Grotius, I.I.i.; *MPMK* 1:96.

34   Grotius, I.III.viii.2; *MPMK* 1:102.

35   Richard Hooker, *Of the Laws of an Ecclesiastical Polity* (1594) I.ix.1. I cite from the edition by John Keble (Oxford, 1845).

36   Thomas Aquinas, *Summa Theologiae,* I.II.90.4a.

37   Hooker, I.viii.4.

38   Hooker, I.iii.5.

39   Hooker, I.iv.2; cf. I.xvi.3–4.

40   Grotius, I.IV.i.3; *MPMK* 1:102.

41   The existence of ineradicable disagreement about ecclesiological matters is as important to

Locke's overall position as is the tendency for disputes about property to threaten the possibility of social life.

42 This is the point of Grotius's famous declaration that what he has been saying—that people have rights—would have a certain degree of validity even if (what is not possible to conceive) there were no God. Rights impose obligations on others, he is saying, regardless of the existence of sanctions, divine or otherwise. Grotius, *Prolegomena,* sec. 11; *MPMK* 1:92.

43 Martin Luther, *Secular Authority: To What Extent It Should Be Obeyed,* vol. 4, *Martin Luther: Selections from His Writings,* ed. John Dillenberger (New York: Doubleday/Anchor, 1961), 370–71.

44 See Bernard Williams, *Ethics and the Limits of Philosophy* (Cambridge, Mass.: Harvard University Press, 1985), 1. This is an enduring question. But taking it as the question with which we are to be concerned blurs important distinctions.

45 Elizabeth Anscombe, "Modern Moral Philosophy," *Philosophy* 33 (1958). In 1928 Max Scheler made similar complaints about modern moral philosophy, but I doubt that he helped to stimulate the contemporary English-language debates.

46 "The Misfortunes of Virtue," *Ethics* 101 (October, 1990).

47 In what follows, I find myself in agreement with Charles Taylor, *Sources of the Self* (Cambridge, Mass.: Harvard University Press, 1989), 514. See my "The Use of Autonomy in Ethical Theory," in Thomas C. Heller, Morton Sosna, and David E. Wellberry, eds., *Reconstructing Individualism,* Stanford, Calif.: Stanford University Press, 1986), 64–75. Christine M. Korsgaard has given a much fuller interpretation of the Kantian position on this matter in "Morality as Freedom," in Y. Yovel, ed., *Kant's Practical Philosophy Reconsidered* (Kluwer: Dordrecht: Kluwer Academic Pubs., 1989), 23–48.

48 For a brief account, see R. G. Collingwood, *An Autobiography* (New York: Oxford University Press, 1939), chap. 7.

49 A somewhat different version of this essay was presented as a Gauss Seminar at Princeton University in February 1990. I have benefitted from the discussion there in preparing the present version.

George R. Lucas, Jr.

Refutation,

Narrative,

" . . . Things are as they are, and will end as they   and Engagement:
must."—Aeschylus

Three Conceptions
What sort of "history" is the "history of philosophy?" How might this history be described or
characterized? Is this history, for example, best   of the History
characterized as the record of refutation of
false views, or as the gradual accumulation of   of Philosophy
ever-greater insight into the truth? Is the sup-
posed canon of great philosophers and their views to be seen as some sort of
intellectual equivalent of a Darwinian competition for survival of, in this
case, the "best and the brightest" of Western civilization? Or does that
history constitute something else entirely? In any case, how might we go
about investigating these questions?

One way both to answer these questions and to develop a comprehensive
characterization of the history of philosophy would be to survey the views of
prominent philosophers through the ages to ascertain what it is they saw
themselves to be about, and how they viewed the activity of their predecessors. A certain circularity, of course, is inherent in this approach; for if
the history of philosophy is a Darwinian struggle of some sort, we will find
ourselves inadvertently listening only to the views of the victors in that
struggle and scanting the views of marginalized or "forgotten" philosophers
who might have seen philosophy and their own philosophical activities as
constituting something entirely different.

Bearing that limitation in mind, I suggest that the major philosophers in
the Western tradition, and those who study their activities and accomplish-
ments, seem to develop two answers to my initial set of questions, both of
which we shall consider briefly. One view of the history of philosophy is that
it is a history of refutation of past errors and mistakes. The intellectual
"Darwinian struggle," if we stick with that metaphor, is the struggle between
rival philosophical positions and their advocates. What we perceive as we
survey the history of this struggle is the successive emergence of victorious

positions—those, presumably, with a greater claim to truth or legitimacy. Examples of philosophers who saw themselves engaged in this sort of struggle—that is, in refuting rival claims that they took to be mistaken or erroneous—include Descartes as the paradigm historical case, and perhaps also Edmund Husserl, Bertrand Russell, Rudolf Carnap, and Hans Reichenbach.

What is interesting about this conception of the history of philosophy, and about this admittedly incomplete list of famous philosophers who seem to embody it, is that the most obvious examples are modern and contemporary. It is hard to locate a good example from among the ancient, Hellenistic, or medieval philosophers in Western thought who understood themselves to be "refuting" their rivals. That is in part, I will argue, because many philosophers, including most from these earlier periods, do not appear to have comprehended *philosophical activity itself* as the refutation of rival views. That is not to say, of course, that such philosophers as Aristotle or Thomas Aquinas were not interested in avoiding error and in discovering the truth; let alone am I suggesting that they did not quarrel or otherwise contend with adversaries. Rather, I mean that many prominent philosophers in the history of Western thought would not have considered characterizing the pursuit of wisdom as the sort of Darwinian contest implied in the refutationist view. Instead of "refutation," one might, in the case of Aristotle, employ words like "transformation," "sublation," or "discovery" to describe his activity. Rival views are not so much refuted and put to flight as they are gradually transformed and absorbed within an emerging and deepening historical narrative. Aristotle is the paradigm historical case of this second view, which I shall term the "narrative" view of the history of philosophy; its greatest modern exponent is Hegel, and its most profound contemporary advocate is Alasdair MacIntyre.

Both of these perspectives on, or conceptions of, what the history of philosophy itself is, however, fail to do justice to the entire sweep of that history. The examples of Aristotle and Hegel transparently indicate that not all philosophy and great philosophers can be encompassed within the refutation model. By the same token, neither Descartes, nor Carnap, nor Reichenbach could be said to have been motivated by a desire to do justice to their philosophical predecessors and opponents, or to have had as their goal the weaving of a broad, synthetic, and inclusive narrative of philosophical truth.

Concurrently, then, with my examination of the models of refutation and narrative, I propose to consider the question of the nature of the history of philosophy as among the same species as questions about the history of any discipline: e.g., what is the history of physics or chemistry the history of, or, what is the history of art, or literature, or music, the history of? In the third section, "Engagement," I will use these reflections to suggest that a comparative inquiry yields certain descriptive facts: namely, that the history of philosophy more closely resembles the history of fields or disciplines like the fine arts and literature than it does the histories of sciences like physics and chemistry—unless one embraces the intellectual anarchism of, say, a Paul Feyerabend, and goes on to argue that (despite appearances) the histories of physics and chemistry are themselves really like the histories of art, music, and literature! From a descriptive standpoint, I will suggest that the history of philosophy is, like art history, the history of successive and episodic engagements that fade more from exhaustion and lack of interest than from refutation of error. Moreover, since most of the activity and achievements of these episodes of engagement, and the individual philosophers who participate in them, do *not* find their way into any Aristotelian-Hegelian "master narrative," no matter how vast its sweep or inclusive its aims, I conclude that the history of philosophy is largely the history of loss to oblivion; in contrast to Hegel in particular, the history of philosophy seems more a record of forgetting than a record of memory and recollection.

The history of philosophy as refutation

In his book, *Connections to the World,* Arthur Danto portrays the history of philosophy in sharp contrast to both the history of science and the history of art. The history of science is progressive, at least inasmuch as successors see themselves building on and advancing the discoveries and breakthroughs of their predecessors, all directed to a common and explicitly acknowledged goal of enhancing our knowledge of the natural world. Art history is a very different sort of entity: it consists of a series of experimental episodes—of *adventures*—with only a loose connective narrative. Rather than recording progress toward a common goal, the successive episodes of art history simply exhaust themselves when the original inspirations and creative genius of the founders are gradually supplanted by imitation, stagnation, and a growing self-reflective preoccupation with the philosophical significance of the artistic movement itself. Ironically, on Danto's account, it is the growing philosophical self-consciousness of artists in a school, period, or movement that signals the movement's death. Like Hegel's "Owl of Minerva," this philosophical self-analysis spreads its wings only when the daylight of genuine artistic creativity dissolves into the dusk of self-absorption that Danto describes as "The End of Art."[1]

The history of philosophy, according to Danto, stands in sharp contrast to both of the preceding genres. Each successive episode in the chronology of the history of philosophy seems to regard itself as a completely new beginning, which appears to require a corresponding complete repudiation of everything that came before. . . . It is characteristic of the great philosophical thinker to discover that everything that went before rested on *some hopeless and fundamental mistake*. So, the past of philosophy is kept alive by the need of those who mean to advance the subject to disengage themselves from their predecessors by some *monumental refutation*.[2]

It is difficult to know just what to make of Danto's set of contrasts. Socrates, on Plato's portrayal at least, *does* (in the *Phaedo*) recount his youthful dissatisfaction with the naturalistic, antihumanistic bent of earlier Ionian and Milesian thought. His account of his subsequent and lifelong quest for self-knowledge and for a deeper understanding of the Highest Good for human life could *perhaps* be portrayed as a "monumental refutation" of his predecessors.

Danto's view of the history of philosophy, however, is unabashedly Cartesian and modernistic. Descartes provides the paradigm example of the philosopher attempting to "disengage himself from his predecessors" and repudiate past philosophical traditions in the quest for a new beginning, a "new foundation," for philosophical thought. Alasdair MacIntyre warns us, however, of a certain Cartesian deception: namely, that by uncritically and unreflectively carrying over his knowledge and use of Latin and French, not to mention a host of tacit beliefs and background convictions inherited both from his culture and from many of his philosophical teachers and mentors, Descartes inadvertently saddled modern philosophy with a highly misleading account of what he had in fact accomplished.[3] Philosophers like Descartes who seem to embody Danto's formula for the history of philosophy often present us with spurious accounts of "monumental refutations," which were in fact no such thing.

Nevertheless, Danto is surely right that philosophers like G. E. Moore, Bertrand Russell, Rudolf Carnap, and Hans Reichenbach—and in a quite different context, Edmund Husserl—all thought it plausible to follow Descartes's example. Each, that is, took pains to argue that his own thought represented a clean break from the past and a new beginning for philosophy, inasmuch as all previous philosophy had (again, in Danto's words) "rested upon a mistake." Each philosopher saw the past history of philosophy as, in some sense, a prehistory of pseudophilosophy, a deplorable record of what Hans Reichenbach termed "systems of naive generalizations and analogies."[4] What matters, from *this* view of the history of philosophy, is the solipsism of the present moment, the now—together with the future "golden age" of true philosophical insight that the present, unfettered by the past, will soon usher into being. This, I shall suggest in the chapter's summary section, portrays philosophy itself as eschatology.

Narrative, historicism, and the history of science

Danto's Cartesian account of the history of philosophy as a sequence of "monumental refutations" simply does not exhaust the myriad different attitudes toward this history displayed in what Diogenes Laertius first termed the "Lives and Opinions" of prominent philosophers. Danto's account clashes perhaps most strongly with that of Leo Strauss, for whom philosophy in its history is finally indistinguishable from the entirety of the record of insights and achievements won by the greatest minds of our civilization—scientists, poets, mathematicians, artists, philosophers, composers, and litterateurs—as a result of their continual attempts in each generation to see beyond the contingencies of particular historical moments to a vision truth that persists despite the vagaries of history and culture.

Specifically, it is perverse, Strauss maintained, to presuppose that those who follow in the course of that history *necessarily* possess more detailed understanding or greater insight into a previous thinker's position on some perennial question than that thinker did himself. Neither are we entitled to presuppose that later positions on the perennial "problem" in question are inherently privileged over earlier positions simply by claiming to include those earlier contributions. Such reasoning is the hallmark of what Strauss defined as "historicism,"[5] the arrogant attempt to dismiss past philosophy as merely a cultural artifact, as "historically conditioned."

Danto's account of the history of philosophy as "refutation," according to Strauss, is thus dead wrong. With regard to the differing positions of Plato, Hobbes, and Rousseau on justice, for example, the history of philosophy "does not teach us that the political philosophies of the past refute each other. It teaches us merely that they contradict each other. It confronts us then with the philosophic question as to which of two given contradictory theses concerning political fundamentals is true."[6] Strauss's Platonism, in which the study of classic texts affords an ascent to a realm of timeless truth, is thus hostile to the eschatological triumphalism embedded in the positions of Descartes, Reichenbach, and Husserl. To adopt such a view of the history of philosophy is to trivialize and undervalue the truth, and the timeless contributions to truth made by the great figures in the history of our culture.

Danto's portrayal of the history of philosophy also fails, however, to encompass a number of perspectives to which Straussians themselves are often hostile. For example, from Aristotle through Aquinas to Hegel, one can trace a line of philosophical authors for whom the history of philosophy is understood to represent a kind of progressively greater insight into the nature of things, more along the lines of Danto's (unabashedly unreconstructed, pre-Kuhnian) view of the history of science. The truth, as Hegel observed, requires more than a mere understanding of the whole. "Truth" also entails a rational understanding of the historical process by which what is actual came to be just *what* it is, instead of something else. To paraphrase the *Rechtsphilosophie*: What is historically actual can always be given a rational narrative—a description of episodes, each of which traces the interaction of human purposive agency and historically contingent events sufficiently enough for us to understand what took place, and why.

This, in turn, should be understood as a more positive interpretation of precisely that "historicist" approach to the history of philosophy that Strauss intended to repudiate. Advocating the logic of that historicist position, Charles Taylor suggests that the truth of an idea lies in its genesis and in an understanding of its historical development.[7] Such understandings, finally, emphasize historical continuity: the Hegelian *Aufhebung* is not literally a negation or rejection, but a superseding of the past moment—a "sublation" that is at once a temporal transcendence of the past and simultaneously an inclusion of it. Since the philosopher's past is literally enfolded in each present philosophical position, there can be no such thing as a "clean break," a "new beginning," or a monumental refutation of what has gone before.

Richard Rorty argues that the historicist's philosophical use of the history of philosophy—what he terms, after Hegel, *Geistesgeschichte*—is really aimed at a kind of self-justification or legitimation of the philosophical concerns and outlook of the author of that history.[8] On Rorty's account, we must understand that philosophers like Hegel, R. G. Collingwood, and perhaps Alasdair MacIntyre are, through a reweaving of the philosophical-historical narrative, attempting to provide a warrant, a rational justification, and a satisfactory explanation of their own concerns and philosophical points of view through an appeal to history.

This remains the case, even in the decidedly pessimistic and antiprogressive narrative accounts of philosophers like Augustine, Vico, and Nietzsche. Each of these philosophers reads the history of philosophy as the dismal record of descent from an age of innocence or nobility into subsequent ages of decay, barbarism, and nihilism. Pessimistic narratives, unlike their neo-Hegelian progressive counterparts, however, seem to entail a certain disengagement from history through the claim, not only that all past philosophy, but all recent and contemporary culture (again, in Danto's words), "rests on a mistake." Nevertheless, neither progressive nor pessimistic *geistesgeschicht-*

liche narratives entail anything like Danto's Cartesian project of refutation or outright rejection of the value of the past.

Rorty's account of *Geistesgeschichte* in fact offers a paradigm case of "edifying conversation": the revelation and clarification of a philosopher's (or a culture's) ideological stance. That stance, however, is by nature radically subjectivized and relativized; it utterly lacks transcendental or cross-cultural resources for evaluating its adequacy; and it is subject to being found incommensurable with, and possibly even unintelligible from, the standpoints of its various rivals.

In contrast to Rorty's strict limitations on the scope of the narrative genre, however, Alasdair MacIntyre's most recent analysis of the structure of narratives in both the history of philosophy and the history of science attempts to adjudicate this issue and to find a middle ground between Strauss's substantive view of philosophical truth and the implied relativism of historicist accounts. MacIntyre strongly suggests, against Rorty, that there *are* norms and substantive criteria of truth that can apply to and adjudicate between competing narrative justifications. Using Aquinas's interpretation of Aristotle's *Posterior Analytics* as a starting point, MacIntyre argues that—even without Strauss's imperialistic notion of "timeless, transcendental, and absolute Truth"—one can adjudicate both rationally and cross-culturally between competing, and even seemingly incommensurable, narrative accounts of scientific and philosophical phenomena.

The superior historical narrative in science or in philosophy (on the MacIntyre-Thomas reading of Aristotle) is that narrative which can plausibly represent itself as a cumulative final state of perfected understanding by "specifying, in part at least, the relationships between prior states of imperfect and partial understanding and that final state."[9] That is, the "true" narrative engages all of its rivals and historically prior accounts, demonstrating thoroughly what each rival account entails, why its adherents would have come to hold it, and what problems or issues it addresses successfully—together with the salient issues or problems that the rival narrative is *unable* to account for, and why. The truth of a narrative is thus contingent on its ability at any historical juncture to encompass all major previous and rival points of view in this manner. This, in turn, implies that the "true" narrative account is always a "master narrative"—a totalizing or summarizing account that reveals its rivals and its predecessors as constituting a nested set of partial narratives converging toward the master narrative itself. Against Strauss's reliance on Plato and Rorty's reliance (in this instance) on Hegel, MacIntyre holds that Aristotle provides paradigmatic instances of this teleological narrative method in science and philosophy in his treatment of rival conceptions of the *summum bonum* in Book I of the *Nicomachean Ethics,* as well as in his historical account of causal explanation in Book *Alpha* of the *Metaphysics.*[10]

In contrast to Kuhn's thesis regarding the incommensurability of rival paradigms in the history of science, moreover, MacIntyre argues that the same teleological nested-narrative structure is revealed in the triumph of, say, relativistic cosmology and quantum mechanics over Newtonianism. Each of these newest "master narratives" in physics, that is to say, is believed to be "true" by practicing physicists insofar as each offers a fully intelligible account both of classical Newtonian successes in their respective branches of physics *and* of its shortcomings. By contrast, no such comprehensive account can be offered from the standpoint of Newtonianism, which can account only for its successes and *ex hypothesi* for the failures and shortcomings of its own historical predecessors and rivals—but not for its *own* current shortcomings and failures (which are simply unintelligible in its own terms), and certainly not for its rivals in the form of relativistic cosmology or quantum mechanics.

Such all-encompassing historical narratives do not merely constitute a "rational justification" from the point of view of the new theories, but in fact provide a demonstration both of their continuity and commensurability with the old theory, and of their explanatory narrative superiority to it. Furthermore, as this example illustrates, future theories or scientific paradigms will supplant present ones, not arbitrarily, but only by in turn demonstrating *their* teleological narrative superiority (and hence, greater claim to truth) to presently reigning theories and paradigms, using precisely the same Aristotelian criteria outlined above. As the narrative structure is the essential component of any scientific revolution, MacIntyre concludes, the longstanding incommensurability debate is largely obviated, and science as well as philosophy is revealed as *essentially,* rather than contingently, historical and narrative in character.[11]

Engagement: the history of philosophy and the history of art

MacIntyre successfully formulates a second defensible philosophy of the history of philosophy—one that (remarkably) preserves the strongest insights of historicists like Hegel, Rorty, and Taylor, on the one hand, and the Straussian antirelativist commitment to a substantive theory of truth in the history of philosophy, on the other. History is neither denigrated and forgotten, nor is it limited to what is being accomplished in the present. Instead, the history of philosophy serves as potential, as the material cause of present philosophical views. Finally, MacIntyre's Aristotelian account of the role of historical narrative in science offers a new avenue around the long-standing incommensurability debate in the epistemology of science.

These are impressive achievements. Surprisingly, however, there remain wide areas and aspects of the history of philosophy that MacIntyre's heroic enterprise fails to encompass—and in so failing, likewise fails, on MacIntyre's own terms, as an adequate "master narrative."

I thus come to another, final exception to Danto's Cartesian account of the history of philosophy. John Dewey once observed that a philosophical position is never so much *refuted* as simply *abandoned*. And, indeed, a historical record of almost casual abandonment in a quite undramatic sense defines the topography of the recent past, as well as of the more remote past, in the history of philosophy.

Whatever became, one might ask, of early twentieth-century metaphysical versions of neo- or critical realism in America, or its counterpart, sense-data theory, in Great Britain?[12] Who reads the evolutionary cosmology of Herbert Spencer, or of Spencer's American popularizer, John Fiske, anymore, apart from a handful of scholars whose motivation is fairly described as purely antiquarian? In this vein, whatever became of the *Microcosmus* of Hermann Lotze? At the beginning of the twentieth century, Lotze was the most widely read and discussed philosopher on the European scene. Are there any personal idealists left on that scene? And lest I seem merely to be picking on what Rorty labels "weakened forms of idealism,"[13] whatever happened to ordinary language philosophy, which H. H. Price described as recently as 1964 as "this potent and formidable deity which now rules the philosophic world?"[14]

Such movements, and countless others like them, were never even accorded the dignity of a decent burial in the form of solid refutation, nor can we claim for most of them the questionable fate of having been "*Aufhebung-ized*" into some narrative Absolute. Far better, it might seem, to have your philosophical position examined and refuted, or else forcibly annexed and transformed within some imperialistic, Hegelian master narrative, than to suffer the even greater humiliation of simply fading away, like an old soldier, from philosophical consciousness into footnote immortality.

In a similar vein, what accounts for the oscillations among what Stephen Pepper identified as "the relatively-adequate [metaphysical] world hypotheses" in a culture like our own, when evidence, data, and the testimony of common experience cannot decide the issue or adjudicate between rival metaphysical claims?[15] Some of these hypotheses—e.g., animism or mysticism—lack (on Pepper's account) a discernible "root metaphor" in our culture, and so they never seem to take hold or catch on among us, despite the fact that these views richly inform and interpret the lives and experiences of countless "rational" human beings in other cultures. This irreducible plurality is troubling enough for the logocentric philosophies of the history of philosophy encountered above.

Why is it also the case, for example, that a single, relatively stable culture in the course of only a few years will first come to hold an idealistic or organicist metaphysical position, and just as suddenly abandon it in favor of a revival of some new form of mechanistic materialism? Such a dramatic transition (Danto would call it a "monumental refutation") is exactly what transpired in Anglo-American philosophy earlier in this century. Followers of the victorious philosophical trend, of course, try to argue that it *is* precisely evidence and logical argument that force such transitions. But this is patently false; evidence and argument play a rhetorical role in establishing the current reign of any given metaphysical fashion. It seems, rather, that after a time, no one is any longer interested in defending the earlier view, or in believing the arguments that once allowed it to prevail, no matter what the evidence or "compelling force" of logic.

Many proponents of the progressive refutationist view of philosophy insist on comparing the history of philosophy with the history of the natural sciences. In the present instance, however, such comparisons suggest that the history of philosophy is parallel in many respects to an anarchistic, antirationalist account of the history of science. According to Paul Feyerabend, for example, scientific theories rise to prominence and then fade from the scene (as did their predecessors) more as a function of "prejudice, conceit, [and] passion"[16] than of their rational or explanatory comprehensiveness. Luck, passion, and the cooling of passion and loss of interest—not logic or falsification—form the warp and woof of the history of science.

Likewise on my account of philosophy's history: philosophers propose their views with an inordinate, even arrogant degree of pomp and circumstance; but history disposes rather unceremoniously of all save a few. The vast majority of these philosophical systems, theories, and movements are never refuted or torn down, nor are they rewoven into some more recent narrative perspective. Rather, they are simply abandoned, like old, unserviceable buildings. Their foundations gradually disappear beneath the debris of subsequent intellectual history unless and until some philosophical archaeologist spades them up again for his own purposes, or stumbles across them warehoused in a library or museum.[17]

My perspective on the history of philosophy (like Feyerabend's perspective on the history of science) is strikingly similar to Danto's portrayal, *not* of the history of philosophy, but rather of the history of art. Like the history of art, the history of philosophy records a series of inconclusive episodes, each exhibiting a common internal structure ranging from brilliant insight and originality to widespread interest and popularity, leading invariably to the kind of stagnation associated with imitative discipleship, scholasticism, and dogmatism, which lead in turn to decay and disinterest.

In *The Ancients and the Moderns*, Stanley Rosen suggests that "modern philosophy begins with an attempt to . . . justify passion."[18] The ancients, by contrast, were passionate in their pursuit of wisdom. My proposed philosophy of the history of philosophy particularly pursues this ancient insight that Rosen emphasizes: namely, all philosophical perspectives or movements, ancient or modern, must be understood as being born in eros, in the passionate interest and engagement of their founders, rather than in the quest for certainty. Socrates, for example, was never *certain* of anything; he decided to abandon Ionian and Milesian *Naturphilosophie* because he found the subject barren and uninteresting; he was passionately engaged in the quest for wisdom as self-knowledge.[19] Thus, philosophical movements perish when it simply becomes the case that no one any longer cares about the issues or problems they address. If "care" [*Sorge*] is the "Being of *Dasein*," as Heidegger remarked, it is all the more the "being" and lifeblood of philosophical systems and authors. The Owl of Minerva takes its flight from the reigning movements in both art and philosophy in the *absence* of care.[20]

Summary: philosophy and art, music, literature

No one of the preceding perspectives alone can claim to be fully representative of the history of philosophy; philosophers and philosophical movements were cited to illustrate all three of the positions described. However, each of these three philosophical perspectives on the *history* of philosophy in turn defines and attempts to legitimate a specific attitude toward philosophy itself. And it is here, in their respective "philosophies of *philosophy*," that disturbing and incompatible differences become apparent.

1. Danto's "mistakes and refutation" version illustrates the tendency of some philosophers to disassociate from and denigrate the history of philosophy and to engage in what Gilbert Ryle used to call "philosophy without footnotes." Those like Carnap, Russell, and Reichenbach who sincerely embodied this view did tend to denigrate and to misunderstand the history of philosophy. Theirs was a report card vision of history, determining, from a privileged (some would say, presumptuous) perspective, just who "got it right." Reichenbach's portrayal of the history of philosophy, for example, as a series of "pseudo-scientific answers" and "naive generalizations and analogies" amounts to a triumphalist eschatology: he engages in the naive glorification of what is being accomplished in the present, and what is to be

achieved in the future, at the expense of what has been achieved in the past. This kind of philosophical eschatology, so prevalent in this century, constitutes nihilism in Rosen's sense: a wholesale repudiation of the past "on behalf of some unknown and unknowable yet hoped for future."[21] Like disillusioned followers of some religious millenialist, philosophers are just now beginning to disabuse themselves of a century of disappointed eschatological expectations for their profession that originated with this view of their history.

2. In MacIntyre's radical revision of Rorty's *Geistesgeschichte* version, by contrast, history is canonized. Philosophy *is* its history, and present philosophical episodes of that history simply represent persistent attempts to weave and reweave the fabric of the past into a suitable garment for the present. According to this view, the past, literally enfolded narratively within each present moment or episode of history, constitutes the material condition and cause of present historical perspectives. And, in keeping with older views on the progressive and cumulative character of scientific knowledge, this view of the history of philosophy stresses continuity, rather than incommensurability, with the past. The history of philosophy is literally (in the words of Hans-Georg Gadamer) "that conversation which we are."

Yet, with the passing of millenia, that cultural conversation (like the lengthening chain of Marley's ghost) becomes increasingly burdensome—and increasingly hegemonic. Who, for example, is permitted to participate in this conversation—and on what terms? Deconstructionists, together with feminist and ethnic voices from the margins of authoritative traditions, often complain (in paraphrase of MacIntyre himself): Whose history? Whose tradition? The history of philosophy on this second perspective threatens to issue in a totalitarian suppression of *la differance,* while the "master narrative" comes to represent the deadened oppressive weight of a thoroughly contingent and wholly unrepresentative past—logocentric, Eurocentric, onto-theocentric, phallocentric. Such a view of philosophy and its history perennially threatens to constrain the present and future to mere reiteration and permutation of the prior achievements of the past, devoid of freedom, with no opportunity for novel development or for intellectual liberation.

3. The aesthetic perspective on the history of philosophy that I propose takes sharp exception to Husserl's denigration of *Weltanschauungen,* and it sides with Nietzsche and with Stanley Rosen's portrayal of Plato and the ancients, holding that philosophy begins in eros as a kind of divine passion.[22] Philosophical positions are never taken up or abandoned because they are, or cease to be, logically compelling. Rather, the life and death of a philosophical movement in history lies wholly in its ability to arouse the passionate interest or to compel the authentic engagement of adherents.

Here, I am in closer agreement with Danto in *Connections:* philosophical views are oddities; they are not, like scientific views, natural kinds standing in experiential opposition to one another. Rather, they are (as a physicist would say) orthogonal to the world and its objects and states of affairs. The question is "whether philosophy is knowledge after all, if there is such a thing as philosophical truth—or whether, instead, philosophy is like a mood, a coloration of the whole of reality . . . [rather than] a separable part of the world."[23]

If philosophy is truly like this, we would expect many more instances of genuine incommensurability between rival philosophical views than MacIntyre's narrative account of the history of science, as applied to the history of *philosophy,* would permit.[24] Indeed, from the standpoint I have outlined, such MacIntyrian "master narratives" may amount to little more than Aristotelian *phantasia,* imaginative stories destined to be replaced by others utterly unlike them. Moreover, no reasons or arguments suffice finally to account for such a replacement, or for why a philosophy or philosopher "catches on," let alone why people subsequently lose interest. They just do.

Despite the long-standing desire of analytic philosophers to draw an analogy between philosophy as properly practiced and the progress of natural science, there is nothing like the kind of "progress" in philosophical positions, let alone on philosophic truth, that this analogy in Danto's "mistakes and refutation" version requires. Whatever sort of discipline it is taken to be, philosophy is simply not the sort of thing that "makes a difference" in the world in the way that the succession of scientific views does.

My account, instead, invites closer comparisons of philosophy and its history with art and art history, music and music history, and literature and its history. In all of these instances, the history of the field is integral to the field—constitutive, without serving as constraining canon. Each area of concern is unthinkable apart from its history, which serves as the principal source of inspiration, but not of confinement. Most significantly, one cannot be argued into or out of some position in that history. Historical transitions in philosophy, as in art or music, occur on the basis of interest and engagement; they are not compelled by logic. It is useless to argue with an individual who is no longer interested in a philosophical movement that he or she should become interested once again. Such preoccupations with self-understanding, apologetics, and angry justification spell the end of philosophy as surely as they spell, on Danto's account, the end of art.

Rorty, in *Philosophy and the Mirror of Nature,* makes "interest" a category for the analysis of historical transitions in philosophy.[25] There is a large difference, however, between what he calls "interest" as an expression of cultural or ideological fashion, on one hand, and the *daimon* of Socrates, the eros of Plato, the *thauma* [wonder] of Aristotle, or, for that matter, the divine madness of Nietzsche or Van Gogh, on the other. Against the postmodern notion of interest as purely relative fashion and passing fancy, my perspective proposes Rosen's category of eros, or passionate engagement, as the motivation for historical transitions in philosophy, as in art, music, or literature—and as the understanding of *philosophy itself* that is to be derived from these observations.

Finally, it is also the case that my perspective on the history of philosophy happens to correspond more closely than does any of its rivals to *how* that history has, in fact, largely transpired. This small historical detail ought not to go unnoticed. It is simply false, because incomplete, that *all* philosophy and philosophers are encompassed as instances of refutation, as it is likewise simply and obviously false that *all,* or even very many, philosophers and their philosophies survive in one or another subsequent narrative philosopher's master narrative. Both of these conceptions of the history of philosophy, paradoxically, function by leaving out most of that history. By contrast, the concept of the history of philosophy as episodic engagement provides, in principle, an account of and a role for every philosopher, whether trivial or profound, and likewise accounts for and gives the larger explanation of the "real" significance of those great philosophers who thought themselves to be engaged either in acts of refutation or of narrative historical recollection. Ironically, then, this third conception of the history of philosophy succeeds on MacIntyre's stated terms, where his own narrative account fails on those terms: namely, the "engagement" hypothesis accounts for all relevant historical facts, including all of *its* rivals, while they are unable to account for it. The engagement view also explains why some philosophers might have (mistakenly) thought themselves to be involved in refutation or narrative recollection, why it would be reasonable for them to think this, but what was wrong with these beliefs, and why.

If "engagement" is the most adequate descriptive characterization for the history of philosophy, as I believe it is, then a number of disturbing conclusions follow. First, this fact about philosophy's history threatens to become one more article in the ongoing "death of philosophy" discussion, since, if true, this characterization of philosophy's history leaves the activity of philosophy itself considerably humbled and without a discernible *telos*. That is, if the history of philosophy is refutation or narrative recollection, then I, as a philosopher, *know* what it is to "do" philosophy and how to go about it—either refuting error and false positions, or patiently weaving the ever-more-inclusive narrative. By contrast, apart from humility and a sense of profound loss and futility, what activity is specified for the philosopher who comes to realize that the history of past philosophical activity is defined by the series: passionate engagement, waning of interest, loss, and forgetting?

Here, I might editorialize that I do not mourn the loss of the *telos* provided by the refutation model. The practitioners of that model have never impressed me. I find their conception of philosophical activity vain, presumptuous, destructive, and wholly unproductive. We are well rid of it. I do, however, mourn the threatened loss of the Aristotle-Hegel-MacIntyre conception of narrative recollection. If one were to ask me, "what do you think philosophers ought properly to be about, normatively speaking?" I would reply that philosophy ought best to be conceived as the humble and painstaking activity, the sensitive, open, and inclusive activity that MacIntyre describes.

Unfortunately, on the conception of the history of philosophy that I find to be descriptively correct, the history of philosophy is the history—not of Hegelian recollection and memory—but of forgetting, and of loss to oblivion. Likewise, the emergence of a "canon" of history's most significant philosophies and philosophers—what Richard Rorty sneeringly dismisses as the "doxography" of great white dead males—is less the result of some presumed triumph of greatness than it is a measure of the loss of richness and diversity that constitute philosophical engagement in any historical epoch. This recognition, and the role to which it consigns virtually all of us who engage in the activity of philosophy, is perhaps the most profoundly humbling and troubling aspect of this last conception of philosophy's history.[26] But this does seem to be the case, as it is an accurate assessment of our own fate. Artists, poets, and musicians, however, do not paint, write, or compose for posterity. Presumably, they do so because the activities in question are intrinsically satisfying and worthwhile—and, in any case, because they find that they cannot do otherwise. If this hard lesson is learned by philosophers, perhaps philosophy itself will once again become an activity that is intrinsically satisfying, rather than an activity pursued, as it often is at present, for reasons of celebrity and vanity. That, I believe, could not but be a good thing.

Notes

1   The comparison with Hegel is no accident but has become central to Danto's controversial thesis concerning the "end" of art. See "Art, Evolution, and the Consciousness of History" and "The End of Art," 187–210 and 81–115, respectively in *The Philosophical Disenfranchisement of Art* (New York: Columbia University Press, 1986). Hans-Georg Gadamer makes a similar point when discussing "the hundred-eyed argosy that in Hegel's apt words

is presented by art," which, when integrated into our self-understanding, "is no longer art but philosophy." See *Reason in the Age of Science,* trans. Frederick G. Lawrence (Cambridge, Mass.: MIT Press, 1981), 19.

2   Arthur C. Danto, *Connections to the World* (New York: Harper and Row, 1989), 3 (my emphases).

3   See Alasdair MacIntyre, "Epistemological Crises, Dramatic Narrative, and the Philosophy of Science," *The Monist,* 60 (October 1977): 458 ff.

4   Hans Reichenbach, *The Rise of Scientific Philosophy* (Berkeley: University of California Press, 1951), 121.

5   E.g., in Leo Strauss, "On Collingwood's Philosophy of History," *Review of Metaphysics* 5, no. 4 (June 1952): 585–86.

6   Leo Strauss, *What Is Political Philosophy?* (New York: Free Press, 1959), 60–61.

7   Charles Taylor, "Philosophy and Its History," in Richard Rorty, J. B. Schneewind, and Quentin Skinner, eds., *Philosophy in History* (Cambridge: Cambridge University Press, 1984), esp. 20–25.

8   "The Historiography of Philosophy: Four Genres," in Rorty et al., eds., *Philosophy in History,* 56–61. *Geistesgeschichte* depends to a large extent on two other genres that Rorty identifies: (1) historical reconstruction (e.g., Margaret Wilson on Descartes, or Charles Taylor on Hegel; the attempt to read and interpret a text or figure on its own terms in proper historical context); and (2) rational reconstruction (e.g., Jonathan Bennett on Spinoza, or Keith Lehrer on Thomas Reid; the process of trying to translate, without undue anachronism, the salient thoughts of a past philosopher into our own idiom). All three genres are legitimate, in Rorty's view, as distinguished from "doxography," the reverential, bloodless, and uninsightful rehearsal of the received canon of great men and their ideas.

9   *First Principles, Final Ends, and Contemporary Philosophical Issues,* The Aquinas Lecture, 1990 (Milwaukee: Marquette University Press, 1990), 25. MacIntyre cites and makes use of Jonathan Barnes's proposal to reconcile the differences in scientific method between what is set forth in the *Posterior Analytics* and what is actually practiced in the *Physics* and the biological treatises. According to Barnes, the *Posterior Analytics* is concerned with the *demonstration* of cumulative, acquired knowledge: the work instructs its readers on how to exhibit and teach knowledge already acquired, not on how to obtain knowledge. Jonathan Barnes, "Aristotle's Theory of Demonstration," in J. Barnes, M. Schofield, and R. Sorabji, eds., *Articles on Aristotle* (London: Duckworth, 1975), vol. 1.

10   *After Virtue* (Notre Dame, Ind.: University of Notre Dame Press, 1984) seems to focus on cultural and historical relativism and incommensurability. The subsequent arguments on this issue in *Whose Justice? Which Rationality?* (Notre Dame, Ind.: University of Notre Dame Press, 1988) are sufficiently unclear as to mislead Martha Nussbaum in a review of this work to accuse MacIntyre of having "Recoiled from Reason" in favor of a notion of social order and cohesiveness derived from Thomistic piety (*New York Review of Books,* December 7, 1989, 36–41). MacIntyre was in fact proposing to abandon not reason itself, but the relativistic notion of mere "rational justification" in favor of this revised criterion of "narrative truth" suggested by Aristotle, and noted approvingly by Thomas. The issue is admittedly complex, and MacIntyre's argument is set forth somewhat more clearly in his recent Gifford Lectures, *Three Rival Versions of Moral Enquiry* (Notre Dame, Ind.: University of Notre Dame Press, 1990); and in *First Principles, Final Ends, and Contemporary Philosophical Issues,* from which the preceding account is largely derived.

11   In addition to the works above, see "The Relationship of Philosophy to Its Past," in Rorty et

al., eds., *Philosophy in History,* 31–48, and "Epistemological Crises," 453–72, in which the positions on Kuhn, incommensurability, and the history and philosophy of science are explicitly developed.

12   Readers interested in finding out what happened to early realism and a host of similar, widely popular philosophical movements in the United States and Great Britain around the turn of the century will find their obituaries chronicled in greater detail in G. R. Lucas, *The Rehabilitation of Whitehead: An Analytic and Historical Assessment of Process Philosophy* (Albany: The State University of New York Press, 1989), chap. 3; and in G. R. Lucas, *The Genesis of Modern Process Thought: An Historical Outline with Bibliography* (London: Scarecrow Press, 1983), chap. 4.

13   The phrase occurs in the conclusion of *The Consequences of Pragmatism* (Minneapolis: University of Minnesota Press, 1982), 214.

14   H. H. Price, "Appearing and Appearances," *American Philosophical Quarterly* 1 (1964): 3–19; quote at 7.

15   Pepper identifies some six metaphysical worldviews, or "world hypotheses," each of which is consistent with evidence and common experience of one sort or another and all of which exhibit underlying root metaphors that interpret and organize these data and experiences. Argument cannot finally decide between them. See Stephen Pepper, *World Hypotheses* (Berkeley: University of California Press, 1942).

16   Paul Feyerabend, *Against Method: Outline of an Anarchistic Theory of Knowledge* (Atlantic Heights, N.J.: Humanities Press, 1975), 175: "science is much more 'sloppy' and 'irrational' [in its history] than its methodological image [would suggest] . . . the difference between science and methodology *which is such an obvious fact of [its] history* indicates a weakness of the latter, and perhaps of the 'laws of reason' as well . . . ideas which today form the very basis of science exist only because there were such things as prejudice, conceit, passion; because these things *opposed reason;* and because they *were permitted to have their way.*"

See also the role of "attitudes" in the rise and fall of Aristotelian physics, in *Science in a Free Society* (London: NLB, 1978), 53–70. E.g., at 60, Feyerabend argues in effect that radical shifts in scientific worldview occur in history "because certain *changes of attitude* had also taken place . . . [which were] partly nonintellectual reactions to new historical circumstances." He disputes the role of logic, argument, demonstration, and "proof" in effecting such changes in attitude.

17   In analogy with Ian Hacking's revealing account of the "rediscovery" of Dresden porcelain, "Five Parables," in Rorty et al., eds., *Philosophy in History,* 104ff.

18   Stanley Rosen, *The Ancients and the Moderns* (New Haven, Conn.: Yale University Press, 1989), 14.

19   I am obviously deeply indebted to the discussion of eros as the origin of philosophy, and as the distinction between the ancients and the moderns, interspersed through Stanley Rosen's brilliant work, *Hermeneutics as Politics* (New York: Oxford University Press, 1987), e.g., the distinction between the "madness" of Socrates and Derrida, 75–77; see also 47, 60ff.

20   There is an untraceable sense in which this perspective on the history of philosophy is deeply indebted to George Allen's beautifully written *The Importances of the Past* (Albany: State University of New York Press, 1986).

21   Stanley Rosen, *Nihilism: A Philosophical Essay* (New Haven, Conn.: Yale University Press, 1969), 140. The reasoning that Rosen denounces here also constitutes an example of what George L. Kline identifies as the "fallacy of the actual future" endemic to religious millenialists and Marxist intellectuals alike; see Kline's presidential address for the 1986

annual meeting of the Metaphysical Society of America, "Present, Past, and Future of Categorical Terms," *Review of Metaphysics* 40, no. 2 (December 1986), 215–35. I am applying such categories to contemporary philosophers.

22   Rosen, *Hermeneutics as Politics,* chap. 5, sec. 2.

23   Danto cites James, rather than Dewey, as the source of this insight. But the views advanced are similar to my own. See *Connections to the World,* 11–13.

24   Feyerabend's cynical portrayal of the "shrinking imagined context" of allegedly refuted scientific theories also challenges the adequacy of MacIntyre's Aristotelian account of commensurability in the triumphant master narratives forming the history of science. See *Against Method,* chap. 15.

25   E.g., *Philosophy and the Mirror of Nature* (Princeton, N.J.: Princeton University Press, 1979), 351. He expands on this motif, calling attention explicitly for the first time to the comparison of philosophy and poetry, in "From Logic to Language to Play," *Proceedings and Addresses of the American Philosophical Association,* 59 (1986), 752.

26   In his detailed commentary in response to an earlier draft of this essay presented at the Pacific Division meeting of the American Philosophical Association on March 29, 1991, in San Francisco, John Dupre of Stanford University helpfully remarked on what he took to be my own "Darwinian" characterization of the history of philosophy as subsuming the rival perspectives on that history discussed here. In his own words: "Each generation spawns an array of philosophical positions, most of which leave no philosophical descendants and are of interest only to the philosophical palaeontologist. The mechanism of selection [according to Lucas] is the passion of the following generation. Those positions which succeed in inspiring such passion are taken up and developed or, at least, refuted. Presumably the latter is also a kind of inheritance, though with a more Freudian twist. The Dantoesque radicals can be seen as macromutations or hopeful monsters; like their biological counterparts, most fail dismally. Clearly an evolutionary view gives a very central role to history. The ancestry of an idea, revealing which of the ideas of the past succeeded in inspiring the passion of future generations and became embedded in future philosophical positions, would be a fundamental fact about it. And questions about the selection process, about what makes some ideas survive while most die, would be of great importance." The final question Dupre cites is of the species often raised by contributors to this volume: e.g., Jerome Schneewind's question for the history of ethics, "why and how did the idea of individual moral autonomy come to occupy a central role in modern moral philosophy?" In addition to this important philosophical cross-examination of intellectual history, however, I am attempting to call attention to that history as primarily loss and forgetting, rather than recollection. I am arguing that the philosophical writing of the history of philosophy must encompass an account, and the point of view of history's victims, as well as its victors, in what Dupre is characterizing as this Darwinian struggle for survival.

Part III

Perspectives

on the

Significance

of Cultural

Memory

Arthur C. Danto

The Shape of

Artistic Pasts:

East and West

In the Robert Ellsworth Collection of Nineteenth and Twentieth Century Chinese Art at the Metropolitan Museum in New York, there is an affecting work by Wan Shang-Lin (1739–1813), who, as a landscape painter, is said (in the neutral prose of this collection's spectacular catalog) "to have been influenced by Ni Tsan [1301–1374]."

The image on Wan's scroll is of a monk in a somewhat austere landscape, identified as Lung-men; but, as we know from the inscription, the image itself is less about its pictorial subject—the Lung-men monk—than it is about a painting of that subject by Ni Tsan, which Wan may or may not have seen. It is intended for an audience that, in effect, can compare Wan's image with a recollected or imagined original—or that, in any case, knows enough about the work of Ni Tsan to be able to make comparisons.

The inscription itself exhibits a vigor singular by contrast with the rather pale and diffident image composed of trees, rocks, and the isolated itinerant. And though in no sense a student of calligraphy, I feel confident that the difference in stylistic address is intentional and meant to be appreciated as such: the disparity between writing and drawing exhibits that difference in affect between memory and waking perception that Hume identifies as a gradedness in vivacity. There is a tentative fadedness in the image, as if dimly recalled. This interpretation, of course, must be mooted by the fact that Ni Tsan's own style, in which strokes have the watery feel of washes, was itself intended to leave unresolved the question of whether the landscapes he was so fond of painting were themselves perceived or dreamt. They are almost languorous in consequence of this mood, which seeks to make as vividly as the subject allows the palpable undecidability of illusion and reality—after all, the question a monk might himself raise regarding the landscape through which he makes his meditative transit. Here is a poem a propos by Ni Tsan himself:

> When I first learned to use a brush,
> Seeing an object I tried to capture its likeness.

Whenever I travelled, in country or town,
I sketched object after object, keeping them in my painting basket
I ask my master Fang I,
What is illusion, what real?
From the inkwell, I take some inkdrops,
to lodge in my painting a boundless feeling of Spring.

The inscription on Wan Shang-Lin's landscape in a certain sense instructs us as to how the subjacent image is to be appreciated; in particular, the inscription serves to connect it and its original, as it connects Wan and Ni Tsan, in a complex artistic network. Wan writes:

I have seen two paintings of the Lung-men monk by Ni Kao-shih [Ni Tsan]. One belongs to Yao Hua tao-jen and one to the governor of Yaochou. Both have some brushwork of excellent quality, but neither can be judged with certainty as genuine. For eight or nine years, these two paintings have been puzzling me. Today is the sixth day of the ninth month, 1800, one day before the results of examination are to be published. We are gathered at the I t'ing Studio. I have been doing some sketches of hermits and suddenly the paintings came to mind. So, from memory, I have done this copy. If it has some similarities, it is as Tso-chan [Su Tung-p'o] says, "similarity in surface only." I feel embarrassed [for the quality of my work].

I

We may infer a great deal regarding the structure of the Chinese artist's world from these examples. There were, of course, no museums in our form of that crucial institution, and certainly none in which artworks from various traditions hang cheek-by-jowl under the same accommodating roof as in the paradigmatic encyclopedic museum we assume as the norm. But it would have been common knowledge in which collections works were to be found; and the assumption is that these could be studied by scholar-artists.

It is clear that there were criteria of connoisseurship, as there always are when there is the practice of collecting and where the issue of genuineness has some importance. We must not suppose that genuineness connotes authenticity, at least in the sense in which imitation connotes inauthenticity. It is no criticism of Wan Shang-Lin's painting *that* it is an imitation, but only one if it is, as an imitation, good or bad. After all, Wan's painting was preserved, not, I think, in the way we preserve copies of Poussin made by Degas (i.e., because Degas himself achieved an independent stature, and anything from his hand has meaning and certainly value in even the crassest sense of that term, though the copy from his hand also has interest because he *created* it). I suspect, by contrast, that Wan's painting would have what value it has even if he did little else beyond imitations of Ni Tsan, who himself did imitations of earlier artists.

There was an important practice of imitating Ni Tsan—as the existence of two copies of the same work in known collections perhaps testifies—even though (or perhaps possibly because), as Wen Fong writes, Ni Tsan was inimitable. According to Wen Fong, the artist Shen Chou (1427–1509) "nurtured a life-long ambition to imitate Ni Tsan," yet, according to one story, every time he applied his brush to paper his teacher would shout, "No, no, you have overdone it again!" So for half a millennium there can be traced a suite of paintings in the style of Ni Tsan, some of them, just as Wan Shang-Lin observes, possessing brushwork excellent enough that the question of genuineness can at least be raised. So the bland art-historical commonplace "influenced by Ni Tsan" scarcely serves to explain the complicated relationship in which the members of this history stand to one another, or to Ni Tsan himself. But neither does the word "imitated Ni Tsan" altogether capture as a description the action glossed by Wan Shang-Lin in his own inscription.

Here, I can but speculate on a tradition to which I am in every essential respect an alien, but at the least we can say that these imitations were not intended to deceive anyone, or to cause in them false beliefs about the provenance of the work. Something rather more like what Aristotle must have had in mind in the *Poetics* defined this practice: "It is natural for all to delight in works of imitation."

Now, in truth, though irrelevant to his tradition, no one the least familiar with Ni Tsan's work could be taken in by this imitation. This is not simply because the authority of Ni Tsan's brushwork is absent, even if all the standard motifs are there: the paired bare tress, for example, or the water and the rocks. Something else is absent, or, if you like, present in this painting, which could not have been present in the original—so what is absent is a quality with which this presence is incompatible. Wan has his monk facing a cliff, which situates him in a kind of enclosure, almost as though he had encountered an obstacle, whatever this may mean in the trackless atmosphere of monastic reality. The paintings of Ni Tsan, however, are marked by their abstract openness, their "boundless feeling." The empty paper becomes a kind of empty, dreamful space from which the possibility of horizons has been subtracted.

I do not know whether this emptiness was invisible to the Chinese artists who imitated Ni Tsan or not. There are, of course, always things that reveal the copyist: things he puts in without necessarily being conscious of doing so, because what is in the original just makes no sense to him, and so he spontaneously compensates. Leo Steinberg, from whom I learned the revelatory utility of copies, points out that in *The Last Supper,* Christ is shown virtually without shoulders—essential (in Steinberg's view) to the larger compositional effect of the work, but anatomically impossible—so that copies of that work almost invariably "correct" the drawing. In late copies, indeed, Christ has the shoulders of a football hero. Possibly Wan Shang-Lin (who was, after all, working from memory) felt there had to be "something there," and so he unconsciously "corrected" his master, thereby transforming the work in an almost metaphysical way.

Or, there may be another answer. Imitations of Ni Tsan may have so concentrated on brushwork and motif that it became impossible to see the other components of the work, or to see the work in any other way. This can happen with work that is (pardon the phrase) "highly influential." I take the following example from Michael Baxandall: try to imagine how Cézanne would look to us if Cubism had never been invented. The meaning of Cézanne to counterfactual artistic traditions in other possible worlds is tantalizingly inaccessible. Suppose, in a similar fashion, that Chinese artists had come to admire the *spatialities* in Ni Tsan; then the quality of his lines might have become almost irrelevant, and someone could have been complimented on the success of an imitation of Ni Tsan, which, to an observer who *was* fixated on lines and brush strokes, would scarcely be seen as such.

But, of course, such an emphasis on spatiality was not the tradition. In the tradition that unites Ni Tsan and Wan Shang-Lin, the brushwork counts for everything. We also have to remember that, at least until well after the introduction of photography into China in 1839, exact resemblance was never an ideal. There was never in Chinese painting the defining ambition of Western art to dupe birds; at the most, one would want the vitality of one's brushwork to match the vitality of one's subject. So it would be enough, perhaps, for something to be considered an imitation of Ni Tsan that it should accomplish this, and, within these limits, the imitator had freedom to do what he wished; it would no more be expected that no one could tell the difference between Wan and Ni Tsan than that no one could tell the difference between the painting of a tree and the tree itself.

"When every boulder or rock shows free and untrammelled inkstrokes, then the painting will have a scholar's air. If it is too laborious, the painting will resemble the work of a draftsman." So wrote Ni Tsan. Here we can begin to see the extreme difficulty—one would almost say the impossibility—of imitation as the Chinese understood it, and so understand its challenge. One must paint as the Master painted and, *at the same time,* be free and untrammeled. The imitation cannot be outward indiscernibility; rather, the work

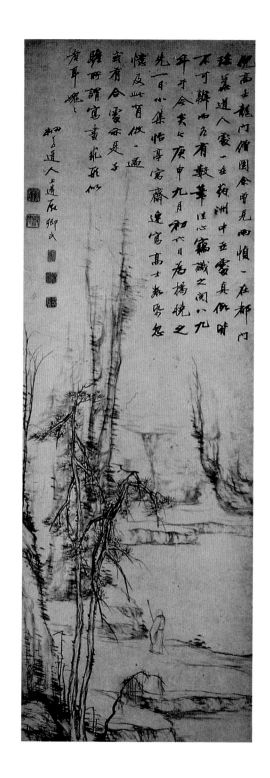

1. Wan Shang-Lin, *Landscape with Monk*. (Courtesy of the Metropolitan Museum of Art, Robert Ellsworth Collection of 19th and 20th Century Art)

2. Ni Tsan, *Empty Groves After Rain*. (Chinese National Palace, Taiwan)

3. Ni Tsan, *Woods and Valleys of Yu-Shen*. (Location unknown; transparency courtesy of Columbia University Library, New York)

4. Ni Tsan, *Mountains Seen from River Bank*. (Location unknown; transparency courtesy of Columbia University Library, New York)

5. Ni Tsan, *Enjoying Wilderness in Autumn Grove*. (Crawford Collection; collection location unknown)

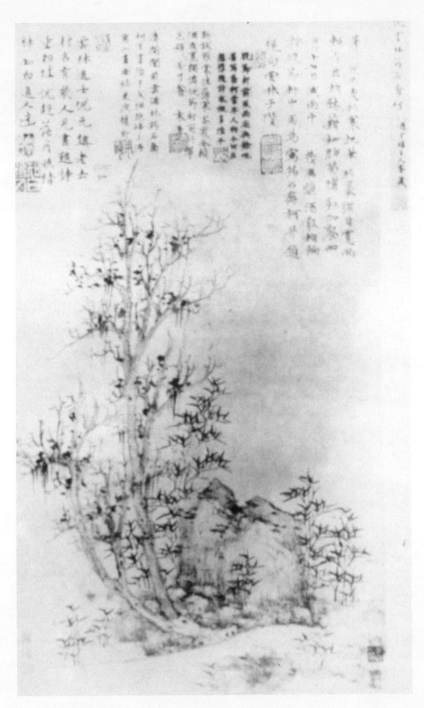

6. Ni Tsan, *Bamboo with Rock*. (Imperial Collection, Beijing)

must flow forth from the same internal resources, and painting in the style of Ni Tsan in consequence becomes a form of spiritual exercise.

We get a whiff of this possibility in our own culture, of course, in the instruction of the Guardians in Plato's *Republic,* though in the reverse direction. Plato worries that we will become what we imitate, and so we must have morally acceptable models. In my view, the Chinese thought was that we can imitate *only* if we in fact become like our model, however this is to be achieved. Outward similarities are what we might expect from a mere craftsman. It is the internal similarities that count. By 1800, Ni Tsan had become a legend and, in a sense, an imperative. Stories were told of him as a noble recluse, the embodiment of great virtues—purity, courage, equanimity in the face of hardship—a man for whom vulgarity was the evil to avoid. Ni Tsan was like one of the Sage Kings! So he was constantly reinvented, cited as a precursor, and celebrated as a hero. In imitating Ni Tsan, one was making a moral stand, creating a narrative for one's life, filling the shoes of greatness. To say simply that one was "influenced by Ni Tsan" thus would be like reading in a life of Saint Paul that he was "influenced by Jesus Christ."

II

The philosophical shape of art history in China differed so from that of art history in the West that Wan Shang-Lin's narrative simply would not have been available for a Western painter of any significance; he could not have represented himself as situated in the kind of history in which Wan felt himself at home. We are, after all, speaking of a stretch of historical time that corresponds almost precisely to that which takes us from Giotto to Jacques-Louis David; hence, a period of periods growing out of and transcending one another in a way that pointed a progressive vector. We have the three Vasarian cycles—anchored in Giotto, Masaccio, and Raphael; Mannerism, the Baroque, in which the Church was able to call on painters and sculptors and even architects to achieve illusory feats of which even a master like Masaccio would have been incapable. And we have the long age of the academies in which, by 1800, the state now rather than the Church was asking that artists articulate the values of the revolution and define the meaning of citizenship again in ways inaccessible to art near the beginning of this period.

Painting was the progressive discipline par excellence, and no one who took himself seriously as a painter would have wished to have been born at an earlier time, or would seek through imitation to reenact the works of earlier masters. To be sure, the Renaissance defined itself through a narrative that connected it with Greece and Rome, but this required a representation of the intervening time as merely dark ages, a time of lost skills that had to be rediscovered, and of ignorance that had to be driven away—a long descent into shadows from peak to peak of light. The next time something like this occurred was in the Pre-Raphaelite movement in England, where again the effort (audacious in conceptions when we think of the actual gifts of its major practitioners) was to dismiss as a kind of aberration everything from Raphael down—to make a new beginning, returning to the masters in an effort to relearn visual truth.

Between Wan Shang-Lin and Ni Tsan was the hapless Shen Chou, the painters of the Lung-men monk in the two versions known to Wan, if these were not (as very likely they *were* not) by Ni Tsan himself; and the many others who sought to preempt for their own life and work the style of Ni Tsan. None of these felt he was making a new beginning, or that between himself and the Master was a dark wood in which the art of painting wandered or languished. Wan's was a vectorless history. Past and future were so of a piece that there was no conceptual room for modernity, and the concept of "influence" had to mean something different from what it would mean to a Western artist—an artist, for example, who copied a predecessor, not caring about similarity, not matching himself against his model, but simply learning how something was done, miming the structure of art history itself to internalize and go beyond what came before. Michael Baxandall writes:

> "Influence" is the curse of art criticism primarily because of its wrong-headed prejudice about who is the agent and who is the patient: it seems to reverse the active/passive relation which the historical actor experiences. If one says that X influenced Y it does seem that one is saying that X did something to Y rather than Y did something to X. But in the consideration of good pictures and painters, the second is always the more lively reality. . . . If we think of Y rather than X as the agent, the vocabulary is much richer and more diversified: draw on, resort to, avail oneself of, appropriate from, have recourse to, adapt, misunderstand, refer to, pick up, take on, engage with, react to, quote, differentiate oneself from, assimilate oneself to, assimilate, align oneself with, copy, address, paraphrase, absorb, make a variation on, revive, continue, remodel, ape, emulate, travesty, parody, extract from, distort, attend to, resist, simplify, reconstitute, elaborate on, develop, face up to, master, subvert, perpetuate, reduce, promote, respond to, transform, tackle. . . . Most of these relations just cannot be stated the other way round—in terms of X acting on Y rather than Y on X.

Raphael is often described as the most influential artist who ever lived, chiefly, I think, because his compositional strategies entered the curriculum and became the way that artists in academies were taught to compose well into the nineteenth century. But very few of the artists so influenced were influenced in the way in which Wan was influenced by Ni Tsan. There were, of course, artists who sought in a certain sense to paint like Raphael, say as Benjamin West did in portraying his family in *tondo* format based on Raphael's *Madonna della sedia*. But even in that case, there is a metaphorical reference being made, and a different order of rhetoric transacted than anything I find in Wan Shang-Lin.

I think one cannot too heavily stress the fact (without necessarily having to affirm so voluntarist a view of our relationship to the past as we find in Sartre, who says such dramatic things as that we *choose* to be born) that the past is very much a function of the present, in the sense that what causes us to act as we do is not so much the things that influence us, as the representations of the past that define us as artists, and through which, say, Ni Tsan was constituted as the "influence" through which Wan Shang-Lin painted. Historical explanations accordingly do not carry us, as from cause to effect, from the influence to the influenced, but rather they must account for the representation—the complex of beliefs, feelings, and values—through which influence and influenced arise together as a historical unit. This may be the deep reason why we might see in Ni Tsan things to which those for whom he was an influence were necessarily blind, and why, in a certain sense, the past yields facets for our admiration to which those contemporary with it, or more directly influenced by it than us, are blind. Monet was constituted a predecessor by the Abstract Expressionists by virtue of certain features of the Water Lily paintings becoming salient in the retrospective light of scale, all-overness, and freedom of brushing that could not have meant to Monet or his contemporaries what they came to mean for artists for whom Pollock opened up the past. Or think, for just these same reasons, how Fragonard's *Figures de fantaisie* were so greatly admired by artists in New York who visited the great Fragonard exhibition a few seasons ago, for whom *Progress of Love* (in the Frick Collection) were simply eighteenth-century paintings, whereas these were so spontaneous and free that some felt that the history of Abstract Expressionism should begin with them. I cannot imagine a future for art in which Fragonard's *Progress of Love*—unquestionably his master-piece—should become an influence and a meaningful (because active) past. Possibly it is the mark of post-modernism that anything can become an influence at any time, a disordered past corresponding to a disordered present and future.

Since Vasari, to be an artist in the West has been to have internalized a narrative that determines the way we can be influenced by the past. The difference between Western and Chinese artists will then be a difference in lived narratives and modes of available influence. Modernism, alike in China and the West, meant the dismantling of these narratives and reconstitution of our relationship to the past.

III

Wan Shang-Lin lived in fortunate times, in that he could practice an art against a tradition that had not radically changed for five centuries. He could represent his work as simply seeking what the masters sought, imitation being as good a means as any. His contemporaries in the West, too, lived in fortunate times, at least in the sense that they saw themselves as belonging to a history which they understood what it would mean to continue. Not long after 1800 in France and in most of Europe, the cosmopolitan museum appeared—the Louvre, the Brera, the Rijkmuseum, the Prado, the Kunsthistorisches Museum were founded within a few years of one another—in which artists could study the masterpieces of their tradition.

As late as the Impressionists, artists were in the spirit of wholeness with their tradition. The Impressionists in particular saw their task very little differently from Vasari, as the conquest of visual appearances, of arranging colors across flat surfaces in such a way as to affect the retina as it would be affected by some scene in the real world to which the painterly array corresponded. They felt themselves closer to visual truth than their predecessors—hence, as continuing a tradition to which they belonged. Their discoveries regarding the colors of shadows belonged to the same progress as linear perspective, aerial perspective, chiaroscuro. They craved academic recognition. Even Rousseau, who saw himself as the great master of the modern, aspired to the Légion d'Honneur.

Modernism came about when this entire tradition was called into question by artists who no longer felt themselves to belong to it. And something of the same sort happened in China over much the same period. To be modern is to perceive the past as the locus of only negative messages, or things not to do, of ways not to be, or, of the paintings in museums as "les morts," as [Pascin] said in explanation of why he never went near them.

I think that modernity begins with the loss of belief in the defining narrative of one's own culture. When that narrative is strong and taken simply as the way things are, it is almost impossible to be influenced by another culture. After all, from the establishment of mercantile routes, works of art were imported into the West. Chinese porcelains appear in the Dutch still lifes of the seventeenth century, but merely as objects to hold fruit, though, of course, as we know, there was a demand for pottery in the Chinese style from the fact that it was broadly imitated around 1700 by the potters of Delft.

A great deal of such importation and imitation can occur without the premises on which cultural complacency rests being greatly shaken. Who can forget the atmosphere of exotisme/érotisme of Odette's drawing room, with its Japanese lanterns and Chinese pots, its screens and fans and cushions of Japanese silks, the innumerable lamps made of porcelain vases (and some Turkish beads), though the marvelous lantern, suspended by a silken cord, was lit from inside by a gas jet "so that her visitors should not have to complain of the want of any of the latest comforts of Western civilization," as Proust writes archly. The superiority of Western civilization was never doubted, and one of the premises of Victorian anthropology was in effect that there is a moral direction in history as there is in evolution, that societies and species evolve toward optimality, and that Western Europe was history's masterpiece just as homo sapiens was nature's masterpiece.

The superiority of Chinese civilization was no less an axiom of those who lived it. The relationship to the outside, fundamentally, would be one of curiosity; the outside was the object of curiosity in the double sense of embodying strangeness, as in "curio," and as something to understand—as an object of scientific curiosity.

The outside in neither sense was something we might aspire to as a form of life. Kant, who must have learned about the South Seas from Captain Cook's *Voyages,* sees them as places where lives of extreme pleasure and indolence can be led, but not, he argues, lives we can rationally will for ourselves. Neither could we rationally will to live the lives that ethnographers began to explore and chronicle throughout the nineteenth century. The presumption, rather, was that these lives were like living fossils, stages through which "we" had advanced; and a complex narrative was assumed in which the savages of Africa and Oceania were "ourselves," seen through the wrong end of the telescope of social evolution—just as they, looking through the right end, could see "themselves" as us. We would be the goal toward which it was the White Man's Burden to conduct them.

There was an empirical question, I suppose, as to whether their stage of social development did not also mark a correlative stage of intellectual development, so that they could not master the form of life toward which they could merely evolve. Our task was that of shepherds, giving them some skills useful to them (and economically valuable to us). The African who aspires to a European form of life would, as a result, be thought of essentially as an object of comedy—an attitude that surprisingly lasted well into the 1950s in such novels as Joyce Cary's *Mister Johnson.* Indeed, the "Other" in

Western art, whether the pygmy, as even in the paintings of Pompeii, the Hottentot, or the Chinese in eighteenth-century French painting, would be like other eighteenth-century paintings, for example, of monkeys doing such things as painting pictures or playing instruments, or of small children conducting flirtations—all as very largely comical, as occasions for reflecting on our own superiority (as when we watch primates doing nearly human things in the zoo). Parallels are to be found in Chinese art as well.

IV

For me, the deep change, and indeed the beginning of modernism, begins in the West when Japanese prints became objects, not of curiosity, but of influence. Consider how much had to be forged before they could be received as influences! Monet collected Japanese prints, as Matisse and Derain collected African masks and figures. But Van Gogh and Gauguin decided to *constitute* the masters of the Ukiyo-I print as *their* predecessors, as Picasso determined that a tradition in the Ethnographic Museum of the Palais de Trocadero constituted the relevant past for the Demoiselles d'Avignon.

In the case of Japanese art, it was not simply that these works stopped being objects of charm and curiosity and exoticism—connoting, as in Odette's overheated interior, pleasures forbidden by the moral world embodied in the bourgeois decor she was anxious, as a high-class courtesan, to put at a distance. It was, rather, that these prints showed the *right way* to represent as art; and, if these prints were right, an entire artistic tradition was wrong and an entire mode of artistic progress was shown to be beside the point.

Part of this change had to do with the treatment of space, part with the ideal of an illusion that three-dimensional space, whose conquest was the glory of Western art, made possible. Gauguin drew everything toward the surface, rejected chiaroscuro, flattened his forms by bounding them with heavy lines—though like Odette, who took it for granted that she should use gas to illuminate her lantern, Gauguin benefited from the easy availability of manufactured pigments to get colors in a relatively pure state, defined as "coming from the tube." (It was by and large chemical pigments that finished off the Japanese print.)

In desituating his own art from his own tradition, accepting as influences the Japanese masters, Gauguin simultaneously was engaged in a piece of cultural criticism: he explicitly said, when he considered relocating to Tonkin, "The West is rotten."

I cannot here discuss the reverse impact of Western representational strategies on China, but the Ellsworth collection presents us with an art-world under powerful transformation—corresponding, I suppose, to the immense social and economic changes China was undergoing during the same period. But, unmistakably, when the Chinese artist allowed himself to employ Western strategies—aiming at likenesses, using illusory space and chiaroscuro, exploiting shadows and illuminational sources, altering the canon of acceptable subjects, behaving in ways Ni Tsan would certainly dismiss as "vulgar"—this, too, was an act of cultural criticism, a calling into question of an axiom of cultural supremacy. My own first impression in walking through the Ellsworth collection was that in some mysterious way, Chinese art had begun to look *modern*, as if "Modern" were a style of historical dismissal.

And, of course, it is. Chinese art and Western art in the nineteenth and early twentieth centuries are almost locked in that kind of ironic relationship we find in O. Henry's famous story, where each character sacrifices what the other admires in it—where the comical denouement would consist in the Chinese proudly displaying a work in faultless perspective to a Western artist—who, in turn, has achieved a perfect Oriental simplicity and lan- guorous ambiguity of form.

V

There have been three strikingly different narrational moments in Western history, moments in which the present means something different because the past to which it is related means something different. The first, of course, is the Renaissance, which is a narrative of recovery—a plot of having, losing, and finding once again. Here the deep historical question is, *why* was it "lost" and *how* was it "found" again. Gibbon's answer—"Barbarism" and "Chris- tianity," respectively—is an answer to a question that presupposes this sort of narrative, though, of course, it has in its own form something of a Christian cadence of paradise, Fall, and redemption to paradise. I am not certain that such a narrative would have insinuated itself in the minds of historical theorists, were it not for the concept of the Fall. The narrative itself, of course, had come to an end; once risen, we are never to fall again. So, in an important sense, *history itself was over,* and we thus passed into an age of academies.

The second narrational moment is the Enlightenment, which, after all, furnished the logical shape of what came to be Victorian anthropology. It was, in Kant's powerful and moving expression, "Mankind's coming of age." History was a vectored progress marked by growth and stages. If contempo- rary culture really is mature and superior (as adults are presumed superior to children by being rational masters of their own lives, whose growth is behind them), then either we can say that history is *over,* or that we have reached a stage beyond which we can only imagine things like the Superman. For Nietzsche simply continues the Enlightenment narrative, agreeing in large measure with its logic, but dismissing the complacency of regarding homo sapiens europanensis as the apex. Zarathustra is there to help us onto the next stage, as those who felt the White Man's Burden undertook the obligation to bring the stragglers abreast of us in the confidence that this was the last redeeming stage of history—what made it all worthwhile.

The third narrative moment is Modernism, which, in my view, begins in the mid-1880s with Van Gogh and Gauguin, who repudiated the entirety of their own artistic pasts and sought their influences elsewhere, in Japan, or Egypt, or Polynesia—the art of which was (in Gauguin's view) finally more "cerebral," or, as Picasso said, more "reasonable," than that with which it had spontaneously been contrasted. Both of these artists, Van Gogh and Gauguin, undertook to enact their beliefs by dramatic dislocation: Van Gogh went to Arles because he was looking for a reality whose visual representations would be like Japanese prints, and Gauguin went to Tahiti, where he had to carve his own Polynesian idols.

The historical problem or central question of modernity, in my view, is: what happened to account for the representation, by these artists, of their own past as less relevant for them than the imagined past of other cultures? What accounts for the profound shift in self-evaluation between the Crystal Palace Exhibition of 1850, and the Exposition Universelle of 1889? The philosophical problem is the logical form of such explanations and the analysis of historical causation, when the effect is narrative representations that may or may not be true. Wan Shang-Lin would still be correctly described as "influenced" by Ni Tsan, even if Ni Tsan did not exist—even as Gauguin was "influenced" by an art that—it was one of the profounder disappointments of his voyage out to Tahiti to discover—did not exist. It is as though we had effects without causes.

I have neither a historical explanation of the modernist narrative to offer nor a philosophical analysis of the logic of such historical explanations. But I do want to say something about how modernism in art realized itself. Political circumstance, for better or worse, aborted this development in China, as it did in the Soviet Union, and as it would have done in Germany had Nazism, with its strong views in regard to modernism as *entartete Kunst,* triumphed.

When Braque and Picasso were coinventing Cubism, Braque afterward wrote that they stopped going to museums. Braque had haunted the Egyptian collections of the Louvre when he arrived in Paris in 1902, and I have already mentioned Picasso's fascination with the Trocadero. There is a story about Braque driving with his wife through Italy, stopping in front of a museum, and saying: "Marcelle, you go in and look around and tell me what's good in there." He was anxious not to spoil his eye with old painting (François Gilot tells us), and nothing could more eloquently express the attitude toward the past that is proper to the modernist narrative. No one, inevitably, puts it better than Picasso:

> Beginning with Van Gogh, however great we may be, we are all, in a measure, autodidacts—you might almost say, primitive painters. Painters no longer live within a tradition and so each one of us must recreate an entire language. Every painter of our times is fully authorized to recreate that language from A to Z. No criterion can be applied to him *a priori,* since we don't believe in rigid standards any longer. In a certain sense, that's a liberation; but at the same time, it's an enormous limitation, because when the individuality of the artist begins to express itself, what the artist gains in liberty he loses in the way of order. And when you're no longer able to attach yourself to an order, basically, that's very bad.

One can interpret these comments in two ways. One is a way recommended by Ernst Gombrich in his influential history of art, wherein he concludes by saying: "There is no such thing as 'art,' there are only the individual artists." Or one can say that the philosophical question of the nature of art becomes urgent, all the more so in that the connection with the past has been broken, leaving only a kind of negative aesthetics: "*not* this; *not* that."

One response to this dilemma has been the creation of a modernist aesthetic, which is essentially ahistorical. Formalist analysis cuts across all times and all cultures, making in effect, every museum a "Museum of Modern Art." All art exists for display and formal delectation, across an aesthetic distance. All art—the Dogon figures, the watercolors of Wan Shang-Lin, the works of Picasso—stand outside life, in a space of their own, metaphorically embodied in the Plexiglas display case, the bare white gallery, the aluminum frame. When one seeks a deeper connection between art and life than this, modernism is over.

That is our present situation. The effort to reconnect to life through reconnecting with the past, as in the referential strategies of postmodernism, is pathetic. Formalism is finally unsatisfying, and the need for a philosophy of art under which art is responsive to human ends is a matter of absolute priority. It is the mark of living in the posthistorical period that we face the future without a narrative of the present.

Note

An early version of this essay was presented at the Sixth East-West Philosophers' Conference held in Honolulu in August 1989 and published in *Culture and Modernity: The Authority of the Past,* edited by Eliot Deutsch (Honolulu: University of Hawaii Press, 1991), and is reprinted here with the kind permission of the author and editor.

Lynn S. Joy

Humanism

and the Problem

The relations between Renaissance humanism as a program of learning and the new science of the seventeenth century have constituted a prevalent theme for historians of science writing from widely different points of view. These different points of view reflect in part the sheer variety of fledgling sciences which historians have seen as contributing to that heuristic mix of natural philosophy, mechanics, medicine, natural history, alchemy, and the mathematical sciences of the quadrivium, all of which underwent a notable period of ferment during the sixteenth and seventeenth centuries. Thus Thomas Kuhn, when seeking the antecedents of modern physics, emphasized the scholarly interests of certain Renaissance natural philosophers in such works as Vitruvius' *De architectura,* Euclid's *Geometry* and *Optics,* the pseudo-Aristotelian *Mechanical Problems,* Archimedes' *Floating Bodies,* and Hero's *Pneumatica.*[1] In quite another vein, Frances Yates called attention to the significance for the new science of the work of the philologist Isaac Casaubon, whose accurate dating of the texts of the *Hermetica,* she believed, had "shattered at one blow the build-up of Renaissance Neoplatonism."[2] Yates's complex portrayal of the possible sources of modern science in the Neoplatonist advocates of the hermetic philosophy as well as in their humanist opponents, and Kuhn's more straightforward discussion of the influence of the classical mathematical disciplines on the development of modern physics both illustrate a basic historiographical problem encountered by those who try to interpret the relations between Renaissance humanism and the new science. The problem is that these relations seem crucially to depend on *which* fledgling sciences the historian chooses to examine in making the connection.

The further problem of defining what one means by Renaissance humanism also confronts historians of science who interpret these relations. Robert Mandrou, for example, in a work widely read in English translation, stated: "The movement of learned men, humanists and scholars which brought about so profound a change in European thought in the sixteenth century did not take the form of a struggle to promote a particular doctrine. . . . In other words, it is futile to try to discover a single humanist 'line'. . . . There was, indeed, no humanism but only humanists and scholars, each labouring in accordance with the spirit that moved him. . . ."[3] Mandrou was not of course the first historian to give an account of the multiplicity of strands of Renaissance thought and social institutions which formed what he called the "scientific spirit" of the seventeenth century. Others including W. P. D. Wightman shared this aim, and Wightman characterized the difficulty of defining Renaissance humanism in equally cautionary terms:

> According to Kristeller the word "Humanismus" was first used to desig-
> nate a form of education emphasising the study of the classical lan-
> guages only in 1808 (F. J. Niethammer). The nearest approach to a
> similar usage in the centuries of its birth was the colloquial term
> *Humanista* current in the Italian universities in the early sixteenth
> century: this name for the teacher or student of classical grammar and
> "rhetoric" corresponded to the long established custom of referring to
> the teachers of other disciplines as "artista," "civilista," etc. The associa-
> tion of "humanitas" with the new emphasis in the "arts" may have been a
> reference to Cicero's use of the expression "studia humanitatis" for a
> similar discipline. At most, then, the Italian Renaissance was "humanis-
> tic" in its explicit recognition of an immensely rich literature in Latin
> and Greek . . . which demanded study for the better understanding of
> the power of the human spirit.[4]

I want to discuss the relations between late Renaissance humanism and the emerging sciences of the sixteenth and seventeenth centuries by focusing on just two specific features of humanism. One was the humanist scholar's preoccupation with the interpretation of ancient texts. The second was what I have elsewhere described as the breakdown during the later sixteenth century of the coherence of the humanist project itself.[5] My chief concern is to understand the profound influence that these two features of humanism may have had on the conceptions of science held by humanistically trained natural philosophers and physicians. I hope to suggest how humanist schol-arship may have provided them with a distinctive form of scientific inquiry. This suggestion is advanced as a historiographical hypothesis which, if true, would offer a fruitful way of explaining much that is puzzling in the standard literature about the relations between humanism and science. However, my hypothesis is not meant to apply to *every* Renaissance science, nor is it intended to give an exhaustive explanation of how the new science of the seventeenth century acquired a distinctive form which differed from that of the Renaissance sciences.

What was the significance for scientific inquiry of the humanists' preoccupation with the interpretation of ancient texts? This question is usually answered by focusing on the obvious gains to be made by Renaissance natural philosophers from the transmission of ancient Greek, Hellenistic, and Latin research and theory in the specialized sciences and in philosophy in general. Such an answer, however, minimizes the much more serious consequences of the use of ancient texts in Renaissance natural philosophy. We should not underestimate the degree to which the activities of translating and commenting on texts involved many thinkers in a kind of intellectual work wholly foreign to our present conceptions of science. Consider the case of the prolific translator of Aristotle's *Physics,* Joachim Périon (1498/9–1559). Périon, a French scholar who prided himself on his Latin style, took it upon himself to improve on what he regarded as Aristotle's inelegant Greek prose by rendering the *Physics* and numerous other works of the Stagirite into Ciceronian Latin. The egregious mistranslations of Aristotle's scientific and philosophical technical terms which resulted from Périon's method would seriously have set back the ongoing philosophical debates about the real merits of Aristotle's views if Périon's humanist contemporaries had not intervened by discouraging the reading of his translations. His inaccuracies might otherwise have skewed the entire sixteenth-century discussion of Aristotle by creating false versions of Aristotle's views and hence by rendering meaningless both the rejection of and continued adherence to those views. Fortunately, the philosophers Francesco Vimercato, Simone Simoni, and Jacques Charpentier and the translator Jacques-Louis d'Estrebay all intervened to prevent any major damage. What was Périon's unforgivable error? His modern reader Charles Schmitt aptly accused him of failing to realize "that philosophical and scientific writings, aiming as they do at truth, have more at stake than the polished verbiage of the rhetor," and also of "turn[ing] his back upon the philosophical usage and interpretative framework of several centuries of intense activity."[6] I call attention to Périon's Ciceronian version of Aristotle's *Physics* as one possible outcome of the humanists' preoccupation with the interpretation of texts in order to emphasize that such a preoccupation often did have very deleterious effects on scientific inquiry, even at the apparently innocuous level of finding Latin nouns that would accurately render the sense of Aristotle's technical terms.

The fact that many Renaissance natural philosophers and physicians engaged in a kind of intellectual work which was wholly foreign to our present conceptions of science does not, nevertheless, mean that this work did not also produce a form of scientific inquiry worth defending in its own right. For, despite occasional setbacks engendered by misguided Ciceronians like Périon, the belief that ancient texts could impart true knowledge of the world was a redeeming feature of the humanists' notion of scientific inquiry. Indeed it was a characteristic, but usually unstated, assumption of many thinkers who were both humanists and natural philosophers or physicians that two distinct categories of truth informed the kinds of research they pursued. The first category was truth with regard to an ancient authority; the second was truth with regard to the natural world. In pursuing truths of the first sort, humanist natural philosophers labored to discern what was the correct interpretation of an ancient text and sometimes also labored to decide which ancient texts, among numerous rival texts, should be treated as canonical within a given field of inquiry. Their presupposition in doing so was that the texts *in themselves* could reveal true knowledge of the world, and as such they could function as more than mere vehicles for the transmitting of theories. Texts were thought to be equal in status to one's sense experience of the world. However, at the same time, many humanist natural philosophers believed that by appealing to their sense experience of the world they could reveal aspects of nature which had been ignored by those of their thirteenth-century predecessors who had practiced speculative metaphysics and those of their fourteenth-century predecessors who had adopted methods of metalinguistic analysis in natural philosophy.[7] Hence the humanists' second category of truth—truth with regard to the natural world— required them, at least in their empirical investigations, to transfer their interpretive skills from texts to sense experience. In doing so, they confronted new kinds of interpretive problems, that of justifying their interpretation of a set of observations and that of determining which observations should count as decisive within a particular field of inquiry.

How did one practice science, given a commitment to two such disparate notions of truth? Could a preoccupation with the interpretation of texts seriously undermine one's efforts to increase the empirical content of natural philosophy? To outline a response to these questions, let us consider the intellectual strategies employed by a prominent sixteenth-century physician and an even more renowned seventeenth-century natural philosopher. Louis Duret (1527–86) was a leading member of a school of physicians that the historian of medicine Iain Lonie has called the "Paris Hippocratics."[8] Professor of medicine in both the University of Paris and the Collège royal, Duret represented the second generation at Paris to carry out a program of reviving the Greek texts of Hippocrates (both those on which Galen had commented and those on which he had not) while simultaneously conducting practical investigations in diagnosis, prognosis, and therapy. He is perhaps best re-membered for his new Greek text, Latin translation, and commentary on Hippocrates' *Coan Prognoses*. This difficult project was first undertaken by Duret's teacher, Jacques Houllier, but it was Duret who contributed most to its realization.[9] What is most striking about Duret's career is the way he managed to integrate his philological labors with his practical work as a physician. Indeed each aspect of his career seemed largely to depend on the other. His interpretation of the Greek text of the *Coan Prognoses* depended on his being able to identify the symptoms described by Hippocrates as symp-toms which he himself had actually observed. Hence his sense experience helped him to be a better philologist. Conversely, his knowledge of Hippo-crates' Greek text enabled him to interpret more skillfully his sense experi-ence, since the observations he made of actual patients were by no means always self-evident signs of their pathological conditions. These observa-tions, like texts, also required interpretation. Duret's encyclopedic knowl-edge of both Galen and Hippocrates supplied him with hypotheses in whose terms he could recognize the significance of what he observed, whereas other, less learned doctors might not even *see* in a patient any pattern of symptoms worthy of note. But Duret's manner of combining philology and practice must not be viewed anachronistically as constituting a hypothetico-deductive method. He was not engaged in theory-testing when he brought text and observation together. Rather he was seeking the best interpretation of the text and the best interpretation of his observations. Each activity enhanced his skill at interpreting the signs—whether words or observa-tions—of the other. Thus sense experience was not used by him as a means of verifying or falsifying the hypotheses obtained from his texts, for his goal was not to verify or falsify any theory, but instead to increase his observational powers and to give a more perceptive interpretation of what he saw. Inter-pretation, broadly conceived, was the chief aim of his science.

Consider next the case of the principal reviver and exponent of Epicurean atomism, the natural philosopher Pierre Gassendi (1592–1655). Gassendi was a French Catholic priest and professor of mathematics in the Collège royal in Paris who in 1649 published the first full-scale Latin translation and commentary on the Greek texts of Epicurus. He later transformed this commentary into his own atomist treatise, the *Syntagma philosophicum* (1658), in which he reiterated many of Epicurus' arguments for the existence and qualities of atoms, showing in various ways how they were superior to the alternative metaphysical principles of Aristotle, Plato, and nearly every other ancient Greek, Hellenistic, and Latin philosophical school.[10] Gas-sendi's manner of combining the interpretation of texts and the interpretation of sense experience is of great interest because he continued the humanists' emphasis on the role of interpretation in scientific inquiry and yet provided a framework for reconceiving the overall goals of the scientific enterprise. He consulted his own and other scientists' observations of various natural phenomena when he deciphered the meaning of Epicurus' crabbed and sometimes incomprehensible Greek texts. This amounted to his annotating each relevant passage of the texts with detailed accounts of natural phenomena which illustrated Epicurus' principles of atomism. Since these principles ran the gamut from assertions about space, time, matter, and motion to descriptions of the psychology of human sense perception, to explanations of astronomical and meteorological phenomena, Gassendi drew on his own extensive knowledge of the history of both ancient and more recent physics to offer concrete examples of what Epicurus might have meant in each passage. Everything from Hero of Alexandria's compressed air machines to Pascal's Puy de Dôme barometric experiment, for instance, found their way into his explication of Epicurus' statements concerning the void.[11]

Conversely, Gassendi also employed atomist principles obtained from the texts when interpreting the experiments and observations cited in his commentary. Atomist principles, such as the principle that atoms are always in uniform rectilinear motion unless hindered by contact with an external body, were applied by him to interpret the phenomena of terrestrial motion, which he puzzled over when evaluating the merits of the Copernican hypothesis and Galileo's new laws of motion.[12] Thus, at one level, his revival of Epicurus furthered the humanist natural philosophers' and physicians' twin goals of scientific inquiry: the interpretation of texts and the interpretation of sense experience. Moreover, like the physician Duret, Gassendi had sought out an ancient intellectual tradition which he reconstructed for the express purpose of becoming a modern member of it. His conjoint interpretation of Epicurus' principles and various well-known natural phenomena *in terms of one another* constituted his becoming an active member of a once-again viable atomist tradition.

Still the aims of Gassendi's Epicurean writings turned out to be more complex than those of some of his humanist predecessors. This was because he reconstructed the atomist tradition in just that historical period when the breakdown of the coherence of the humanist project—already evident in the later sixteenth century but even more evident during the early decades of the seventeenth century, when Gassendi acquired his scholarly training—began to be seen as a strong reason for abandoning altogether the humanists' program of learning.[13] What did Gassendi perceive to be the inadequacies of this program? They seem to have arisen from several sources:

(1) the humanists' inability to justify the authority assigned to the ancient initiators of various philosophical traditions;
(2) their inability to justify the choice of one competing philosophical tradition rather than another;
(3) their inability to justify the multiplication of philosophical texts and commentaries which was an outcome of humanist scholarship, either as an end in itself or as a means of acquiring new knowledge.

Gassendi tended to be less critical of some humanists' doubts about the appropriate social and political roles which they ought to perform, but his reticence here may simply have reflected the prudence that caused him to select a career which, while socially and politically circumscribed, would allow him maximal freedom of expression on other topics.

Gassendi's response to this crisis of late Renaissance humanism was to reconstruct Epicurean atomism in such a way that it would not be viewed merely as the revival of just one more ancient tradition. He clearly recognized that, in view of the proliferation of revivals of ancient traditions, what was needed now was a means of evaluating each tradition's merits and a means of justifying one's choice of a tradition by establishing its superiority to all of its ancient as well as more recent rivals. It was no longer enough for a scholar simply to interpret the texts of a single tradition and to interpret his own sense experience in the light of those texts. Rather the fundamental problem lay in adjudicating among competing traditions to determine which tradition deserved one's allegiance. Gassendi's characteristically humanist solution to the problem of competing traditions was to return to the texts. Through the comparative interpretation of the principles of the rival philosophical schools, he strove to justify his allegiance to one conception of nature above all others.

Gassendi's ambitious undertaking had a significant unanticipated consequence for the future development of seventeenth-century science. Because he chose to argue in his *Syntagma philosophicum* that an atomist conception of nature was, among all of its rivals, the only viable conception of nature on which to base an empirical science, he helped to bring about the acceptance of a materialist, mechanical view of nature which we now regard as a key feature of the new science of the seventeenth century. But this new science certainly did not require its practitioners to devote themselves to the interpretation of texts in the same way as the humanist natural philosophers and physicians had done. Of course it was still open even to mathematical natural philosophers like Newton to undertake textual researches in, for example, the alchemical literature or in biblical chronology. However, the newly mathematized physics of Newton's *Principia* could no longer be characterized as having been formulated for the express purpose of elucidating an ancient text. For, while the wisdom of the ancients might still heuristically *inspire* investigations in the new science, it could no longer supply the kind of justification of the truth of scientific theories which became possible once natural philosophers had committed themselves to conducting their empirical investigations on the assumption that nature was a law-governed, mechanical system composed of a single, fundamental type of matter.

Why not? What kind of justification was now required which the humanist natural philosophers and physicians had not emphasized in their form of scientific inquiry? Within the metaphysical framework of a materialist, mechanical conception of nature, the mathematical natural philosopher found himself free to entertain the possibility that sense experience, because it comprised the link between the material world and ourselves, should be the ultimate arbiter of the truth of scientific theories. Given his prior acceptance of an atomist explanation of the causal mechanism of sense perception, the mathematical natural philosopher could envision an alternative role for sense experience, the role of a justifier of theories. Theories for him were justified if they were confirmed by the evidence of the senses. This role differed from the humanists' understanding of sense experience as an ambiguous object that, like a kind of text, was itself in need of careful interpretation before it could be taken seriously as a source of knowledge.[14] There thus occurred a major transition whose importance has not hitherto been sufficiently remarked, from a humanist mode of classifying and categorizing the presentations of the senses, which left open the possibility of rival interpretations of the significance of these presentations, to another mode of classifying and categorizing, which regarded the presentations of the senses as unambiguous points of reference for the testing of theories. This transition occurred in part within the scientific theories of Gassendi, his predecessors, and his contemporaries, and in part at the level of the metaphysical presuppositions of those theories.

The humanists' interpretation of texts could now be viewed as largely irrelevant to science because it was extraneous to the more fundamental testing of theories against our sense experience of the material world. Gassendi's reconstruction of the philosophy of Epicurus supplied his contemporaries with a conception of nature and an explanation of the workings of sense perception which, once it was accepted as the metaphysical framework for their scientific investigations, allowed them to verify and falsify theories while resting secure in the belief that sense experience was a privileged and unambiguous source of truth. This achievement may seem to some historians of science to be wholly unoriginal because it might be viewed as indistinguishable from the empiricist tendencies of many other seventeenth-century thinkers. But recall that Gassendi, in his effort to repair the inadequacies of late Renaissance humanism, had constructed his atomist conception of nature from texts! Recall further that his solution to the problem of the proliferation of ancient traditions, which was threatening to undermine the credibility of humanist scholars, was a historian's solution. He had, after all, written a history of the ancient and modern philosophical schools by comparing their rival texts, and he had given a *historical* justification of the superiority of the Epicurean tradition. His endorsement of both the metaphysics and physics of that tradition was thus based on his belief that they constituted the best principles of their kind in the history of philosophy *so far*. Yet nothing ruled out some future natural philosopher's revision of this history and the consequent adoption of a quite different and even incompatible conception of nature—provided that the alternative conception of nature could be shown to be preferable to the conceptions of all other historically recognized traditions. Finally, consider that Gassendi's solution to the problem of traditions produced an important version of the materialist, mechanical conception of nature that became the basis for the new science of the seventeenth century. Therein lies the significance of his achievement, and therein we may observe perhaps the most striking feature of the relationship between late Renaissance humanism and the new science.

The career of Gassendi demonstrates that the humanists' conception of truth with regard to an ancient authority, when it was established by means of historical arguments involving a rigorous comparison of rival texts, could become the precondition for the new science's conception of truth with regard to the natural world. The humanists' interpretation of texts could become the sine qua non of an empirical natural science. Whether today one is a relativist or an objectivist, and whether one is a constructivist or a realist, this single fact about the relations between humanism and science ought to give us pause. It should give us a cogent reason indeed for reopening the question of what really was the significance of the Scientific Revolution.

Notes

1 Thomas S. Kuhn, *The Essential Tension* (Chicago: University of Chicago Press, 1977), 55–56.

2 Frances A. Yates, *Giordano Bruno and the Hermetic Tradition* (Chicago: University of Chicago Press, 1964), 398–99. Yates here also acknowledged that the significance of Casaubon's dating of the *Hermetica* was first pointed out by Eugenio Garin in his *La cultura filosofica del Rinascimento italiano* (Florence: Sansoni, 1961), 143–54.

3 Robert Mandrou, *From Humanism to Science, 1480–1700*, trans. Brian Pearce, original French ed. (Paris: Éditions du Seuil, 1973), English ed. (Harmondsworth: Penguin Books, 1978), 62–63.

4 W. P. D. Wightman, *Science and the Renaissance,* 2 vols. (Edinburgh and London: Oliver and Boyd, 1962), 1: 12.

5 Lynn Sumida Joy, *Gassendi the Atomist, Advocate of History in an Age of Science* (Cambridge: Cambridge University Press, 1987), 41–65. For a book-length study of this breakdown, see Anthony Grafton and Lisa Jardine, *From Humanism to the Humanities* (Cambridge, Mass.: Harvard University Press, 1986).

6 Charles B. Schmitt, *Aristotle and the Renaissance* (Cambridge, Mass.: Harvard University Press, 1962), 73–82.

7 On fourteenth-century natural philosophers who engaged in metalinguistic analysis, see John E. Murdoch, "The Analytic Character of Late Medieval Learning: Natural Philosophy Without Nature," in Lawrence D. Roberts, ed., *Approaches to Nature in the Middle Ages* (Binghamton, N.Y.: Center for Medieval and Early Renaissance Studies, S.U.N.Y., 1982), 171–213.

8 Iain M. Lonie, "The 'Paris Hippocratics': Teaching and Research in Paris in the Second Half of the Sixteenth Century," in A. Wear, R. K. French, and I. M. Lonie, eds., *The Medical Renaissance of the Sixteenth Century* (Cambridge and New York: Cambridge University Press, 1985), 155–74.

9 Ibid., 162.

10 For a detailed discussion of Gassendi's handling of Epicurus' arguments concerning atoms, see Joy, *Gassendi the Atomist,* 130–94.

11 Ibid., 189.

12 Pierre Gassendi, *Epistolae tres de motu impresso a motore translato* (1642 and 1649), in Pierre Gassendi, *Opera omnia* (6 vols., Lyons, 1658), 3: 478–563.

13 Concerning this breakdown, see Joy, *Gassendi the Atomist,* and Grafton and Jardine, *From Humanism to the Humanities.*

14 A notable number of sixteenth- and seventeenth-century humanists found themselves so distrustful of the veracity of sense experience that they embraced the views of Pyrrhonian skeptics such as Sextus Empiricus and Academic skeptics such as Cicero. Gassendi, while very familiar with the writings of both of these Hellenistic skeptics as well as the writings of more recent skeptics like Gianfrancesco Pico della Mirandola and Pierre Charron, did not ultimately find skepticism an acceptable position. However, his close friends Gabriel Naudé and François de la Mothe le Vayer did. See Richard H. Popkin, *The History of Scepticism from Erasmus to Spinoza,* 2d ed. (Berkeley and Los Angeles: University of California Press, 1979), 87–150; and Joy, *Gassendi the Atomist,* 28–39, 130–64.

Robert Cummings

Neville

The Symbiotic

Relation of

Philosophy and

Theology

My general theme is an old one, traceable to Hegel and even to Plato. Philosophy provides a critical analysis and clarification of the presuppositions of theology and religious practice, and it also provides a cultural platform allowing distance from religion and some objectivity. At the same time, religion provides a substantive personal and cultural content for philosophy, continually recalling it from preoccupations with method and dehumanizing self-distancing. The main cultural traditions of India and China do not distinguish philosophy from religion, except as illustrations of the more general distinction between reflective and practical aspects observed in any cultural enterprise. The sharp distinction drawn in the West, while perhaps overdrawn, reminds us of the corrective services that philosophy and theology provide each other.

My specific approach lifts up problems peculiar to the state of culture in late modernity when some thinkers believe that modernism is being succeeded by postmodernism. You can tell from my description that I believe the modernism-postmodernism distinction is less important than is often alleged. Indeed, I believe that modernism is a very specific form of late modern culture, one greatly determined by the philosopher Kant and excessively preoccupied with finding certainty and rejecting historical determination in order to avoid mistakes. Postmodernism is the cultural movement that rejects that particular form of late modernity. My own historical connections with pragmatism and process philosophy are alternatives to modernism and never were especially concerned with certainty or with keeping philosophy or theology pure and untainted by the past. Postmodernism is thus a therapy for someone else's disease, if in fact modernism itself were all that bad.

By philosophy here I do not mean only the academic subject but also and more importantly the development and criticism of philosophical ideas in many branches of culture, for instance, in politics and religion. And by theology I mean not only the academic subject but also the reflective elements in all aspects of religious life, including the directly practical. In particular, I shall look to theology as it understands some of the revolutionary changes taking place in religion.

Power and narrative

My argument begins with an interpretation of two major philosophical themes of European modernity, the idea of power and the idea of narrative, or story. Both ideas are enormously complex and have interacted in exceedingly important ways.

The idea of power took its modern form from the Renaissance invention of mathematical physics. There were many versions of the new physics, each with its theory of force or power. Newton's won the day, and power was interpreted as inertia. A thing in motion tends to remain in motion unless deflected by some countervailing thing in motion; degree of force or power is measured by what it takes to deflect inertial motion, and Newton provided a mathematical metric to express degrees of power. The explanatory power of the new physics was so great that it displaced the older approaches. In particular, by representing both structure and change in a mathematical language, the new physics was able to ignore all reference to value in nature, and it displaced those older languages for which worth and the recognition of worth are crucial variables.

The explanatory reference to power was not limited to the topics of physics but quickly became a theme and metaphor for many other topics. Human beings, for instance, came to be understood as machines whose behavior is a function of the pursuit of will, a kind of inertial force of self-continuance formed by desire, passion, or arbitrary choice. Human behavior is subject to rational understanding when we assume that persons are impelled toward goals, consciously or not. The combination of the factors of life is comprehensible as an organization designed to accomplish a person's will, and the person's career is intelligible in terms of coping with the structures of the environment relevant to inertial pursuit of goals. Life is to be understood as the modification of inertial will by one's resources and environment. Thomas Hobbes was one of the first to depict the person as an inertial machine. But even without his crude, mechanistic psychology, most subsequent modern philosophers accepted the consequence of his view— that individual subjectivity is intentionally directed inertial will, albeit not necessarily conscious. The brilliance of the modern view is that human behavior is thus subject to mechanistic explanation because rational analysis can be made of the organization of means to achieve goals, and the goals themselves are set by vectors of inertial forces. Human beings are understood as problem-solvers, where the problem is a function of the obstacles that stand in the way of achieving the will's goal. Problem-solving is the successful exercise of power. Even the contemporary psychological functionalists and proponents of artificial intelligence share this view, which had been made the basis of the social sciences by Adam Smith and Karl Marx.

According to the modern commitment to inertial power, the determination of the will's goal is only to be understood as the vector outcome of antecedent forces. There is no way to register the ancient world's concern with the merit and justification of the will's direction. Merit and justification are issues to be raised only about instrumental choices, assuming the larger inertial goals, such as the continuance of life (Hobbes's version) or the pursuit of wealth (Locke's version). Nor is there a way, within the modern conception, to register the problematic of sin, the suggestion that the direction of the will is flawed because it is formed in some serious disrelation to God or to the ultimate conditions of existence.

Political theory, too, adopted the modern metaphor of power. The social contract theory (not to say Machievelli's views) understands that social structure is necessary to compromise or vector together the diverse and often conflicting inertial interests of citizens. Modern political philosophy does not judge primary human interests, or even primary goals for a polity. Rather, it judges the efficiency and rationality of a society, particularly its government, in allowing the individuals' inertial powers to be pursued with least deflection. Most forms of capitalism assume that primary economic desires are not rational but that the secondary desires for attaining the primary ones are. A market is "free" in order to respect the subjective integrity of will itself. Freedom, in the modern sense, divorced from any responsibility more profound than service to the instruments of due procedure, is a function of the prevailing metaphor of inertial power.

The crude residue of the power metaphor in current concerns for social justice is to be found in the mentality suggesting that injustice consists in dominance or oppression, that is, in imbalances of power, especially the powerlessness of the poor and oppressed. Shaped by the metaphor of power, the apparent goal of justice is to give power to the relatively disempowered to seek their own interest, whatever that might be. This residue of the power metaphor abjures any attempt to articulate a true or valid interest for people, save those interests that are instrumental for exercising power. There are two core elements of truth in the modern conception of justice. One is that victims of injustice usually are also powerless, and habitual perpetrators of injustice need power to sustain themselves. The other is that justice in some way requires power for all individuals to participate in public life, a crucial ideal for democracy. Nevertheless, the modern way of expressing these core truths, by means of the metaphor of power, excludes the consideration of the worth of ends; it legitimates only deliberation about means. Furthermore, the belief that empowering the victims by itself leads to greater justice for them or for others is sheer delusion, manifested again and again in our century.

How the idea of power moved from the themes of subjectivity in the human machine and the employment of the social contract to rationalize individual power to the social rhetoric of dominance, oppression, and empowerment is a complex story, certain episodes of which I shall rehearse shortly. At this point, however, I am pleased to say that European and American *religion* averted the impact of the metaphor of power up until this very century. For doing so, religion paid the price of being viewed by the intellectual establishment as not cognitive, not entirely rational, and as something to be explained away in nonreligious terms, such as those of psychology or the sociology of knowledge. Exclusion from cognitive respectability has been painful to many theologians, but it has not inhibited religion from periods of great creativity and influence. In our own time, however, theology has suddenly adopted the mentality of the power theme.

To understand this development, it is necessary to recur to another of the original Renaissance themes, that of narrative. By narrative I mean the understanding of people and history in terms of the interaction of individual stories. Not a chronicle of episodes, nor an exemplification of people as types, narrative in the modern sense supposes that each person's life hangs together as a meaningful unit in story form and that narrative involves the interweaving of these stories. The story of someone's life depicts the shifting direction of intentionality as life's events are addressed.

Many sources of the modern narrative theme exist, including the Renaissance recovery of ancient humanism and Luther and Calvin's recovery of Augustine's *Confessions*. William Haller has noted that the late-sixteenth-century English Puritan preachers departed radically from the Everyman typology of earlier allegorical preaching and, instead, instructed their hearers that everyone has a story responsible to God, a story of ancestry and conditions, but principally of the shifting intentions of the heart or will. Thus was the modern "individual" born, and Haller attributes Shakespeare's success in part to the audience prepared by Puritan preaching.

Religion in the modern era has understood well the importance of narrative for its own expression. The Protestant Reformation, the Catholic Counter-Reformation, and the rise of Hassidism with the reactions for it, have fostered articulation of the individual's story as the way to understand identity in terms of the interaction of personal intentionality and circumstance, both social and physical. The story-formed identity of individual and group is what is conceived by modernity to stand in significant relation to God.

Furthermore, as Thomas J. J. Altizer has documented so thoroughly, the implicit model of the story-formed self that developed for human beings was mirrored in the developing model of God as self. Just as human beings were imagined to have a depth of self of the sort that consists in and is revealed by the unfolding of a personal story, so God was thought to have an analogous, interior, story-formed depth. To be sure, antecedents for the personalization of God existed prior to the modern period. Yahweh was thought to be a jealous, personal God, insistent that Israel follow him rather than the other gods; in this belief, the Hebrew religion bore many resemblances to Mesopotamian and Greek polytheism. As monotheism became the norm in Hebrew thinking, and Yahweh came to be conceived as creator of the world and lord of all nations, the sense of divine intentionality, with judgment, mercy, and love, was carried along. Yet the transcendence of the creator God made it difficult to sustain much of a feel for divine subjectivity, and mediators were thought necessary to convey God's intentionality, as in the appeals to Wisdom and the Logos. In early Christian thought, the humanity of Jesus, coupled with divine origins, divine authority, and uncompromised, divinely begotten nature, allowed the personal characteristics of God to be wholly embodied in the actions and fate of Jesus. Apart from such particular revelations, the transcendent creator was a mystery.

In all of this early history, however, the story form of Yahweh's history with Israel was not a matter of divine inner subjectivity but a chronicle of episodes of promise, betrayal, forgiveness, restoration, and the rest. In Augustine there was a significant beginning to the notion of subjective depth in the self, modeled on a conception of God as memory, love, and will; yet, in Augustine's God those are more principles than an unfolding story. With Thomas Aquinas the conception of God was again returned to principles, especially that of *esse* or the pure act of existence. Only in the Renaissance and Reformation with its assorted reactions to scholastic theology, and with parallels in Jewish life, did God come to be conceived as a person in the modern sense. Within Christianity, the Christocentrism of the Reformation thinkers tended to assimilate the personal qualities of Jesus as Christ to the Trinitarian Godhead as a whole. In the grand philosophy of Hegel, the culminating model of the internally developing, story-formed self, intentional and responsive to external conundra, came to define both the metaphysical principles of the universe constituting divinity and the nature of the human person. That grand synthesis incorporated even the inertially defined nature of modern physics into the historical self of the Absolute. Hegel was first and last a theologian, and since then has been the orienting point for nearly all of European theology.

The Hegelian synthesis summed up the more pervasive cultural assumption of modernity—that history is to be viewed as a story of progress. Its form is a story of the episodes in which the powers of the morally superior prevailed over other powers, over the vicissitudes of nature and disease, over the limitations of human ability to travel and live outside the human niche, over ignorance, barbarism, parochialism, and irrational violence. The most common current focus of the idea of progress is that we now are living in a dramatic narrative in which the powers of right and justice are in contest with those of political and economic oppression; progress hangs in the balance as we righteous ones struggle to make the story come out for justice.

The Hegelian synthesis of course did not last. The narrative side abandoned the rigors of scientific understanding for imagination, and the scientific side thought of the narrative form precisely as imaginative, romantic fiction. Marx was the last major thinker of the European world to attempt to wed narrative to science. In retrospect, we view most of the nineteenth century of European and North American culture to be a war between science gone to scientism and romanticism gone to bourgeois aggrandisement of the ego. Their sometime marriage resulted in effective imperialism. More often, they were two independent, incompatible, and equally foundational themes for organizing and understanding culture, both of them crucial for the construction of the modern Western world.

The end of narrative and power

By our own time, both modern projects have come to an end, beginning with the narrative form for understanding either self or God.

Freud in his way, and Marx in his, pointed out that certain very important elements in a person's story are functions of analogues of inertial forces, not of intentional motives for which a story of responsibility can be told. Therefore, individuals are not to be understood as having story-form identities, but rather as having identities construed in significant part as vectors of forces. The powers of these intrapersonal forces shape the social story as well. And they lead to a counterfeiting of the true achievements of the deep, story-formed self. Perhaps the great ironic symbol of our time is the person walking down a crowded street with a Sony Walkman, listening to the immediately accessible language of the blues made public, encapsulated in the deepest psychic feelings of the private world. The psychic depth that supposedly comes from the extended story of a person before God in the world is transmogrified into a momentary and repeatable feeling, immediate and exempt from criticism, expressed in a public medium that reduces the individual to Everyman with the Blues, alone again with no historical relations. Altizer says the fate of the individual in our time amounts to an abandonment of the Judeo-Christian historical identity and an acquiescence in the Buddhist no-self.

The grand conception of God as the Absolute Self similarly became implausible. Among the reasons for this development are the continuing problems of theodicy: this is not the kind of world an absolutely good, knowing, and powerful God would create; World War I held a mirror to European culture, and what was seen was not the Israel of God. Meanwhile, liberal theology, anxious to make religion compatible with the inertial-power worldview of modern science and to enlist religion in the improvement of a progressing but far from perfect world, undermined the sense of personal relation with a personal God. By no means is it necessary, or even common in the world's religions, that religious life means a person-to-person or I-thou relation with God; but religious life had meant that in modern Christianity, and in much of modern Judaism. And that relation became impossible in the twentieth century. At most, recent popular Christianity entertained a person-to-person relation to a ghostly Jesus, usually in the garden when the dew is still on the roses. When in the 1960s Altizer, Rubenstein, van Buren, Vehanian, and others repeated Nietzsche's claim that God is dead, some Christians and Jews complained, for nostalgic reasons; but hardly anyone else cared. The other religious people knew that the God of the Great Self was a misrepresentation, and that a new representation must be found if religious communities were to sustain themselves.

The fate of the physics of inertial power in the twentieth century was to choke on its own success. Since Francis Bacon, science saw itself as the engine of technological control over human destiny and maintained the fiction of general progress until technology's own instruments were used to put an end to this illusion of and teach once more the ancient doctrine of original sin. The great theoretical achievements of the twentieth century, those conceptions that showed the theories of Newton and his peers to be local special cases of a far vaster truth, gave rise to nuclear destructiveness that completed the joining of nature's vast elements with the unnatural passions of Lear's older daughters. What is physics now but a paradigm negotiating its way through a thoroughly political contest of intellectual and economic dominance?

The combined critique of power and narrative lies in the deconstructionists' use of the notion of logocentrism. Their claim is that Western culture since Hellenic times has been formed by a few dominant ideas or patterns of ideas. The themes of inertial power in physics and of narrative are examples of those ideas. The dominant ideas constitute a logos that centers the culture and gives it meaning. For the logos to be meaningful, it has to be determinate and exclusive. Its meaning consists precisely in those alternative ideas or perspectives that it excludes. And because the dominant idea of a culture excludes from purview the real alternatives to its way of centering reality, it is incommensurable with regard to them and cannot defend itself as superior. In the end, every candidate for the logocentric idea is arbitrary, incommensurate with its alternatives, and no better or worse than the others. Most deconstructionists, being Marxists from nostalgia, recommend the nondominant perspectives, or at least insist that they be placed alongside the dominant ones. No cultural structure can legitimate itself on the deconstructionists' view, however, because any structure depends on being centered on certain exclusive ideas. The practice of deconstructing the dominance of any logocentric candidate is thus presented as an intrinsically necessary subversive task for any society. This accounts for the high moral tone of most deconstructionist writing, despite its obligation to treat any moral idea as logocentric. Deconstruction becomes the voice of philosophical truth and cultural honesty when ideas themselves are viewed under the aspect of their power alone, regardless of their truth or interest.

Theological revolution

In the current theological contributions to social revolution, these ideas of modernity have three principal embodiments, but they are only partial truths and largely mistaken. The first is the supposition that people's most important characteristics regarding justice are the power relations that hold among them and that these are distributed according to social class. The second is the interpretation of the situation of justice and injustice in our time as part of a cosmic narrative of progress, now at a crisis point, where the forces for empowering the victims must overcome the devices of the oppressors. Individuals within the drama are defined by the narrative itself, not by their individual circumstances; they are responsible by virtue of being on one side or another, not because of what they do. The third embodiment of modernity arising from deconstructionist themes is that, once the folly of reducing justice to power dynamics and individual life to participation in a cosmic narrative is recognized, real life has no historical or actual commitment but is like a free-floating, critical, gnostic angel. Against each of these elements of modernity in contemporary theology, I have a counterproposal that is far more revolutionary.

Without denying that people do fall into various classes, and that sometimes these are mediators of large-scale structures of power, I want to suggest an alternative conception of the human social condition, namely, that people are related to one another by an ontological covenant. The idea of covenant has deep biblical roots and has had several theological revivals. The version I propose for our current thinking has five main characteristics.

1. First, as covenantal, relations among human beings are more than "natural," where "natural" means what birds, snakes, lions, and lambs might do by virtue of their inertial will. Specifically, a covenantal relation includes, in addition to the natural elements, two kinds of representations. Each individual acts in reference to representations of himself or herself as a member of the covenantal society. In addition, there are representations of certain relations among people, between individuals and social institutions, and between both of those and the rest of nature, that are normative and ought to be respected as such. These representations, both of self in social roles and of norms for social life, are conventional in the sense that they are subject to the developmental contingencies of history. Yet the former are constitutive of what it is to be a person: persons are beings that integrate representations of themselves with their responses to other things. The latter are norms identifying some of what is valuable and how the values of certain things oblige us. Although the margins of such norms as reflected in the Ten Commandments and the Golden Rule are historically variable, they express observations about worth and obligation that appear quite universal across cultures.

2. Second, the covenantal character of human life is ontologically constitutive. That is, the conditions of self-representation and responsiveness to representations of value are intrinsic parts of being human. In the old theological language of the second creation story in Genesis 2, although animals were created merely naturally, human beings were created by means of the covenant. God prepared the natural garden of Eden for Adam, whom he imported. Adam was made to name the animals, creating conventional language, and to accept a caretaker role with regard to nature. He was biologically divided down to human proportions and presented with Eve, another person, relations with whom were essential to being human. The consequence of acknowledging that the covenant is ontologically constitutive is that, although it can be broken, it cannot be ignored. We can misrepresent ourselves and can deny or distort our appreciations and obligations. But we are then in self-deceit and sin, not free of the covenant. Here is a far subtler analysis of injustice than the simple view that the wrong people have the power.

3. Third, as creatures in covenant, people relate to one another by both natural and institutional media. They participate in various natural systems

of metabolism and environmental interaction, and they play roles in economic, domestic, political, ethnic, artistic, and religious systems. No individual, however, is reduced to one or all of these systems, but has essential features for relating himself or herself to them so as to be responsible. The idea of responsibility is crucial to the covenantal understanding of human life. Whereas according to the class analysis typical of modernity, an individual is an abstract token or counter in a concrete class struggle; according to the covenantal analysis, a person's participation in a social structure is but one part of the individual's reality and likely offers openings for the exercise of the person's responsibility. Whereas in modernity's power analysis, a person is either a victim or oppressor, that is, passive or active with respect to power; in the covenantal analysis, a person is nuanced in many ways with respect to activity and passivity, and in very many ways is responsible for how to relate to environing systems that in turn relate to other people and nature.

4. Fourth, because every person, indeed, every natural thing and social system, is a center of worth and value, and because each thing enjoys that value because of the many relations in which it stands to other things, morality is essentially ambiguous and fragmentary. A person may be good in the economic system but wicked politically. An event might be a triumph for some of the actors but a disaster for others. Of course, we should always choose the greater good where discernible and avoid the greater evil; often, the moral course is clear, especially with regard to the commonly recognized elementary values. Nevertheless, the best of actions will have evil consequences too; no project will ever be completely finished, no life ever fully self-realized. Everything is fragmentary, incomplete, and excellent according to a kind of local snapshot. This is part of what finite existence means. Therefore, no single cosmic story can be told. And, although it is often clear in the proximate view how to tell the good from evil people, and the better from the worse course, we know that in the long view the judgments will get more complex and perhaps even become reversed. The depiction of moral life as a cosmic drama is a bourgeois illusion, an idolatrous expansion of the local to divine proportion.

5. Fifth, because the covenantal status of human beings is in the nature of things—the way we are created—and because we ruin it by deceit and sin, and because that ruin perverts nature and our institutions, and because even our virtues are ambiguous and fragmentary, we are thrown back on the creator for forgiveness and fulfillment. Divine infinity bears our sorrows and sins, loves those we strive to destroy for the greater good, completes our partial lives, and embraces our days in a vaster life that trivializes your death

and mine. Or if there be no God, the ambiguous fragmentariness of finite reality is as absurd as Camus said, and it is unintelligible that there be a world at all. Without faith, one might despair in that contingency. Regardless of despair, the broken covenant constitutes us in a truth about how to represent ourselves and obliges us to respect the irreconcilable worths of things.

I have gone on at length about the covenantal analysis of the human condition in order to provide a contrast to the class analysis that has come to seem almost that of common sense. To sum up, the covenant hypothesis sees human beings as constituted by representations of self and of moral matters, as well as by natural elements; it treats the covenant as ontologically constitutive of human existence; it analyzes social institutions and the natural environment as elements relating individuals but not exhausting them so as to dissolve personal responsibility; it appreciates the fact that finite life is both ambiguous and fragmentary; and it gives thanks for that finite creation as such, hoping for fulfillment in the divine. Perhaps it is becoming apparent how this conception reconnects the current situation with the historical depths of the Judeo-Christian past. Before exploring that, however, it is important to look at the conception of history as narrative.

The second modern theme embodied in most Christian theology fueling social revolutions is the myth of cosmic narrative. I admit that the belief that one is devoting oneself to a great cosmic cause, with the movement of history behind one's puny efforts, is a great motivator. It ranks with other theological views suggesting that martyrdom in a holy war gets one straight to heaven, regardless of sins. Yet like the other it is a great lie. There is no cosmic narrative, rather a great many small narratives interwoven, with overlapping and sometimes contradictory significance. Nor is the fictional narrative told about the West true, that it is a steady progress from paleolithic to primitive to bronze age, iron age, literate age, antiquity, feudalism, renaissance, modernity, enlightenment, high technology, to ourselves. Even the use of technology waxes and wanes. The moral qualities of Western civilization are dappled with spots of corruption, many of which are of our own time.

Most particularly we are self-deceived to think that our moral efforts, which have also been great in the twentieth century, are part of a historic struggle between good and evil. We may indeed minimize racism and gender prejudice in North America, change the social roles of women to give them due advantage, and restructure the international economic system so as to support those now in poverty with means of their own and human dignity. We may disarm the nations possessed of the power to destroy beyond their right, and establish policies of international law, properly enforced, so as to inhibit war. Yet if we do so it should be by a million piecework efforts, not by a juggernaut movement that destroys everything in its path to the goal. And even those small efforts will be destructive as well as constructive.

Is there an alternative to the grand narrative for understanding our historical situation? Nothing with the integrity and simplicity of a story. Rather, the ambiguities of the covenant are our best hope. Each person, each creature and system in nature, each organization and institution in society has a complex worth of its own. Each is indeed lovely and, as the theological tradition puts it, is loved by God just in being created. When, therefore, we strive to eradicate the AIDS virus, defeat the Nazis, undermine oppressive wealth, eliminate means of nuclear offense, incarcerate people prone to violence and abuse—all good things to do, we should do so with a consciousness that all of those people and things also are lovely and holy creatures. From their perspective, our efforts are destructive if not wicked. Therefore, all of our moral efforts ought to be hedged round with an appreciation of the intrinsic loveliness of the entirety of creation, including perhaps especially those things inimical to health and justice as we best define them. This is only to say that, given the realities of the covenant, we should love all things even as their creator does. The theological language is most accurate.

The linchpin of Martin Luther King, Jr.'s social theory was that nothing should be done that could not be done in love toward those people and institutions that stood in the way. He recognized that massive, institutionalized, social evils exist, and that a mass effort must be focused to remove them. He did not acquiesce in inaction because of the complexity of the moral issues. He did not fear to speak many languages to many different people, articulating their roles in the struggle. Yet he did not allow the struggle to be seen as one between classes of people, in which people were defined by their class for good or ill. The struggle was against evil aspects of institutions in which people were caught up in some parts of their lives. Even those institutions had their comforts: King was more at home in the South where he was a nigger than in the North where he was an educated Negro. The strategies he developed from Gandhi's nonviolent activism were pragmatic ones. I doubt he would hold to them in all circumstances. Yet they were normative, because in his circumstances they allowed for the pursuit of justice with love for all and an appreciation of the costs of one's particular good.

A deeper appreciation of the covenant lies in King's life. The reason for his activism was occasional; that is, the opportunity for addressing racism was occasioned by the events leading up to the Montgomery bus boycott and the forces that rallied round for generalizing the struggle. No manifest destiny here. No grand story. Merely rectifying this particular wrong. And his dream was for freedom and community, not victory. Furthermore, his strategy supposed that the events are never over so as to constitute a story; there is always more to do, and successes can only be partial. Finally, he understood that martyrdom is not justified by the subsequent wholesale success of your cause, because it is almost impossible to tell what wholesale success would consist in. Rather, the sacrifice of a life is justified by its excellence as received into the infinite life of God. Just as there is no excuse for shirking moral action because it is ambiguous and unending, so there is no guarantee that the right will triumph in one's own story. Failure, even inevitable failure, does not detract from the excellence of one's efforts because that excellence, like every lovely thing, has its true home in the infinite Creator.

Rather than the motive of a cosmic narrative in which we line up with the triumphant powers of goodness, we should take a more local commitment to the goods we can see obligatory in our own part of the world. Where real causal connections can be made, we expand the scale of moral efforts. But where they are postulated by myth, we should abjure them as the devil's temptations to do damage beyond the reach of our love.

The covenant conception of history has an important implication for learning. Instead of seeking terms of analysis that block individuals into classes, or into dramatis personae of a large narrative, we need social analyses that identify the different ways in which persons participate in many different systems, how they are responsible in that participation, and how the values of things are altered as they are passed through the various systems. A great failure of most current analysis is that it abets the ideological simplifications of class struggle. Each one of us must balance the merits of a social cause against the deficits its pursuit has in other areas. Just about all of life is a balancing of competing claims, none of which we can satisfy purely. Yet they all make sense as elements in our position in the covenant.

The third embodiment of the power and narrative themes of modernity is in deconstruction, and it is a paradoxical embodiment. On the one hand, the deconstructionists are preoccupied with power and have adopted a fairly simple Hegelian view of the negative dialectic in narrative form. On the other, the preoccupation of all modernity with power and narrative is itself a prime example of logocentrism, and so is subject to deconstructive criticism. As has often been remarked, deconstruction will eventually deconstruct itself and cease to exist.

The mode of being of critical consciousness, then, associated with deconstruction, is what I earlier called a free-floating, critical, gnostic angel. That is, the deconstructionist can identify with no social form because each is arbitrary and logocentric. Actual effort—indeed, revolutionary effort—

can be expended to ablate an oppressive form; yet, not connected to a real community, that critical effort has no historical actuality of its own. Deconstruction looks on embodiment much the way the gnostics did.

The alternative to gnostic deconstruction is a critical consciousness that accepts the finitude of historical ambiguity and limited perspective. It sees the finiteness of the critical perspective as itself part of creation and has the courage to judge from within that basis. Furthermore, such finitist critical consciousness begins with a fundamental identification with the covenant: criticism is a form of love, appreciating the loveliness of all things but suggesting ways of overcoming unnecessary subordination of the importance of one thing to another. Paul Tillich, who may yet turn out to be the theological genius of the twentieth century, called this courage to embrace the ambiguous and fragmentary, and to go on with moral and spiritual life, the essence of faith. Our grand stories of progress have failed. Yet the creation is as rich and obligatory as ever. One has faith when one accepts all of this and takes responsibility for critical consciousness and moral action within the limits of one's corner of the garden. If deconstruction is the culmination of the age of modernity, especially of one of its branches, modernism, then its theological fault is faithlessness.

True faith is the mature acceptance of the finite conditions of the covenant and the courage to live up to one's excellence within the limits of one's lights. Perhaps my language is too individualistic here. Like the faithlessness of deconstruction and its siblings, faith is corporate courage as well as individually located. The religiously motivated social movements of our time have often been expressions of corporate courage. As Saint Paul said, we need to encourage one another. The courage is fake, however, when it is mere identification with success and progress. The faith is real when it acknowledges the limits of the finite and the distance between the finite and the infinite. Part of that distance stems from the fact that all of our efforts must fail in some respects, and our own lives will be incomplete no matter how long and powerfully we live. Faith is the confidence that we can ruin nothing that God cannot redeem.

I promised earlier to say how theology needs concepts more revolutionary than the merely modern themes that stimulate many of the current social revolutions. Let me conclude with some reflections on this argument.

First, revolution in the modernist sense has been conceived as a dialectical negation, a rejection of the old in favor of forms that negate it. To the contrary, a more radical revolution is one that breaks open the present to accept the past and move toward a better future. The theological idea of the covenant defended here in fact is a retrieval of an ancient theme that leads straight to the future goal of a community of mutual respect. Theology has impoverished itself when it has rejected the language of its tradition. Instead, it must recover that and reshape it to the critical advantage of the present.

Second, the idea of covenant requires abandoning the tired modern idea that people are seekers of inertial self-interest. They rather are complex creatures participating in many different systems, most likely misrepresenting themselves in their participation and perverting the true worths of things. People are not just selfish, as modernity suggests, but in fact destructive of the self and of the entire community of persons, society, and nature that constitutes the human creation. That is sin, not immaturity, not illness, not selfishness, not frustration at self-realization. That our problems are those of sin, not mechanical "mal-function," is truly revolutionary for the modern age.

Third, moral action and social change should not be conceived as devices aimed to fulfill oneself or one's group. There is nothing to suggest that fulfillment is possible except at the expense of most of one's environment and even of most of the dimensions of one's life. Rather than fulfillment, we should rather seek excellence in that part of the covenanted creation local to our actions, accepting the fact that excellence is itself limited, fragmentary, and perhaps also vicious on its dark side. Our aim in social justice should be justice, not success with our plans. Hence, the revolutionary motive power in justice is love, not the anger of struggle.

Nothing I have said about the idea of covenant as an analysis of the human condition, nor about the finite and nonteleological approach to social action, nor about faith in the worthiness of virtue, is particularly new. Its novelty comes only in its use as a para-postmodern critique of modernity. In the actual social revolutions and changes now being guided by Christian theological reflection, my terms are present alongside the themes of modernity. Perhaps the modern themes are stronger; they surely determine the rhetoric in most instances. Yet the covenantal themes are both closer to the rhetorical roots of the tradition and are far more realistic about the human condition. People are not just power machines, and the grand narrative, particularly that aspect depicting progress, has been given the lie by history. For theology to be truly revolutionary, it must first revolve to its origins and repossess its early insights. Then it can guide the volatile forces of change with nuance, realism, and true faith.

The symbiotic relation between theology and philosophy is peculiar in our time because of a reversal in its usual working. In our time, theology, in appropriating its ancient idea of covenant, provides the critical ideas that can reorient philosophy after the collapse of the modern themes of power and narrative. Theology thus is both critic and source of imaginative novelty, relatively speaking. Philosophy, for its part, has provided the cultural substance whose presuppositions need to be articulated and criticized, philosophy in the modern secular sense. There are some cultural leaders, of course, who reject philosophy out of hand as abstracted, effete, and irrelevant. They are mistaken because philosophy determines our sense of possibility, as the bondage of current advocates of praxis to the themes of power and narrative illustrates. Other cultural leaders, including some in philosophy, reject theology out of hand because its intellectual commitments are incredible and religion is identified too often with injustice. They, too, are mistaken because it is from the theological traditions of the West and elsewhere that the elementary motifs connecting human beings with one another, with the earth, and with their institutions can be recovered.

In a deeper sense, the old theme is valid today. Religion is what calls us to engage the world, and theology is the understanding of this engagement. Philosophy is the critic that asks about the truth of our religious substance. The age of modernist philosophy is over, just as much as is the age of religious fundamentalism with which it is associated. As theology seeks new religious forms for the social construction of the covenant, philosophy seeks new ground from which to understand and critically analyze religious substance. Philosophy also does much else than attend to religion's problems, and theology is not to be held in suspension until philosophy gets its new forms in motion. Yet the critical and creative interplay between them is as rich and needy as ever.

Part IV

Culture

Memory and

Textual

Interpretation

Eva T. H. Brann

The Six

Silences of a

Keats's "Ode on a Grecian Urn" is a singable, **Grecian Urn**
a sayable, and, finally, even a sententious
poem—and yet it represents and enjoins si-
lence insistently and variously. In fact, I discern six modes of silence:

(1) The silence that surrounds the urn's provenance as the "foster-
child of silence."
(2) The silence of the urn itself as a bearer of legends, as a "silent
form."
(3) The silence within its pictures, those "melodies . . . unheard."
(4) The silence of its world, the town whose streets "for evermore/
Will silent be."
(5) The poet's silence about the contents of the urn.
(6) The final silence enjoined by the urn's epigraph.

It is my purpose in the next few pages to detail the nature of these silences
and to speculate on what they betoken.

(1) Quietness and silence are not, to be sure, anything so generative with
respect to the urn as husband and progenitor, but they *are* its groom and
foster parent. Keats has a fine feeling for the rearing of an antiquity: Seclu-
sion and the long passage of time—that is, the parentage of an artifact
insofar as it is truly antique, while perennial intactness is its state.

(2) The urn, reared by silence, is itself a silent being, a "silent form"
striking a beautiful pose, a "fair attitude." Archaeologists are wont to see
vases anthropomorphically, especially amphoras such as this one. For this
kind of a pot has a mouth, a neck, two armlike handles, shoulders, a belly,
and a foot. This Grecian creature, in turn, bears a silent legend, a wordless
story, a visual inscription. The vase expresses its tale "more sweetly than our
rhyme," but not very explicitly. Its stubbornly tacit telling elicits a storm of
questions, ten questions of the What?, Who?, Where? sort. For although the
vase is a historian—a "sylvan historian," which is to say, a recounter of
pastoral idylls—it gives us no places, names, or dates (Brooks 156). Its idylls
are genre scenes.

There are three interpretations of the scenes displayed on and by the urn. A drawing, attributed to Keats himself, of the Neoattic amphora in the Louvre signed by Sosibios shows the typical Neoattic decorative system: a "brede" of dionysiac dancers in single file all around the body of the vase (Vendler 17). In the "Ode on Indolence," Keats sees three figures in his dream state:

> They pass'd, like figures on a marble urn,
>> When shifted round to see the other side;
>>> They came again; as when the urn once more
> Is shifted round, the first seen shades return;
> And they were strange to me, as may betide
>> With vases, to one deep in Phidian lore.

These dream figures, too, seem to form a continuous braid with those that appear as the vase is turned, just as do the figures on the Sosibios vase. The strangeness of these Greco-Roman figures on the dream urn (the Neoattic sculptors produced marbles in Athens for the Roman market) yields on the Grecian urn to the familiar Attic "Phidian lore." It is generally thought that Keats borrowed one of his subjects, "that heifer lowing at the skies," from a sacrificial cattle scene on the Phidian Parthenon frieze (Vendler 113). But the compositional scheme, the discontinuity of the scenes, he apparently borrowed from Attic pottery. Archaic or classical amphoras are not "overwrought" with figures; they bear two pictures, one front and one back, framed in the earlier black-figure style and free in the classical red-figure.

Therefore, a suggestion that the urn bears three scenes, an orgiastic pursuit, a courtship, and a sacrifice (Vendler 123) may be set aside. The text can be read to support the classical choice: two distinct events. One is the love chase of the second stanza (interpreted as identical with the "mad pursuit" of the question in the first stanza). The other is the symmetrically placed scene of sacrifice in the fifth stanza. As stanzas one and five speak *to* the urn as a sentient being, stanzas two and four muse *on* it as the bearer of tales.

The main point is that the urn is questioned vainly about the particulars of these scenes. Their location might be the valley of Tempe, or the mountains of Arcadia—Tempe, the lovely wild Thessalian gorge of the river Peneus at the periphery of Hellas, Arcadia, the rustic, wild, "bear country" in its interior—the vase from the Attic center speaks of the romantic provinces. One may conjecture about the names of the figures in the love chase: Daphne (whose father is in fact Peneus) was chased by Apollo and was saved by being turned into a laurel tree; perhaps the boughs that cannot shed their leaves are laurels. But Daphne's tale is one of fear, not of happy love, and on the vase there is nothing to mark the god. Nor can we locate the little town "by river or sea-shore,/Or mountain-built." In other words, just as nothing about the urn is particularized—neither its date (which may be the fifth century or the first century B.C.), nor its shape, nor its decorative scheme (which may be a continuous braid or two discontinuous pictures)—so the pictures are genre representations, incapable of responding with particulars to the queries of the poet. What?, Where?, Who?, When?—that storm of questions is re-buffed by the urn's implacable generality. Spitzer (88, n. 15) cites the poem "Kore" by Goethe (written about the time of the "Grecian Urn," 1820), in which similar questions are rebuffed in the name of the "inviolateness" of the work of art: the urn will not give mere secular information.

(3) The third silence is the silence within the pictures, the "unheard" melodies and "ditties of no tone," the silent panting, the toneless lowing. Just as the silent urn can express its "flowery tale more sweetly than our rhyme," so the unheard melodies depicted in its tale are the sweeter for their silence. It is this silence of pictured sound that makes the poet meditate *on* the urn rather than speak *to* it.

"Heard melodies are sweet, but those unheard/Are sweeter": the mind runs to all the paradoxes of our tradition—to Heraclitus' saying that "the unseen harmony is better than the seen" (Kirk and Raven 193), to the silent Pythagorean music of the spheres (Spitzer 78), to Plato's invisible forms. But those forms are intelligible beings, the Pythagorean music consists of num-ber ratios, and the Heraclitean harmony is the all-collecting *logos*. They all are hypersensual. Keats's unheard melodies, on the other hand, are not above the senses but are eminently visual: visible, frozen music, sound transposed into visibility. The silence of and in the pictures is the silence of sight.

(4) The fourth silence belongs to the world the urn inhabits, the world of antiquity. Keats's accurate sense for the soundless romance of the antique comes out especially in the fourth stanza, in the most poignant conceit of the poem (Brooks, p. 161): the little town whose "streets for evermore/Will silent be," because its inhabitants have wandered onto the vase in a sacrificial procession. Here, the poem breaks out of the surface of the artifact into its world—its antique world, that is, the setting that it carries along insofar as it belongs to bygone times. Here is what I mean. When you visit the ruins of ancient towns, you see them devoid of figures: "not a soul to tell/Why thou art desolate, can e'er return." Every ancient figure—man, woman, or beast—that we know comes to us on or as an artifact, be it of clay, marble, or words. Ancient cities are essentially silent and unpeopled, as any connoisseur of the melancholy charm of ancient sites knows.

(5) The fifth silence is the poet's own silence about the contents of the urn. A vase is often a burial pot or a grave marker or a cinerarium. To think of an

antique urn is to think of a funereal function. Spitzer, probably having in mind Keats's line "silent as a consecrated urn" from *Endymion* (III 32), says that the Grecian urn is "obviously consecrated to the ashes of a dead person" (73, 78 n. 8). Again, he cites an apposite poem by Goethe, the first of the Venetian epigrams (1790). Goethe says that the pagan was wont to decorate sarcophagi and urns with signs of life:

> Symbols, drums strike up, we see and hear the marbles.
> Thus fulness overcomes death and the ashes inside
> Seem in their silent precincts yet to rejoice in life.

The urn tacitly holds death within, as it allusively speaks of death in its idylls. Arcady is the place of ecstasy, but its name is also a reminder of the presence of death: the death's head with the legend "*Et in Arcadia ego,*" "Even in Arcady am I [death]," belongs to the traditional English conception of Arcadia (Panofsky 310).

Moreover, the poet himself alludes obliquely to death. "When old age shall this generation waste," the urn will survive to be a friend to mankind. Death is a tacit presence in the ode.

(6) The sixth silence, finally, is the urn's reply in the last stanza to the poet's assault of questions, the unspoken epigraph that enjoins silence.

Ancient monuments do often speak. Statues and grave markers carry epigraphs, often elegiac distichs. The most famous speaking stone of antiquity was the marker erected for the fallen Spartans of Thermopylae; Simonides wrote its inscription. The translation—I do not know its author (Spitzer 91)—rings true to the character of an epigraphic two-liner, although it does not quite preserve the Greek elegiac meter. (I follow the now accepted reading that understands the urn to be uttering not just the aphorism but the whole distich, Vendler 312, n. 18.)

–	˘	˘	–	˘	–	˘	–	˘	–
Tell	them	in	La	ce	dae	mon,	pas	ser-	by,
Beau	ty	is	truth,	truth	beau	ty,—	that	is	all

˘	–	˘	–	˘	–	˘	–	˘	–
That	here	o	be	dient	to	their	laws	we	lie
Ye	know	on	earth	and	all	ye	need	to	know.

All that this comparison shows is how well Keats's odic meter lends itself to an epigraphic climax: it is the urn's second, verbal legend, the complement to the "leaf-fringed legend" of the beginning stanza.

I say "climax," but several critics say "come-down" (Brooks 152). T. S. Eliot, for example, calls the epigraph a "serious blemish" because it is either incomprehensible or untrue.

It seems that the saying is not unmeaning and that it is, in fact, to be taken as the burden of the ode, as its teaching, even its preaching. After all, the poet addresses the urn when it is about to utter, as "cold pastoral," an address in stark contrast to the mood of its pastoral idyll, representing love "forever warm." The address "cold pastoral" means that the urn does not bear only sylvan history, pastoral scenes, but a pastoral letter, an instructive communication to the fold.

What, then, is the gist of its teaching, true or false? What does it mean to say that truth and beauty are completely convertible and that this apothegm is the sum of necessary knowledge?

That beauty is truth, or the portal to truth, is not a new or strange thought. It is, for example, to be found in Shaftesbury and through him in Akenside (Brann 1988: 10), as well as in Schiller (Spitzer 87, n. 14). The notion, so obviously congenial to poets and aestheticians, has an ancient origin in a severer philosophy. In Plato's *Phaedrus,* beauty is understood as Being made manifest (250); sensual beauty gives direct access to the forms, not through the "murky organs" of rational speech, as an ancient commentator explains (Hermeias in Hackforth 94), but immediately, through vision. The meaning, through variations, is that beauty is revelatory, that an object of beauty says something, that it carries significance. But in the Platonic case—and in Schiller's—being and truth themselves are beyond beauty. Beauty merely signifies and gives access to the realm of perfect knowledge: "Only through the morning-gate of the beautiful/Did you penetrate into cognition's land . . ./What we once experienced here as beauty/Will one day come to meet us as truth" (Schiller).

Keats's urn, however, goes much further when it announces in addition that truth is beauty, that is to say, that truth and beauty are mutually convertible terms, hence identical. And it adds the preachment of faith and authority: "that is all/Ye know on earth, and all ye need to know." The urn's silent form does indeed "tease us out of thought." Bowra (143) cites, by way of comparison, Keats's epistle to Reynolds:

> Oh never will the prize,
> High reason, and the love of good and ill,
> Be my award! Things cannot to the will
> Be settled, but they tease us out of thought.

In the presence of beautiful things like the urn, we are coaxed to renounce speech and reason, to refrain from importunate questioning, and, since a "Question is the best beacon towards a little speculation," even to forgo thought (Vendler 111). "Truth beauty," the converse of "Beauty is truth," is a metric throwaway and an *apparently* unmeaning, if not false, addendum for the sake of symmetry, but it amounts in fact to a startling injunction, startling, that is, in a verbal text: Silence! No questions! No words!

The "Ode on a Grecian Urn" belongs to a tradition going back to antiquity, the tradition of "iconic" poetry (Brann 1988: 7), poetry in which *eikones,* visual works of representational art, are described. A subgenre of this type, surviving into modernity, is the *Bildgedicht,* or picture-poem, in which a work of art is described and is made to speak to the reader through a pseudoinscription (Spitzer 92, n. 17). Deeply involved in this tradition is a special aspect of the old rivalry between poetry and painting (Brann 1991), between the invisible word and the speechless picture. Can these preempt each other's function? Can pictures narrate stories as well as words can paint pictures? Which art encompasses the other, thus exceeding it in imaginative scope? But above all, which one is the higher and truer?

Keats's iconic poem gives a remarkable answer. The visible in its silences is truer than the audible and the verbal. Poetry and music fall below sculptured marble (Vendler 305, n. 3). To be sure, there is a certain irony in the thesis, since it is only through the poetic word that the urn is present to the visual imagination, yet there is nothing ironic about the preference for visual beauty. Why does Keats subordinate speech to sight?

Only one other ode has an odd number of stanzas, the "Ode to Autumn," which has three. (The "Ode to Melancholy" originally had four stanzas; Keats canceled the first.) A poem with a central stanza is apt to display an axial symmetry, as the "Ode on a Grecian Urn" indeed does. Stanzas one and five, two and four correspond. Consequently, it also has a precise, literal center:

> More happy love! more happy, happy love!
> For ever warm and still to be enjoy'd. . . .

At the heart of the poem is unconsummated love—unconsummated but not therefore imperfect. This "art is a therapy because it temporarily calms the desiring that turns neurotic for not having" (Lockridge, 406). What draws Keats to the visual beauty of the vase seems to be its peculiar healing temporality, its special stasis. This stasis is not that of timeless eternity, but rather it is *like* eternity: a sempiternal moment, a frozen passage, not-yet turned into "for ever," an unwearied anticipation, an unsated expectancy, a permanent potentiality. This beauty knows death but holds it in abeyance; it is neither alive nor dead, neither in nor out of time. The word "still," which occurs twice in the poem, characterizes this stasis as "still enduring," "yet to come," and "silent." "Thou *still* unravish'd bride of quietness" surely summons all three meanings.

Words and music pass in time; timeless truth is not of the senses. What Keats's demiparadise of marble beauty offers is the silent stasis of a visual moment, of an ahistorical antiquity, of an unnamed idyll, of a never-ending pursuit, of an unheard music, of an unconsummated love, of an ineffective death, of a nonintellectual form. This is not philosophy's but imagination's paradise—the attempt to establish a pure, high, and incorruptible realm of sensation:

> I am certain of nothing but of the holiness of the Heart's affections and the truth of Imagination—What the imagination seizes as Beauty must be truth—whether it existed before or not—. . . .
>
> The Imagination may be compared to Adam's dream—he awoke and found it truth. I am the more zealous in this affair, because I have never yet been able to perceive how any thing can be known for truth by consequitive reasoning—and yet it must be. Can it be that even the greatest Philosopher ever arrived at his goal without putting aside numerous objections. However it may be, O for a Life of Sensations rather than of Thoughts! It is "a Vision in the form of Youth" a Shadow of reality to come—and this consideration has further convinced me for it has come as auxiliary to another favorite Speculation of mine, that we shall enjoy ourselves here after by having what we called happiness on Earth repeated in a finer tone and so repeated. And yet such a fate can only befall those who delight in Sensation rather than hunger as you do after Truth. Adam's dream will do here and seems to be a conviction that Imagination and its empyreal reflection is the same as human Life and its Spiritual repetition. But as I was saying—the simple imaginative Mind may have its rewards in the repetition of its own silent Working coming continually on the Spirit with a fine Suddenness—to compare great things with small—have you never by being Surprised with an old Melody—in a delicious place—by a delicious voice, felt over again your very Speculations and Surmises at the time it first operated on your Soul—do you not remember forming to yourself the singer's face more beautiful than it was possible and yet with the elevation of the Moment you did not think so—even then you were mounted on the Wings of Imagination so high—that the Prototype must be here after— that delicious face you will see. [To Benjamin Baily, November 22, 1817] (Forman 67–68).

Nothing could be more explicit. The rational truth of philosophy is to be replaced by the rarefied truth of the imagination. Or, put in another, complementary, way: This poet's homage to silence intends to alleviate the burdens of romanticism by means of the categories of classicism: particular history by generic antiquity, death by marble beauty, cloying consummation by frozen pursuit, temporal sensation by silent stasis.

Appendix

John Keats
Ode on a Grecian Urn

Thou still unravish'd bride of quietness,
    Thou foster-child of silence and slow time,
Sylvan historian, who canst thus express
    A flowery tale more sweetly than our rhyme:
What leaf-fring'd legend haunts about thy shape
    Of deities or mortals, or of both,
        In Tempe or the dales of Arcady?
    What men or gods are these? What maidens loth?
What mad pursuit? What struggle to escape?
    What pipes and timbrels? What wild ecstasy?

Heard melodies are sweet, but those unheard
    Are sweeter: therefore, ye soft pipes, play on;
Not to the sensual ear, but, more endear'd,
    Pipe to the spirit ditties of no tone:
Fair youth, beneath the trees, thou canst not leave
    Thy song, nor ever can those trees be bare;
        Bold lover, never, never canst thou kiss,
Though winning near the goal—yet, do not grieve;
        She cannot fade, though thou hast not thy bliss,
    For ever wilt thou love, and she be fair!

Ah, happy, happy boughs! that cannot shed
    Your leaves, nor ever bid the spring adieu;
And, happy melodist, unwearied,
    For ever piping songs for ever new;
More happy love! more happy, happy love!
    For ever warm and still to be enjoy'd,
        For ever panting, and for ever young;
All breathing human passion far above,
    That leaves a heart high-sorrowful and cloy'd,
        A burning forehead, and a parching tongue.

Who are these coming to the sacrifice?
    To what green altar, O mysterious priest,
Lead'st thou that heifer lowing at the skies,
    And all her silken flanks with garlands drest?
What little town by river or sea shore,
    Or mountain-built with peaceful citadel,
        Is emptied of this folk, this pious morn?

And, little town, thy streets for evermore
    Will silent be; and not a soul to tell
        Why thou art desolate, can e'er return.

O Attic shape! Fair attitude! with brede
    Of marble men and maidens overwrought,
With forest branches and the trodden weed;
    Thou, silent form, dost tease us out of thought
As doth eternity: Cold Pastoral!
    When old age shall this generation waste,
        Thou shalt remain, in midst of other woe
    Than ours, a friend to man, to whom thou say'st,
"Beauty is truth, truth beauty,"—that is all
    Ye know on earth, and all ye need to know.

Note

This essay is an extension of a chapter from *The World of the Imagination* (Rowman and Littlefield, 1991). Parts of that book served as text for a segment of the NEH Summer Institute at Clemson University. I want to thank the members of the seminar for new insights, and also George Lucas and Patricia Cook for making my stay fruitful and pleasant.

References

Bowra, C. M. "Ode on a Grecian Urn," in *The Romantic Imagination*. Oxford: Oxford University Press, 1952.

Brann, Eva T. H. "Pictures in Poetry: Keats' 'Ode on a Grecian Urn.'" *San Jose Studies* 14 (Fall 1988): 6–13.

———. "Poetry and Painting: Non-Mutual Sisters," part 4, chap. 1B, in *The World of the Imagination: Sum and Substance*. Lanham, Md.: Rowman and Littlefield, 1991.

Brooks, Cleanth. "Keats's Sylvan Historian: History Without Footnotes," in *The Well Wrought Urn*. New York: Harcourt, Brace and World, 1947.

Forman, Maurice B. *The Letters of John Keats*. Oxford: Oxford University Press, 1952.

Hackforth, R. *Plato's Phaedrus*. Cambridge: Cambridge University Press, 1952.

Kirk, G. S. and Raven, J. E. *The Presocratic Philosophers*. Cambridge: Cambridge University Press, 1963.

Lockridge, Laurence S. "Keats and the Ethics of Immanence," in *The Ethics of Romanticism*. Cambridge: Cambridge University Press, 1989.

Panofsky, Erwin. "*Et in Arcadia Ego:* Poussin and the Elegiac Tradition," in *Meaning in the Visual Arts*. Garden City, N.Y.: Doubleday, 1955.

Spitzer, Leo. "The 'Ode on a Grecian Urn,' or Content vs. Metagrammar," in *Essays on English and American Literature*. Princeton, N.J.: Princeton University Press, 1962.

Vendler, Helen. *The Odes of John Keats*. Cambridge, Mass.: Harvard University Press, 1983.

George L. Kline

Changing Russian

Assessments of

This essay is a specialized case study in the philosophical uses of historical traditions. The tradition I am concerned with is dual: the tradition of Spinoza's thought, and the tradition of his German academic commentators. The uses of this tradition by Russian authors are of two sorts: the uses of Spinoza by Russian thinkers, and the uses of both Spinoza and his German commentators by Russian academic scholars.

Spinoza and Their

German Sources,

1796–1862

The Russian authors who wrote about, quoted from, or referred to Spinoza during the years from 1796 through 1862 fall into two categories: thinkers, five in number, whose involvement with Spinoza was casual and even superficial (1796–1857); scholars, four in number—mainly academic historians of Western philosophy—whose involvement was somewhat more extensive and whose treatment was much more detailed (1819–62). The second group exhibits the *changing* assessments referred to in my title.

Two members of the first group, Radishchev and Khomyakov, were also gifted, if minor, poets. Among their contemporaries there were at least three major Russian poets: Derzhavin in the late eighteenth century, Baratynsky and Pushkin in the early nineteenth. However, unlike their German counterparts—in particular, Lessing, Schiller, and Goethe—whose work the Russian poets knew, admired, and sometimes translated, the Russian poets, major as well as minor, seem to have taken no interest in "Romantic pantheism" generally or the thought of Spinoza as interpreted, say, by Goethe, in particular.

The difference between the thinkers and the scholars with regard to Spinoza is striking. The brief mentions of, or quotations from, Spinoza by the five Russian thinkers are all either laudatory or neutral. In contrast, the treatment of Spinoza by the first two scholars is sharply critical, occasionally bordering on abusiveness. It is only the last of the four scholars who offers a full, sympathetic, and balanced account of Spinoza's thought.

The "German sources" referred to in my title—half a dozen early nineteenth-century historians of philosophy—were of primary importance for the scholars. However, the thinkers also got their Spinoza mostly through the German translations of S. H. Ewald (1787–96) and Berthold Auerbach (1841). It was not that these Russians were innocent of Latin; all nine of them appear to have had a passable reading knowledge of the language. But they were all fluent in German, so it was natural for them to consult the existing German translations. There were, in any case, no Russian translations of Spinoza at the time; the first (of the *Ethics*) did not appear until 1886.

The five thinkers, with the dates of their documented "brief encounters" with Spinoza's writings, are Alexander N. Radishchev (1796), Peter Ya. Chaadayev (1828–30, 1831), Ivan V. Kireyevsky (1830, 1832, 1852), Alexander I. Herzen (1843–47, 1850, 1856–57), Alexis S. Khomyakov (1847, 1856). The four scholars, with the dates of their treatments of Spinoza, are Alexander I. Galich (1819), F. M. Nadezhin (1837), Archimandrite Gavriil (1839), and S. G. Kovner (1862).

I

Alexander Nikolayevich Radishchev (1749–1802), who had become familiar with natural-law theory during his study at German universities (1766–71), used that theory as a basis for attacking the abuses of serfdom and of imperial and bureaucratic power in his celebrated *Journey from Petersburg to Moscow* (1790). Catherine II, alarmed by the events in Paris in 1789, overreacted to Radishchev's book, mistaking his reformism for radicalism and his warning of the possibility of revolutionary violence in Russia for advocacy of such violence. Radishchev was condemned to death, but the sentence was commuted to Siberian exile, during which he wrote the treatise, *On Man, His Mortality and Immortality*, begun in 1792 and completed in 1796, and published posthumously. It is in this work rather than in the *Journey* that Spinoza's name appears, in a context which suggests that Radishchev is implicitly defending Spinoza (along with Hobbes) against the common charge of atheism. "Man has a conception of the Supreme Being," Radishchev declares, continuing, "Call it what you will, but Hobbes felt it and so did Spinoza. . . ."[1]

Peter Yakovlevich Chaadayev (1794–1856) was declared officially insane after the publication in 1836 of a Russian translation, in the journal *Teleskop*, of the first of his *Lettres philosophiques* (which had circulated privately since its composition, in French, in 1829). The reason for this harsh verdict was its unsparing critique of Russian history and culture, along with its strongly expressed admiration for Western culture generally and the Roman Catholic

Church in particular. He quotes Spinoza in the Fourth Letter, written in 1831, but not published until after Chaadayev's death. The source of that letter's epigraph is identified only as "Spinoza, *De Anima*," perhaps the result of confusing *anima* with *mens* as it appears in the title of part II: "De naturâ, et origine mentis," regularly abbreviated in the running heads of that part as "De mente." However, the passage comes not from part II but from part I, the proof of prop. 32. Chaadayev's French version reads: "La volonté n'est qu'une manière de penser. Que l'on s'imagine la volonté comme finie ou comme infinie, toujours faut-il reconnaître une cause qui la détermine à agir: elle ne doit donc être envisagée que comme un principe nécessaire et non comme un principe libre."[2] The translation is accurate enough, except for the free rendering of *modus* as *manière* and of *causa* as *principe*.

The other quotation, in the same letter, is identified only by the name 'Spinoza'; in fact, it is from the note to prop. 17 of part I of the *Ethics*. Complaining about those thinkers who "reduce divinity to a being similar to themselves," Chaadayev adds, quoting Spinoza:

> "They attribute to God"—as a great and experienced thinker has said— "a reason similar to that which they themselves possess. Why? Because they know of nothing in their own nature more perfect than their reason. But Divine Reason is the cause of everything and human reason is but an effect: what, then, can these two reasons have in common? At best," this thinker said, "what there is in common between the constellation of the Dog which shines in the sky and the dog which runs about in the street: merely the name."[3]

This translation is freer than the first; indeed, it amounts to a paraphrase of Spinoza's text. But it does not distort his meaning.

Chaadayev was not enough of a medievalist to have noticed—or at least to have mentioned—that the relation between the constellation *Canis* and the animal *canis,* as an analogue of the contrast between Divine Intellect and human intellect, is to be found in Boethius.

Chaadayev's reference to Spinoza as a "great thinker" is reinforced by two other comments dating from the period 1828–30. In the course of a searching critique of pantheism—which in the Fifth Letter he was to call a "grievous doctrine"[4]—Chaadaev remarked that "Schelling is held to have done no more than develop Spinoza's system, putting the finishing touches to modern pantheism."[5] But Chaadayev also admitted that the pantheist Spinoza was, in all likelihood, a very pious human being: "[R]eading him, one feels carried away, despite oneself, by something extraordinarily devout, something which penetrates through the mathematical arrogance of his argument; this is all the more striking because it is so unexpected."[6]

Ivan Vasilyevich Kireyevsky (1806–56), later to become one of the two leading Slavophiles (the other being Alexis Khomyakov), spent several months in Berlin early in 1830 and attended a number of Hegel's lectures on the history of modern philosophy. In two long letters to his family in Moscow (March 15 and 26–30, 1830), Kireyevsky reported that he had had a number of pleasant and stimulating conversations with Hegel, Gans, Michelet, et al., some of them during a dinner party at Hegel's home. He expressed his high excitement at the thought that he was surrounded by "the first-class minds of Europe." Kireyevsky found Hegel's manner of lecturing—frequent coughing and the swallowing of many of his words—repellent, but he was intrigued to learn what Hegel, a man of striking "individuality," would have to say about the great modern philosophers. Unfortunately, Kireyevsky gives us no details; he merely reports that, as of early March, Hegel had finished lecturing on Descartes and was beginning to discuss Spinoza.[7]

Two years later, back in Moscow, Kireyevsky published in the first issue of *Evropeyets* ("The European"), a journal which he had just founded, an essay called "The Nineteenth Century," in which he offers a quick survey of the development of modern philosophy from Descartes to Schelling—including Leibniz's preestablished harmony, French and English materialism, Kant's critical philosophy, Fichte's idealism, and Spinoza's "realism."[8]

Twenty years later, now a full-fledged Slavophile, Kireyevsky offers a more substantial as well as more critical account of Spinoza's thought. After sketching the extreme rationalism (*rassudochnost'*) of Descartes's position, Kireyevsky adds:

> It is thus not surprising that his disciple and successor in the dominant line of philosophical development, the celebrated Spinoza, should have forged his rational conclusions concerning the first cause and the supreme order and structure of the universe so skilfully [*sic*] and compactly that, in the whole of creation, he was unable to see, through that dense and unbreakable network of theorems and syllogisms, the traces of the Living Creator or to detect the inner freedom within man.[9]

Rassudochnost', the term which Kireyevsky uses to characterize Descartes's kind of rationalism, is an abstract noun formed from *rassudok* (roughly, *Verstand*, but with an even more pejorative connotation than Hegel gave this term). It is the term regularly used by the Slavophiles to castigate West European cultural and philosophical "rationalism." It means something like "one-sided, superficial, analytical rationality."

The fairly frequent references to Spinoza in the writings of the prolific essayist, memoirist, and critic Alexander Ivanovich Herzen (1812–70) may be divided into two classes, although certain passages fall into both classes: (1)

passages that emphasize the boldness of Spinoza's thought and the strength of his character, and (2) passages that characterize Spinoza's thought as a whole or in certain of its aspects. Herzen is a true Romantic in this as in other senses; all of his mentions of Spinoza are decidedly favorable.

Herzen's references to the audacity of Spinoza's thought and the firmness and even nobility of his character are often formulated to make an invidious distinction between the relative tolerance with which independent thinkers like Spinoza and Lessing have been treated in the West and the intolerance with which independent Russian thinkers like Chaadayev (and Herzen himself) have been treated in Russia.[10]

In an early diary entry (not published until after his death) Herzen asserts that Leibniz "lacked Spinoza's incorruptible honesty."[11] Three years later Herzen spelled out at least part of what he had in mind:

> To leave something unsaid or incompletely expressed means to leave open the possibility of being misunderstood; one should rather avoid all equivocal expressions—scientific [i.e., theoretical] honesty requires this. Such is Spinoza's language. One may not agree with anything he says, but one must pause in respect before his courageous and candid speech, and this is the reason why he has been hated ten times as much as other thinkers who have said the same thing that he has said.[12]

In this connection, Herzen asserted flatly that "Since Bruno philosophy has had only one great biography, that *del gran Ebreo* of science (Spinoza),"[13] a man who "sacrificed everything to philosophy."[14]

Herzen left Russia, to go into permanent exile in Western Europe in 1847. Writing (in Russian) from Paris in 1850, he placed Spinoza in the perhaps surprising company of David Hume, singling out the two thinkers as admirable exceptions to the general rule that philosophers tend to hold back or conceal their deepest and most shocking insights. "Will you find many," Herzen asks rhetorically, "like Spinoza and Hume who fearlessly go where the truth leads them?" Although he does not specify what it is that he finds shocking in Hume's thought, I assume that it would be the skeptical account of causality and, especially, the critique of miracles and the cosmological and teleological arguments for the existence of God, as well as Hume's blunt "Epicurean" formulation of the problem of evil in the *Dialogues Concerning Natural Religion*. In any case, Herzen draws an invidious contrast with other major thinkers: "What finessing, what circumlocution, what sugaring of the pill the best minds like Bacon or Hegel resorted to in order to avoid plain speaking . . . !"[15]

In the context of critical remarks about Schelling's philosophy in an early letter to his good friend Ogarev, who had just announced his "conversion" to

Schellingianism, Herzen identified Fichte and Spinoza as the "extremes united by Schelling."[16] By "Fichte" he presumably meant something like "extreme individualism" and by "Spinoza" something like "pantheistic impersonalism." In a diary entry of a decade later, Herzen added that Spinoza

> considered thought the highest act of love, the goal and life of the mind. Without discussing his doctrine as a whole, I note the lightning-bolts of genius which flash repeatedly across his works, e.g., "Homo liber de nullâ re minùs, quàm de morte cogitat, et ejus sapientia non mortis, sed vitae meditatio est" [IV, 67]. "Beatitudo non est virtutis praemium, sed ipsa virtus" [V, 42]. His view, *sub specie aeternitatis,* of what is temporal, the wholeness of what is diverse [which] lives eternally in his reason, leaves his predecessors far behind. For him thought was an enterprise which was loftily religious and purely moral.[17]

In another place Herzen noted approvingly that Spinoza had long ago "proved" that nothing which actually happens is to be either "praised or blamed," but is to be "analyzed like a problem in mathematics, i.e., by trying to understand it."[18] In a section of his memoirs written in 1856–57, but not published until after his death, Herzen summed up his view of both the boldness and the central vision of Spinoza's philosophy: "Spinoza, with all the power of his outspoken genius, preached the need to consider as essential only that which 'moth doth not corrupt,' that which is eternal and unchanging, [namely] substance, and not to rest one's hopes on what is contingent, particular, or personal."[19]

The leading Slavophile theorist Alexis Stepanovich Khomyakov (1804–60), who in the 1840s had been Herzen's friend and ideological adversary, commented twice about Spinoza's philosophy, once in 1847 and again in the late 1850s. For Khomyakov, Spinoza is "perhaps the major thinker of the modern period," a "genius" who had introduced the category of "unbelieving religiousness." Spinoza's pantheism is derived in a general way from the "indeterminate" monotheism of the Jewish tradition and in particular from the cabala. (This latter opinion was repudiated by S. G. Kovner in 1862, as we shall see.)

According to Khomyakov, "the origin and principle of Spinozism lay in that Judaism in which Spinoza grew up: as a result, his pantheism (which is essentially atheistic) still had a religious character and was even capable of exercising a beneficent influence upon certain noble natures (such as Steffens)."[20]

In a later, more technically philosophical work Khomyakov referred to the Spinozistic substance as "matter-and-spirit (*dukh*),"[21] adding: "The identity of thought and matter leads us again to the ancient structure built by that

Jew of genius (*genial'nyi zhid*) Spinoza (the word *Zhid* [which Khomyakov uses in place of the more decorous *Yevrei*] does not have a pejorative significance for me, but a purely scientific [i.e., theoretical] meaning)." Khomyakov objects to the "necessitarianism" that he finds manifested in Spinoza's rationalism and in Feuerbach's materialism. But he emphasizes that Spinoza "stood far above" the materialist claim that matter is an autonomous "principle of energy": "It seems that the materialists are not even capable of understanding this great thinker; their minds are seemingly incapable of the effort of pure thinking. . . . They are like the wife of a country priest, for whom a light steam over a nourishing meat-pie is the ultimate representation of the spiritual."[22]

II

The study of Spinoza's thought by Russian academics did not begin until the second decade of the nineteenth century. However, Johann Georg Schwarz (1751–84), a German Rosicrucian and occultist who went to Russia in 1776 as a private tutor and became a professor at Moscow University (in 1779), set up a "pedagogical seminar" under the auspices of the university where he "trained future teachers by means of a critical study of Spinoza" and other Western thinkers.[23] Unfortunately, Schwarz left no written evidence either of his own interpretation of Spinoza's philosophy or that of his students.

Alexander Ivanovich Galich (1783–1848) spent four years abroad, most of it at German universities. He studied for two years with G. E. Schulze at Helmstedt and then spent a year at Göttingen. He returned to Russia and, in 1813 or 1814, defended his dissertation. He taught Latin and Russian at the newly established lycée in Tsarskoye Selo, where Pushkin was one of his pupils. He then taught philosophy at the St. Petersburg Pedagogical Institute and, from 1817, at the newly founded St. Petersburg University. However, he was dismissed in 1821 in a ministry of education purge of professors with "advanced" or "subversive" views.[24] It was charged that both his university lectures and his two published volumes on the history of Western philosophy contained "opinions harmful to the welfare of the state, a disdain of the political authorities established by God, and impertinent judgments concerning the edicts and councils of the government."[25]

Galich was a prolific author. He wrote a series of potboilers on rhetoric, logic, and Russian synonyms, and he compiled a philosophical lexicon.[26] In addition, he wrote a comparatively lively *Istoriia filosofskikh sistem* (*History of Philosophical Systems*) (1818–19), and a substantial work in psychology and philosophical anthropology, *Kartina cheloveka* (*An Image of Man*) (1834). Although *An Image of Man* won the Demidov Prize awarded by the Russian Academy of Sciences, the first third of it (more than two hundred pages) represents an abridged translation of Suabedissen's *Grundzüge der Lehre von dem Menschen* (Marburg, 1829).[27] Galich's other published works in philosophy include *Opyt nauki iziashchnogo (As Essay on the Science of the Beautiful)* (1825) and *Cherty umozritel'noi filosofii (Characteristics of Speculative Philosophy)* (1829), a compendium of Schelling's principal ideas.

The two works that Galich valued most highly (he had spent fourteen years writing the first of them) were *Filosofiia istorii chelovechestva (A Philosophy of the History of Mankind)* and *Vseobshchee pravo (Universal Law)*. But before either book could be published, the manuscripts were destroyed by fire (in 1839 or 1840). Galich, then fifty-seven, felt that he was too old to be able to reconstruct his lost intellectual "children." He became depressed and began to drink heavily, committing a kind of slow suicide.[28]

In the *History of Philosophical Systems,* Galich does not attempt to conceal his dependence on German sources. His bibliography (vol. 1: 15–16) includes at least eight German histories of philosophy. He offers critical comments on most of them and concludes that because of their inadequacies he prefers the work of Socher (1755–1834), whom he identifies simply as a professor at the Catholic University of the Kingdom of Bavaria (in Munich).[29] Together with Ast, Galich declares, Socher "has served as the foundation (*osnovanie*) for the composition of the present textbook" (1:vi). Part of this text, especially in the first volume—he adds—is mine; another part, especially in the second, "belongs to Ast and [W. G.] Tennemann (*prinadlezhit Astu i Tenemanu*)" (ibid., iii). Perhaps Galich shifted his emphasis from Ast and Tennemann to Socher in the course of composing the second volume. In any case, he there announces that "Socher has remained my principal guide (*glavnyi rukovoditel'*) wherever, after checking, I could follow him . . ." (2:iii). This second volume contains Galich's discussion of Spinoza.

However, the standards of scholarly scruple that later were taken for granted had not been firmly established in Russia in Galich's day. In particular, the distinction between "drawing upon a foreign source" and outright plagiarism had not been clearly fixed. Thus, we should not be surprised to find that much of Galich's discussion of Spinoza is lifted bodily, without quotation marks or references, from German sources, mostly Socher and Ast.[30] At least 70 percent of Galich's text is a direct translation of Socher; another 10–15 percent appears to be a paraphrase of Ast. But not a single passage is in quotation marks, and in this section (2:39–51) neither Socher nor Ast is mentioned by name, and neither of their histories is explicitly referred to.

As an example of Galich's "borrowing" and of his uncritical reiteration of Socher's highly negative assessment of Spinoza's thought, I quote a passage in my translation of Galich's Russian and in Socher's German. Galich asserts that Spinoza's system is "wholly incompatible with the moral sense," and goes on:

> That men greeted this system with a sense of loathing, that they saw in it a subverter of faith and morals, that they called it atheism, pantheism, Jewish cabala—such alarm proves that its falseness was vividly perceived by everyone. Anxious minds, outstanding minds, laid bare its harmful effects, attempting to affirm even more strongly the truths that oppose it, thus furthering the spread of the refuted heresy—all of this was a beneficial result of the kind usually entailed by errors which are openly expressed. However, the root of Spinozism was not yet undermined. To be sure, Spinozism is so abstract and difficult to understand that it will never find adherents among a wide public. But for thinkers it remains a menacing aerial phenomenon which they cannot regard with tranquility.[31]

Here is the corresponding passage in Socher. After referring to the "direkter Widerspruch [of this system] gegen das sittliche Interesse," he goes on:

> Dass man es mit Abscheu aufnahm, dass man den Umsturz der Religion und der Sittlichkeit darin fand, dass man es bald atheistisch, bald pantheistisch, bald jüdisch-kabbalistisch nannte, zeigt, dass man seine Unrichtigkeit tief und allgemein fühlte: dass man die Schädlichkeit der daraus abgeleiteten Folgen aufdeckte, die engegenstehenden Wahrheiten prüfte und strenger zu beweisen suchte, war eine wohltätige Folge, welche der unverhüllt aufgestellte Irrtum gewöhnlich nach sich zieht: aber damit waren die Grundsätze desselben noch nicht untergraben. Zwar konnte es seiner Abgezogenheit und Schwerbegreiflichkeit halber nie ein grosses Publikum finden; aber den Denkern musste es doch immer durch seine imponierende fürchterliche Gestalt ein Meteor bleiben, welches sie mit ruhigem Blicke nicht ansehen konnten.[32]

Socher's polemical passion is excessive, but one of his reasons for rejecting Spinoza's position is intellectually respectable. As a Kantian in ethical theory, he sees the opposition between moral freedom and natural necessity as fundamental. He would understandably view Spinoza's assimilation of freedom to necessity (more properly "self-necessitation" as a form of self-causation; but Socher obviously failed to recognize that distinction) as threatening the distinction between right and wrong, between what is in conformity to duty (*pflichtmässig*) and what is contrary to duty (*pflichtwidrig*).

Polemics aside, Galich's choice of Socher as a "principal guide" was reasonable. In a half-dozen compact pages,[33] Socher offers a well-organized, intelligent, and objective account of the fundamentals of Spinoza's position. That Galich's own polemical ardor may have cooled with the passing of time is suggested by the fact that fifteen years later he included Spinoza's name (although he did not explicitly discuss Spinoza's position) along with those of Malebranche, Leibniz, and Geulincx in a list of thinkers who have made major contributions to what he calls "speculative anthropology (*umozritel'noe chelovekoslovie).*"[34]

Although I have been unable to find a copy of F. M. Nadezhin's *History,*[35] I mention it here, both because it candidly acknowledges its single German source, the *History* of Ernst Reinhold, son of the more celebrated Karl Leonhard Reinhold[36] and a former student of Jacobi, and because this source seems to me admirable. It was not, of course, available at the time that Galich wrote his *History.* Ernst Reinhold's account of Spinoza's philosophy is thorough, careful, and competent; he offers many direct quotations in the original Latin, and he concludes with a generous assessment of Spinoza's positive influence on the "poetically speculative spirit" of Schelling.[37] If Nadezhin did not have direct access to Spinoza's works, Reinhold would have provided him with a substantial and reliable account of Spinoza's metaphysics, epistemology, and ethics—although not of his social and political philosophy or his critique of the Bible, both of which topics Reinhold omits.

Archimandrite Gavriil, whose secular name was Vasily Nikolaevich Voskresensky (1795–1868), offers in his *History* an account of Spinoza that in many ways is reminiscent of those of Galich, Socher, and Ast, although it is somewhat more critical in its expository portions.[38] (Gavriil's only other philosophical work is *Filosofiia pravdy [Philosophy of Justice]* [1843], a fairly elementary exposition of natural-law theory, social and political philosophy, the theory of rights, etc. Hobbes, Locke, Rousseau, et al. are discussed in its historical sections, but Spinoza is not even mentioned.)

The sources upon which Gavriil drew in his *History* are not as clearly identifiable as Galich's. His approach is more eclectic and "pluralistic"; he mentions among his sources: Brucker, Tiedemann, Tennemann, Ernst Reinhold, and Ast (*History,* pt. 3, 36ff., 52ff.). He also makes brief mention of Galich's book (p. 41). But I have found no passage which appears to be a direct translation or paraphrase of one of his foreign sources, in the way that Galich translated Socher and paraphrased Ast.

In two places Gavriil's references to Spinoza are primarily classificatory, hence relatively neutral. But they do show that he numbers Spinoza among the major thinkers. Thus, he speaks of the historian of philosophy as bringing to life, by a kind of "magic"—"Plato, Socrates, Aristotle, Spinoza, Kant and all the other philosophers" (22). He refers to the "school of [modern] idealists"—Descartes, Spinoza, Malebranche—"whose quarrels the powerful intellect of Leibniz tried vainly to compose" (30). Among the idealistic *dualists* he includes Plato, Descartes, Malebranche, and Leibniz; among the idealistic *monists,* Parmenides, Zeno, Bruno, Spinoza, Schelling, and Hegel.

Gavriil charges Spinoza with failing to reconcile infinite and eternal substance with finite and perishing modes. But his main attack is levelled at Spinoza's ethics, including both its determinism and the equating of right and power in political philosophy. "This Jew (*Iudei*)," Gavriil declares, "does not accept freedom or the Divine Law which obliges us and which refutes his ravings." For Spinoza, Gavriil exclaims indignantly, "there is no difference between Fénelon and Robespierre, a learned academy and a madhouse, a judge and a criminal, a devastating earthquake and the all-renewing spring"[39]—since all of these things follow with equal necessity from the nature of the one infinite Substance (150, 151).

I have not been able to discover any further scholarly treatments of Spinoza's thought in Russia between 1839 and 1862, although, as we have seen, several Russian thinkers expressed themselves about Spinoza during those years.

The monograph by S. G. Kovner, published in 1862,[40] is a very different piece of work from those of Galich and Gavriil. When Kovner published his monograph, he was a third-year student (presumably of medicine) at St. Vladimir University in Kiev. Nicholas Berdyaev, in an unsigned review of the later, expanded book version (1897) of Kovner's monograph, identifies him as a medical doctor and an "amateur" in philosophy.[41] Kovner's only other published work was a massive history of medieval medicine (1893),[42] which demonstrates his mastery of half a dozen ancient and modern languages in addition to Russian: Greek, Latin, Arabic, Hebrew, French, and German. This book carries the dedication: "To the memory of my late friend Abram Aronovich Kupernik, founder and first trustee of the Kiev Jewish Hospital."

Kovner's monograph offers a detailed account of Spinoza's life and background based mainly on that of Berthold Auerbach,[43] but also draws directly on Colerus (heavily used, of course, by Auerbach) and on Spinoza's correspondence. Kovner's exposition, analysis, and critique of Spinoza's philosophy is mainly inspired by Kuno Fischer.[44]

Kovner's treatment strikes me as admirably fair, balanced, and perceptive. It offers the first full account in Russian of Spinoza's life and the only comprehensive exposition, sympathetic assessment, and effective defense of his philosophy to have appeared in Russia up to that time. Kovner stresses— and perhaps occasionally overstresses—the remarkable unity of Spinoza's life and thought.[45] An overstatement may be seen, for example, in Kovner's claim (perhaps inspired by Colerus) that Spinoza's unselfish *conduct* refutes the charge that his *system* is "atheistic" in the eighteenth-century sense of "egotistical." (See appendix, 188.)

The one idiosyncratic element in Kovner's interpretation—treating the attributes as *beskonechnye sily prirody* ("infinite forces [or 'energies'] of nature") (see appendix, 189)—is obviously, and rather uncritically, derived from Kuno Fischer, who called the attributes *Kräfte, Grundkräfte,* and *wirkende Kräfte.* More convincing, though equally indebted to Fischer—and ultimately, through Fischer, to Jacobi—is the interpretation of Spinoza's system as a species of the genus "pantheism," namely, *naturalism,* coupled with a firm denial that it is either atheistic, theistic, fatalistic, or a (cabalistic) theory of emanation.

Kovner's monograph also offers the Russian reader a small anthology of well-chosen selections from Spinoza's principal works, rendered in fluent, forceful, and—on the whole—accurate Russian versions. Since neither Galich nor Gavriil offered any direct quotations at all from Spinoza's works, this must have been of special value to Russian readers not fluent in Latin or German, at a time when no work of Spinoza's had yet been published in Russian translation. Kovner translates a great many brief passages, amounting in the aggregate to nearly a dozen pages and gives almost as many more in close paraphrase. The quoted passages are taken from the *Ethics, Theologico-Political Treatise, Political Treatise,* and *Treatise on the Improvement of the Intellect,* as well as from half a dozen of the letters.

Perhaps the greatest weakness of Kovner's translations and paraphrases is his inconsistency in rendering key terms. Thus he renders *mens* by three different Russian terms: *um* ("mind" or "intellect"), *dukh* ("spirit" or "mind"), and *dusha* ("soul"). And he renders *intellectus* by four different terms: *um, razum* ("reason"—elsewhere used to render *ratio*), *dukh,* and *poniatie* ("concept"). His rendering of *scientia intuitiva* is free but acceptable: *razumnoe sozertsanie* (= "rational [or "intellectual"] contemplation"). There is one serious omission in a key passage: Kovner gives no Russian equivalent of Spinoza's *totâ* in the celebrated phrase "cognitionem unionis, quam mens cum totâ Naturâ habet." He has simply "ideia edinstva dukha s prirodoi" ("the idea of the unity of the mind with nature").[47]

With Kovner's study of Spinoza, slavish dependence on German sources, as well as a destructively critical attitude toward Spinoza's philosophy, began to be replaced by acute and responsible Russian scholarship. From this time on, Russian studies of Spinoza became increasingly comprehensive, objective, and illuminating. Elsewhere I have offered a brief account of a part of this development.[48] A fuller account must be left for another occasion.

Appendix

(A translation of the concluding pages of S. G. Kovner, "Spinoza, ego zhizn' i sochineniia" ["Spinoza, His Life and Works"], supplement to the *Universitetskie izvestiia* [Kiev], no. 11–12 [1862], pt. 2, 83–87.)

Until [the work of] Kuno Fischer, the dominant opinion was that [Spinoza's] doctrine is a pure pantheism. Thus, one doctrine was constantly and totally confused with a very different one. Fischer has proved beyond any doubt that the relation of Spinozism to pantheism is that of species to genus and that all of the previous critics of Spinoza sinned against the truth by ascribing to the genus what belongs only to the species, or vice versa. In fact, the sole sense of pantheism is that God is the eternal order of the universe. There is in Spinoza's doctrine, too, an identification of God with the eternal order of the universe. This was enough to cause some [commentators] to see in this doctrine a decisive pantheism. But, in essence, this defines only the generic meaning of Spinoza's worldview. Those who would declare pantheism to be its characteristic feature are cruelly mistaken.

And this error inevitably involves another: once having taken the genus for the species, people have usually fallen into the opposite error—taking a certain form of pantheism for pantheism as such and transferring to the latter all of the specific features of the former. As a result of such blunders, many people consider Spinoza to be the founder of pantheism, whereas it is a positive and well-known fact that pantheism traces its origins to very ancient times and embraces a multitude of philosophical systems, one of which is indeed Spinoza's doctrine.[49] Now the question is: what is the specific meaning of this doctrine? At different times there have been the most varied opinions on this matter. Some interpreters have said that it is [1] pure atheism; others have viewed it as [2] fatalism, and still others as [3] a cabalistic worldview. But [in fact] it is neither the first nor the second nor yet the third.

[1] *Spinoza's doctrine is not atheism.* By "atheism" we normally understand the denial of God and a selfish attachment to separate and transient things.[50] Anyone who charges Spinoza with denying God fails to understand even a line of his writings. This charge is based, for the most part, on the following line of argument: Spinoza calls Substance "God" or "Nature"; therefore, he deifies the visible world, [i.e.,] all existing things and thus each separate thing. This obviously amounts to a direct denial of God.

But such a doctrine has nothing in common with Spinozism. Spinoza's God is the inward and eternal cause of all that is (*sushchee*), an infinite being which has infinite existence and excludes every determination as a limit, and every limit as a negation. Such a lofty conception of God clearly precludes any confining of God within the narrow bounds of a separate existence of whatever kind, or even within the whole finite world viewed as a chaotic aggregate of separate things. Rather than saying that Spinoza denies God, one might rather say that he denies man— as Heine[51] aptly remarked.[52] In fact, strictly speaking, for Spinoza only Substance exists; it alone has true being. All separate things are only *modi*—contingent, transitory phenomena.

Even more absurd is the claim that the foundation of Spinoza's system is egoism. Its absurdity becomes evident upon even the most superficial acquaintance with Spinoza's life and doctrine. Who does not know that unselfishness was the fundamental trait of his character as well as the cornerstone of the entire [theoretical] structure that he erected? Only malice and ignorance could accuse him of atheism. He himself, by the way, anticipated such an accusation: "Yes, it has come to this," he exclaimed, "people who openly confess that they can form no idea of God . . . unblushingly accuse the philosophers of atheism."[53]

[2] *Spinoza's doctrine is not fatalism.* There is no doubt that Spinoza's theory of the world is a theory of necessity, but this is by no means a fatalistic necessity. Let us explain this by means of

an example. All of the radii of a circle, as is well-known, are equal; this is a necessary property of the circle. But no one will claim that this necessity is imposed on the circle from without as the result of some kind of mysterious and inevitable predetermination of fate. On the contrary, everyone will agree that this necessity is internal and follows directly from the nature of the circle itself.

In the same way, the necessity preached by Spinoza is not an irrational force located somewhere beyond the world, exercising a blind dominion over beings which lack will. No, it is not a predetermination, a destiny, or a *fatum,* but rather an internal law of nature which governs the universe. How far Spinoza was from intending to formulate a fatalistic theory of the world is best seen in the following passage: "There is nothing more absurd than subjecting God to fate, for we have shown that he is the first and only *free* cause of the essence as well as the existence of all things."[54]

[3] *Spinoza's doctrine is not a theory of emanation.* Such a theory represents the world as an outflow or flowing-out of Deity that takes place through a special process. It thus presupposes a state in God that was prior to this process of flowing out. But this transforms God into a changeable and inconstant being, eliminating all absoluteness and all necessity in the Supreme Being. For this reason, the opinion that Spinoza's worldview is intimately related to cabala and its doctrine of emanation is wholly without foundation. This point is further confirmed by Spinoza's curt and contemptuous remark about the latter: "I have read, and moreover have known, certain cabalistic windbags," he writes in chapter 9 of the *Theologico-Political Treatise,* "and I could never wonder enough at their mad extravagances."[55]

[4] Finally, *Spinoza's doctrine is not theism,* whatever form that position might take. Theism teaches that God is a personal being, separate from nature and thus beyond or above the world. Such a notion is diametrically opposed to Spinoza's view. His Substance is absolute, infinite, and without limitation, because *omnis determinatio est negatio.*[56] Thus, there can be no determination in Substance; it is *indeterminate.*[57] If it is indeterminate, it is, by the same token, *indifferent* and thus *impersonal* as well.[58] Furthermore, Substance is not an external but an internal cause of all that is, and thus, according to Spinoza, it cannot in any way be separate from nature or exist beyond or above the limits of nature.

Of all the species of theism only one, namely, *monotheism,* has a certain affinity with Spinoza's position. Monotheism at least asserts the unity of God, although it limits this unity by representing God as opposed to the world. In this sense, Spinoza is a true son of Judaism, with the sole difference that his God is not separate from nature, not a supernatural being confronting the world, but instead forms a single, indivisible, and harmonious whole with it. As a Jew, Spinoza is a follower of the *one* God; as a philosopher, he *thinks* this one God and, by the same token, destroys every dualism between God and the world because—as Kuno Fischer has aptly remarked—thought always destroys dualism.[59] That Spinoza endeavors solely to *think* God and not to imagine Him is proved by Letter [56]: "To your question," he there writes, "as to whether I have as clear an *idea* of God as I have of a triangle, I answer Yes. But if you ask me whether I have as clear an *image* of God as I have of a triangle, I shall answer No, for we cannot *imagine* [i.e., have an image of] God, but we can indeed *conceive* him."[60]

After what has been said, [we may ask] what comprises the essence or special characteristic of Spinozism. First, Spinoza's *naturalistic worldview.* For him everything is nature. Substance is infinite nature, its attributes are the infinite forces or energies of nature, the *modi* are phenomena of nature, the mind is just as much a phenomenon of nature as is the body. In a word, for Spinoza there is nothing supernatural. Second, the *causal connection of all things:* Substance is cause, the attributes are forces or energies, things are effects.

Evidently there can be no question here of ends or ideals, of good or evil, because in the continuous causal connection of all things each particular phenomenon is the cause of certain [other] phenomena and the effect of [still] others. It is determined by certain phenomena and in its turn determines and conditions others. And even if each thing, taken separately, is in itself contingent and transitory, since its origin does not depend on itself [alone], and the principles of its existence are not contained within itself; still, in the universal order and connection of the whole of nature, all phenomena are equally necessary and equally natural.

Notes

An earlier version of this chapter appeared in French translation by Jacqueline Lagrée as "Les Interprétations russes de Spinoza (1796–1862) et leurs sources allemandes," in *Spinoza entre lumière et romantisme: Les Cahiers de Fontenay*, nos. 36–38 (1985), pp. 361–77.

1   Alexander Radishchev, "On Man, His Mortality and Immortality," trans. Frank Y. Gladney and George L. Kline, in James M. Edie et al., eds., *Russian Philosophy* (Chicago, 1965; 2d ed., 1969; Knoxville: Tenn., 1976, 1984), 1: 78, 79. Radishchev's son Pavel reports that his father "revered Spinoza and Helvétius as virtuous and well-intentioned men who had thought profoundly" (quoted in David M. Lang, *The First Russian Radical: Alexander Radishchev* [London, 1959], 217, from P. A. Radishchev, "Aleksandr Nikolaevich Radishchev," *Russkii vestnik* 18 [1858, no. 12]).

2   *Pierre Tchaadaev: Lettres philosophiques,* ed. François Rouleau (Paris, 1970), 99. Here is Spinoza's text: "Voluntas certus tantúm cogitandi modus est. . . . Quocumque . . . modo, sive finita, sive infinita concipiatur, causam requirit, à quâ ad existendum, et operandum determinetur; adeóque . . . non potest dici causa libera, sed tantùm necessaria . . ."

3   *Peter Yakovlevich Chaadayev: Philosophical Letters and Apology of a Madman,* trans. Mary-Barbara Zeldin (Knoxville, Tenn., 1969), 81. Spinoza's text reads as follows: "Porrò, ut de intellectu, et voluntate, quos Deo communiter tribuimis, hîc etiam aliquid dicam; si ad aeternam Dei essentiam, intellectus scilicet, et voluntas pertinent, aliud sanè per utrumque hoc attributum intelligendum est, quàm quod vulgò solent homines. Nam intellectus, et voluntas, qui Dei essentiam constituerent, à nostro intellectu, et voluntate, toto coelo differre deberent, nec in ullâ re, praeterquam in nomine, convenire possent; non aliter scilicet, quàm inter se conveniunt canis, signum coeleste, et canis, animal latrans" (*Opera,* ed. Carl Gebhardt [Heidelberg, 1924] 2: 62–63).

4   *Chaadayev: Philosophical Letters,* 92.

5   *Pierre Tchaadaev: Oeuvres inédites ou rares,* ed. Raymond McNally, François Rouleau, and Richard Tempest (Paris, 1990), 23.

6   Ibid., 52.

7   Ivan V. Kireyevsky, *Polnoe sobranie sochinenii,* ed. M. O. Gershenzon (Moscow, 1911), 1:30–37 (hereinafter *Sochineniia*). Several years earlier, Kireyevsky (then age seventeen through nineteen) had been an active member of the short-lived Moscow "Society of Wisdom Lovers" (1823–25), another member of which later recalled: "We prized Spinoza particularly and valued his works much above the New Testament and the rest of Holy Scripture" (A. I. Koshelëv, *Zapiski* [Berlin, 1884], 12, quoted in V. V. Zenkovsky, *A History of Russian Philosophy,* trans. George L. Kline [London and New York, 1953], 1: 132).

8   "Deviatnadtsatyi vek" (1832), *Sochineniia* 1: 91–92.

9   Kireyevsky, "O kharaktere prosveshcheniia Evropy i o ego otnoshenii k prosveshcheniiu

Rossii" ("On the Character of European Civilization and Its Relation to the Civilization of Russia") (1852), *Sochineniia,* 1: 196.

10 Alexander Herzen, *From the Other Shore* (1850), trans. and ed. Isaiah Berlin (New York, 1956), 12

11 *Dnevnik,* entry for August 22, 1844, in A. I. Herzen, *Sochineniia v deviati tomakh,* ed. V. P. Volgin et al. (Moscow, 1958), 9: 192.

12 "Kaprizy i razdum'e" ("Caprices and Second Thoughts"), sec. 3 (1847), *Sochineniia* 2: 374.

13 *Pis'ma ob izuchenii prirody (Letters on the Study of Nature),* letter 5 (1845), ibid. 2: 251.

14 *Dnevnik,* August 9, 1844, ibid. 9: 190.

15 *From the Other Shore,* pp. 115–16.

16 Herzen to Nicholas Ogarev, August 1, 1833, *Sochineniia* 9: 245.

17 *Dnevnik,* September 18, 1843, ibid. 9: 119–20. Herzen also quotes the "Beatitudo" passage, saying that it represents Spinoza's "great idea," in *Diletantizm v nauke (Dilettantism in Science)* (1843), ibid. 2: 90 n. 2. Nicholas G. Chernyshevsky, a devout Feuerbachian, noted that Feuerbach—"the greatest of the present-day German thinkers, whose genius is in no way inferior to Hegel's [!]," long remained faithful to Hegelian principles. In the same way, "Spinoza, whose genius was far higher than that of Descartes, for a very long time regarded himself as the latter's most faithful disciple" ("Essays on the Gogol Period of Russian Literature, Sixth Essay: Belinsky" [1856], in N. G. Chernyshevsky, *Selected Philosophical Essays* [Moscow, 1953], 467).

18 "Kaprizy i razdum'e," sec. 2 (1846), *Sochineniia* 2: 363.

19 "N. Kh. Ketcher," *Byloe i dumy (My Past and Thoughts),* ibid. 5: 253.

20 A. S. Khomyakov, "O vozmozhnosti russkoi khudozhestvennoi shkoly" ("On the Possibility of a Russian School of Art") (1847), *Polnoe sobranie sochinenii,* 3d ed. (Moscow, 1900), 1: 89, 90. Henrik Steffens (1773–1845), a Norwegian-born geologist and mineralogist, was inspired by Spinoza and by Schelling, whose lectures at the University of Jena he attended in 1798–99. Steffens taught at various German universities. Schelling wrote a foreword to his *Nachgelassene Schriften* (1846). A Russian translation of certain of Steffens's writings, *O postepennom razvitii prirody (On the Gradual Development of Nature),* was published in Odessa in 1834.

21 *Mens* (and also *intellectus*) are often rendered by the Russian word *um.* However, since *dukh* is an exact equivalent of the German *Geist,* the term used to render *mens* by most German translators of, and commentators on, Spinoza in the late eighteenth and early nineteenth centuries—among them S. H. Ewald (1787–96), Joseph Socher (1801), Ernst Reinhold (1829), Berthold Auerbach (1841), and Kuno Fischer (1854). Khomyakov, like Galich and Gavriil before him, sometimes rendered *mens* by *dukh.*

22 "On Recent Developments in Philosophy (Letters to Yu. F. Samarin)," trans. Vladimir D. Pastuhov and Mary-Barbara Zeldin, in Edie et al., eds., *Russian Philosophy* 1: 228, 243, 250.

23 Andrzej Walicki, *A History of Russian Thought from the Enlightenment to Marxism,* trans. Hilda Andrews-Rusiecka (Stanford, Calif., 1979), 22.

24 Biographical details are drawn from A. Nikitenko, *Aleksandr Galich: byvshii professor Skt.-Peterburgskogo Universiteta (Alexander Galich: Former Professor at St. Petersburg University)* (St. Petersburg, 1869), and N. S. Gordienko, "Lektsii A. I. Galicha po logike, metafizike i nravouchitel'noi filosofii" ("A. I. Galich's Lectures on Logic, Metaphysics, and Moral Philosophy"), *Voprosy filosofii,* no. 5 (1958): 112–16.

25 Quoted from Russian imperial archives by Gordienko, "Lektsii," 112.

26 The potboilers: (1) *Teoriia krasnorechiia dlia vsekh rodov prozaicheskikh sochinenii (A*

Theory of Rhetoric for All the Genres of Prose Composition) (1830); (2) *Logika, izlozhennaia po [G. M.] Kleinu (Logic Expounded According to [G. M.] Klein)* (1831); *Leksikon filosofskikh predmetov (A Lexicon of Philosophical Subjects)* (1845, 1847; two parts published, but the work left unfinished); (4) *Russkie sinonimy (Russian Synonyms)* (an unfinished work). See Nikitenko, *Aleksandr Galich,* 60.

27   Gustav G. Shpet, *Ocherk razvitiia russkoi filosofii (An Outline of the Development of Russian Philosophy)* (Moscow, 1922), pt. 1, 135. This work is reprinted in Shpet, *Sochineniia* (Moscow, 1989).

28   Nikitenko, *Aleksandr Galich,* 61–62.

29   Joseph Socher, *Grundriss der Geschichte der philosophischen Systeme von den Griechen bis auf Kant* (Munich, 1801).

30   D. Friedrich Ast, *Grundriss der Geschichte der Philosophie* (Landshut, 1807); the discussion of Spinoza is on 369–78. A revised and enlarged edition was published in 1825, in which several brief remarks favorable to Spinoza were added. For example, in the opening paragraph Spinoza is identified as "der spekulativste aller neueren Philosophen" (*Grundriss der Geschichte der Philosophie,* 2d ed., 325). This edition, of course, was not available to Galich when he was writing his own history.

31   Alexander Galich, *Istoriia filosofskikh sistem* (St. Petersburg, 1819), 2: 47–48. Galich has added two or three sentences in the passage, which have no counterpart in Socher's text. The phrase "thus furthering the spread of the refuted heresy" is his. And immediately preceding this phrase, Galich inserts the titles of two polemical writings directed against Spinoza, one in French, the other in Latin. Neither of these is given by Socher.

32   Socher, *Grundriss,* 234.

33   Ibid., 229–34.

34   Alexander Galich, *Kartina cheloveka (An Image of Man)* (St. Petersburg, 1834), 26.

35   F. M. Nadezhin, *Ocherk istorii filosofii po Reingol'du (An Outline of the History of Philosophy According to [Ernst] Reinhold)* (St. Petersburg, 1837). Nadezhin's only other work of which I am aware is *Opyt nauki filosofii (An Essay on the Science of Philosophy)* (St. Petersburg, 1845), which was scornfully dismissed by both the Westernizer Belinsky and the Slavophile Kireyevsky (Shpet, *Ocherk,* 168).

36   Ernst Reinhold, *Handbuch der allgemeinen Geschichte der Philosophie für alle wissenschaftlich Gebildete* (Gotha, 1829), pt. 2, first half, 222–86. Although such historians of Russian philosophy as Shpet have made it clear that the Reinhold in question is Ernst and not his father, Karl Leonhard (*Ocherk* 163), confusion persists. L. Skvortsov identifies Nadezhin's Reinhold as "K. L." (and misspells "Nadezhin" as "Nadezhdin"—the more usual form of this Russian name) (*Filosofskaia entsiklopediia* [Moscow, 1962], 2: 379).

37   Reinhold, *Handbuch,* 286.

38   Archimandrite Gavriil, *Istoriia filosofii (A History of Philosophy)* (Kazan, 1839), pt. 3, 143–51.

39   Perhaps it is passages such as this one that Shpet has in mind when he remarks that Gavriil's critical judgments are sometimes pithy in the polemical style of the Russian theological academies (*Ocherk,* 120–21).

40   "Spinoza, ego zhizn' i sochineniia" ("Spinoza, His Life and Works"), supplement to the *Universitetskie izvestiia* (Kiev), no. 11–12 (1862), pt. 2, 1–87. This prizewinning student essay, Berdyaev informs us in an 1898 review, was supplemented for publication by the addition (in Russian translation) of passages on Spinoza by George Henry Lewes, J. van Vloten, and René Worms, and the reprinting of a Russian critique of Spinoza by A. Volynsky (originally published in the Russian-Jewish journal *Voskhod* in 1885). Since

Berdyaev characterizes this book, published in Warsaw in 1897, as posthumous, we can fix Kovner's dates at ca. 1840–ca. 1896. Berdyaev, unsigned review of books by Jodl, Rehmke, and Windelband, as well as Kovner, in *Mir Bozhii*, July 1898, sec. 2, 74–79. This review is identified as Berdyaev's in *Nicolas Berdiaev, Bibliographie*, compiled by Tamara Klépinine (Paris, 1978), 104.

41   Berdyaev, *Mir Bozhii*, 76.

42   S. G. Kovner, *Istoriia srednevekovoi meditsiny (A History of Medieval Medicine), Universitetskie izvestiia* (Kiev), 1891–93).

43   Berthold Auerbach, "Das Leben Spinozas," in *B. v. Spinozas Sämtliche Werke* (Stuttgart, 1841), 1: ix–cxxv.

44   Kuno Fischer, *Geschichte der neuern Philosophie* (Heidelberg, 1854), 1: 235–595.

45   Kovner, "Spinoza," 4f., 66ff.

46   In addition to the passage translated in the appendix ("Spinoza," 87), Kovner refers to the attributes as "forces" (*sily*) in two other passages (46, 47).

47   Ibid., 40. Kovner may have been influenced in his choice of *dukh* over *um* by Auerbach's translation of this phrase as "der Gedanke der Einheit . . . , welche der Geist mit der ganzen Natur hat" ("Das Leben Spinozas," 4: 216). But the omission of "all" or "the whole" (= *totâ*) is entirely Kovner's doing.

48   See my *Spinoza in Soviet Philosophy* (London and New York, 1952; reprint 1981), introduction, 5ff.

49   Kuno Fischer, *Geschichte der neuern Philosophie* (Mannheim, 1854), 1: 554. (This note and parts of notes 52 and 53 below are Kovner's. All other notes, and the bracketed portions of notes 52 and 53, are mine.—GLK.)

50   Here and in several other passages Kovner uses the Russian term *predmety* (literally "objects") to render Spinoza's *rēs* (plural). However, elsewhere he uses the more usual *veshchi* ("things"). In this appendix I have regularly translated both *predmet* and *veshch*' as "thing."

51   Heine wrote: "Statt zu sagen [Spinoza] leugne Gott, könnte man sagen, er leugne den Menschen." See his *Zur Geschichte der Religion und Philosophie in Deutschland*, a work originally titled *Der Salon von Heine* (1835; 2d ed., 1852), in *Sämtliche Werke*, ed. Jost Perfahl (Munich, 1972), 3: 449.

52   Spinoza's doctrine can even be called 'acosmism' [and was indeed thus called by Hegel, both in the *Enzyklopädie*, 3d ed. (1830), sec. 50 n., and in the posthumously published *Vorlesungen über die Geschichte der Philosophie, Sämtliche Werke*, ed. H. Glockner (Stuttgart, 1928), 19: 373].

53   *Tractatus Theologico-Politicus*, chap. 2 [in *Opera*, ed. H. E. G. Paulus (Jena, 1802), vol. 1], p. 173 [Gebhardt, 3: 30. Perhaps inadvertently, Kovner has omitted the phrase that falls between "Dei ideam non habere" and "non erubescant"—namely, "et Deum non nisi per res creatas (quarum causas ignorant) cognoscere."]

54   *Ethics* 1: 33 n. 2; 2: 76.

55   *Tractatus Theologico-Politicus*, 3: 135–36.

56   Spinoza, of course, did not use this formulation; what he said was simply that "determinatio negatio est" (Letter 50, 4: 240). The widely repeated misquotation was apparently first made current by Hegel in the posthumously published second edition of his *Wissenschaft der Logik* (1833), ed. G. Lasson (Hamburg, 1934, 1967), 1: 100, although as early as 1817 Hegel had used the expression in a review of Jacobi in the *Heidelbergische Jahrbücher der Litteratur*, no. 1 (1817), 6. (I thank Hans-Christian Lucas for kindly bringing this reference to my attention.) It did *not* appear in the *first* edition (1812) of the *Logic*. *Omnis*

194   George L. Kline

determinatio est negatio also appears in the first edition of Kuno Fischer's *Geschichte der neuern Philosophie* (1854) 1: 338, which is doubtless where Kovner picked it up. Fischer appears to have recognized his error; at least, in later editions, e.g., the fourth edition of 1898, he omits the erroneous formulation.

57   In this sentence Kovner, following Spinoza's lead, uses the noun "determination" (*opredelenie*) and the adjective "indeterminate" (*neopredelennyi*) in their etymological senses of "limitation" and "unlimited." (*Opredelenie* is a calque on *determinatio*; *predel*, like *terminus*, means "limit.") In certain early letters (dating from 1665 and 1666), Spinoza used *indeterminatum* as a synonym for *infinitum* ("perfect without limitation") and *perfectum* (Letters 21 and 36: 4: 129, 184–86).

58   Kovner employs an untranslatable play on the terms *bezrazlichnyi* ("indifferent") and *bezlichnyi* ("impersonal"). The Russian terms are linked etymologically in a way that their English counterparts are not. *Bezlichnyi* (literally "faceless") is derived from the nouns *litso* ("face" or "person") and *lichnost'* ("person" or "personality"). The etymological sense of *bezrazlichnyi* ("not-distinguishing-between-*persons*) has been generalized into "nondifferentiating" or "indifferent."

59   The cutting edge of Fischer's brusque remark, which appears to be directed against Kant, echoes Hegel's remarks in the *Differenzschrift*.

60   The emphases in this quotation are Kovner's; the text is to be found in *Opera* 4: 261.

In "The Shape of Artistic Pasts: East and West," Arthur C. Danto argues that "Since Vasari, to be an artist in the West has been to have internalized a narrative that determines the way we can be influenced by the past. . . . Modernism . . . meant the dismantling of these narratives and reconstitution of our relationship to the past." Danto argues that "modernity begins defining narrative of one's own culture," the co outside their own traditions or create somethi .oss of belief in the at artists must look tely new in order to resituate themselves in regard to their own traditions. We can find such attempts to reorient modern thought to its own past in the writings produced by the various authors we now classify as literary "modernists," writers such as T. S. Eliot, Ezra Pound, and James Joyce. Joyce's *Ulysses,* published in 1922, provides a specific site for the investigation of one writer's response to the relation between modern literature and historical traditions, especially in the ways in which Joyce's text responds to tradition in the form of myth.

"History," says Stephen Dedalus, "is a nightmare from which I am trying to awake."[1] Stephen seeks to awaken not only from his own personal nightmares, but from the various historical traditions—English, Roman Catholic, Irish—he views as his "masters":

> —I am a servant of two masters, Stephen said, an English and an Italian. . . .
> —And a third, Stephen said, there is who wants me for odd jobs (*U*1.638–41).

All of the major characters in *Ulysses* are embedded or enmeshed in their own personal histories, which are in turn embedded in larger historical traditions—Leopold Bloom's identity as a Jew, for example—and behind all of the more or less contemporary and identifiable personal, cultural, and political histories that define the characters of *Ulysses,* Joyce spreads the larger cloth of myth and the historical traditions implied by or embedded in mythic narratives, a framework that remains for the most part hidden to the characters (though Stephen Dedalus does consider the possible meanings of his very un-Irish surname). Much speculation on Joyce's writing concerns itself with his use of mythic paradigms as the textual substrates of his works (e.g., the Daedalus myth in *Dubliners* and *A Portrait of the Artist as a Young Man,* the *Odyssey* in *Ulysses,* and the story of Finn MacCumhal in *Finnegans Wake*). This essay will explore Joyce's use of myth and tradition in *Ulysses* by investigating his development of an "intertextual memory," a textual repository of memories from other texts that models itself on the ways in which we ourselves are constructed by traditions, unconsciously shaped by the voices and echoes of mythic paradigms we may not even be aware of.

"Never know whose thoughts you're chewing," Leopold Bloom muses as he eats his lunch in *Ulysses* (U8.717–18), and at times the reader may feel the same way about this text that incorporates, alludes to, and plays with so many other texts and traditions. Jacques Derrida has called Joyce's writing a "hypermnesiac machine" because in texts such as *Ulysses* and *Finnegans Wake* Joyce inscribes so many of those texts and traditions—popular, literary, mythic, scientific, and otherwise—that make up the cultural consciousness of the modern Western reader (147). In fact, *Ulysses* often includes or inscribes other texts in such a way that the reader at times does not know whose thoughts she is chewing and may not even realize she is chewing them at all.

In *Ulysses,* Joyce brings his hypermnesiac machine to bear on everyday life, specifically the lives of Stephen Dedalus and Leopold Bloom. As early as November 1923, two opposing viewpoints on the significance of the book were forming, represented at that point by Richard Aldington and T. S. Eliot. In his essay, *"Ulysses,* Order, and Myth," Eliot outlines a conflict between himself and Aldington over the novel's use of a "mythical method" (178) and takes Aldington to task for treating "Mr. Joyce as a prophet of chaos" and for viewing *Ulysses* as "an invitation to chaos" (175–76). Eliot, on the other hand, hopes to enlist *Ulysses* in his struggle to encourage a "classical" element in modern literature as a hedge against the perceived decay of master narratives that is a central topos in modernist writing. For Eliot, Joyce's use of the *Odyssey* as "a continuous parallel between contemporaneity and antiquity. . . . is simply a way of controlling, of ordering, of giving a shape and a significance to the immense panorama of futility and anarchy which is contemporary history" (177). It is, Eliot claims, "a step toward making the modern world possible for art" (178), and has "the importance of a scientific discovery" (177).

Following Aldington, some readers have found *Ulysses* (in C. G. Jung's

words) an "infernally nugatory" book in which "nothing happens"—it "begins in the void and ends in the void" (7)—a book that represents the
abstract, objectifying, empiricist worldview of "white-skinned man who
believes in the object, who is cursed with the object" (Jung 20). This reading
of *Ulysses* as an ultimately frustrating, even nihilistic, text is echoed in recent
readings of *Ulysses* as a book concerned only with language and the slipperi-
ness of referentiality, a view that at times comes curiously close to arguing
that in its "play" with language, *Ulysses* mimes or *represents* exactly that
which cannot truly *be* mimetic or representative of anything. In this way,
Hélène Cixous can claim that Joyce's works can join that group of "writings
whose subversive force is now undermining the world of western discourse"
(15).

By reading *Ulysses* as a book of memory, we can see how Joyce makes use
of tradition to constitute everyday life as a deep, if not necessarily rich,
palimpsest of mythic and narrative paradigms. Such a reading may have the
virtue of avoiding the either/or choice of reading the novel as a superficial
and "infernally nugatory" book or as a text that depends on an obscure
"mythic method" to convey its ultimately reassuring and stabilizing meaning.

Ulysses is seeded or loaded with allusions, overt and covert, to other texts,
to events both ancient and contemporary, and even to personal details of
Joyce's life. The unparalleled level of intertextuality in *Ulysses* and *Finnegans
Wake* invites readers not only to take note of the allusions themselves, but to
ponder the significance of such an overwhelming density of allusion. Joyce's
intertextuality, his method of layering or "seeding" the text with traces of
older texts and traditions, is based on memory and the reader's inevitable
orientation within a web of texts that forms a culture or at least part of a
culture.

The remarkable intertextuality of *Ulysses* is in itself a form of memory—
intertextual memory—that subtly comments on the events of June 16, 1904,
and on the very act of reading the book. The past is present in Joyce's textual
echoes—not just echoes of Homer, of course, but also Shakespeare, Dante,
Swift, Maria Susanna Cummins, Maeterlinck, and many more—and these
intertextual resonances are often not explicit or easily recognizable by characters or, more intriguingly, by readers. Intertextuality in Joyce's works
seems to acknowledge a cultural memory theoretically available to any
reader of *Ulysses*: all of us are made up not only of our own experiences, but
also by the shared experiences and imaginings of cultural traditions. Joyce
acknowledged this aspect of his own mind when he commented to his
brother Stanislaus that "if I put down a bucket into my own soul's well,
sexual department, I draw up Griffith's and Ibsen's and Skeffington's and

Bernard Vaughn's and St. Aloysius' and Shelley's and Renan's water along with my own. And I am going to do that in my novel (inter alia) and plank the bucket down before the shades and substances above mentioned to see how they like it: and if they don't like it I can't help them" (*Letters* 2: 191).

According to Colin MacCabe, Joyce once advised Jacques Mercanton, who was translating *Ulysses* into French, "'the fewer quotation marks the better' and that even without them the reader 'will know early in the book that S.D.'s mind is full like everyone else's of borrowed words'" (MacCabe 117). Derrida writes that to read Joyce is to be "*in memory of him,*" in the sense that the "hypermnesia" of Joyce's work "*a priori* indebts you, and in advance inscribes you in the book you are reading" (147; original emphasis).

Allusion, like memory, works by signifying or recalling something which is no longer present. As Michel de Certeau writes of the disruption of the text by "the quotation of voices": "A lapse insinuates itself into language. The territory of appropriation is altered by the mark of something which is not there and does not happen (like myth)" (154). The substrate of intertextuality, then, can function as a shadow comment on the story before us, insinuating itself into the way we read, like a troubling but elusive memory, disturbing any easy appropriation of meaning and complicating the varieties of meanings suggested by the text.

The intensity of allusion or intertextuality in *Ulysses* exceeds what we might think of as "useful" or usual even in a modernist text. While Eliot, conscious of the density of reference in "The Waste Land," provides notes to help the reader absorb the "meaning" of his hidden references—the "memories" of ancient myths and customs inscribed in or under the otherwise bleak lives of his modern urban somnambulists—and thus attempts to help the reader complete the text's meaning, Joyce does no such thing. Although the novel's title obviously alludes to the Homeric story, it does so obliquely— *Ulysses* rather than *Odyssey*[2]—and Joyce refused to make his book correspond in any *exact* way with his Homeric paradigm. The title's overt suggestion of an "arche-plot" behind the events of June 16, 1904, has led more to disagreement and confusion about the relationship of the *Odyssey* and *Ulysses* than to a sense of clarification or a clear echo of meaning.[3] The reader's memory of the book's title—*Ulysses*—hovers over the "territory of appropriation," stimulating the reader's desire to remember the title by finding echoes of it in the text, by equating the book's characters with those of Homer or by seeking similarities between the novel's chapters and the books of the epic. At the same time, this intertextual memory always remains problematic, the connection as often absent as it is present, as often ironic as it is satisfying. The title functions as a suggestive, troubling memory of another text that does not determine, but rather suggests, ironizes, and shapes the reader's experience. The so-called parallels between the two books provide a wealth of tantalizing suggestions, but they do not settle anything for the reader and in fact often complicate the reader's understanding of the text.

The Homeric parallel to *Ulysses* is part of a larger, intertextual memory that provides numerous paradigms of completion "under" *Ulysses.* Joyce's book is a palimpsest, then, in which we read an ambiguous modern ending inscribed over layers of older, closed texts such as *Hamlet* and *The Divine Comedy.* The book contains so many other stories, even stories from Joyce's own life, that the reader cannot possibly take them all in, and the text makes no particular effort to expose its most hidden intertextual suggestions or to articulate the relevance of those that are more explicit. Yet *Ulysses* provides these subliminal suggestions to the reader, perhaps in the hope that the suggestions encode in the text memories or echoes of other stories, other texts, other endings that will resonate on some level of the reader's mind.

While most of the texts alluded to in *Ulysses* suggest closure of some sort, their possible meanings as hidden models for the book's plot vary greatly. Joyce's references to traditionally closed texts like the *Odyssey* often suggest the possibility of a textual Ithaca; on the other hand, such references often seem ironic and even mocking by forcing a contrast between the closure they suggest and the openness and self-referentiality of the modern text in which they occur. Thus, Umberto Eco reads the intertextual echoes of older, closed texts in *Ulysses* as "an example of a paradoxical equilibrium among the forms of a rejected world and the disordered substance of the new . . ." (Eco 63), and as

> the incredible image of a world that supports itself, almost by miracle, on the preserved structures of an old world which are accepted for their formal reliability but denied in their substantial value. *Ulysses* represents a moment of transition for contemporary sensitivity. It appears as the drama of a dissociated consciousness that tries to reintegrate itself, finding, at the core of dissociation, a possible recovery by directing itself in opposition to its old frames of reference. (Eco 55)

Myth, then, operates below the surface in *Ulysses,* creating a gap between itself and the surface and suggesting a variety of supplements to the possible interpretations of this surface. The interpretive difficulty lies in judging the significance of the parallels between the text of *Ulysses* and the older plots it "remembers." For example, do the mythic parallels between *Ulysses* and *The Odyssey* redeem Joyce's characters, rescuing them from the paralysis of Dublin by infusing their lives with an archetypal richness, or do they mock the world of twentieth-century Dublin, ironically undercutting the imperfect modern counterparts of the faithful Penelope and the cunning, bold wanderer Odysseus?

Rather than belabor the Homeric parallels to *Ulysses* further, I wish to provide another example that will further illustrate this dilemma in *Ulysses* and, at the same time, suggest an additional mythic substrate or subtext for the novel (specifically, for the thirteenth episode, conventionally referred to as "Nausicaa," according to the Homeric parallels Joyce laid out in his letters and notes). In the "Nausicaa" episode of *Ulysses*, Leopold Bloom finds himself near a chapel on a beach at twilight, tired by the day's activities and anxious about his wife's adulterous affair with one Blazes Boylan. In fact, Bloom has, unlike Homer's hero, deliberately delayed his return home so as not to interrupt a meeting between Blazes and Molly at the Bloom residence. We learn later in *Ulysses* that the Blooms have not had "complete carnal intercourse" in almost eleven years (U17.2278–84), and prior to the "Nausicaa" episode, Bloom has evidenced a proclivity to avoid confronting his sexual problems by engaging in provocative pseudonymous correspondence with a woman he has never met and by running from a possible encounter on the street with Boylan. Instead, Bloom indulges himself with fantasies of women idealized either as pure and goddesslike or as lascivious whores.

On the beach in "Nausicaa," Bloom encounters Gerty MacDowell, a young woman whose view of the opposite sex, like Bloom's, has been clouded by idealized images provided, in her case, by pulp fiction. Gerty has come to the beach with two girlfriends and the three little boys they are taking care of. Though she and Bloom never really meet and never speak to each other, they exchange meaningful gazes, each "painting" the other in the colors of their own fantasies, each privately masturbating. The first part of the episode is filtered through Gerty's thoughts, while we experience the remainder immersed in Bloom's stream of consciousness.

In an investigation of some of Joyce's sources, Michael Patrick Gillespie has claimed that "While the prose style of 'Nausicaa' at first appears to be an obvious parody of pulp romances, experiences with preceding chapters suggest that models for its structure come from more diverse sources" ("Sources" 334). One of these "diverse sources," another "romance," albeit dating from the second century, is *The Golden Ass* by Apuleius, also known as *The Metamorphoses of Lucius*, which intersects with *Ulysses* in the "Nausicaa" episode. In this intersection or collision between "present" twentieth-century Dublin and "absent" second-century Thessaly, *The Golden Ass* serves as an intertextual memory for Joyce's "Nausicaa."

Admittedly, the existence of a correspondence between *The Golden Ass* and "Nausicaa" is not obvious or overt, as is the relationship between *Ulysses* and *The Odyssey,* yet Joyce did not hesitate to bury extremely obscure allusions in his texts, presumably with the confidence that these hidden signs would somehow function as part of the text's dynamic. As he revised, Joyce often went back through his chapters and embedded more and more of these subtle allusions into the text, thereby increasing its symbolic density and subtlety. Joyce's revisions to "Nausicaa" imply an attempt to load the episode with hints that point toward another mythic parallel beyond the more obvious parallel of Bloom and Gerty as Ulysses and Nausicaa, another mythic echo that adds more complexity to the occurrences on Sandymount beach on June 16, 1904.

The *Golden Ass* is a collection of myths and stories bound together by the story of Lucius. While we might argue that Bloom makes an ass of himself in "Nausicaa," Lucius has literally become an ass, since he was transformed by a witch who caught him spying on her. Dismayed by his situation, Lucius roams the world in search of a cure, meeting many adventures and hearing many stories on the way. He finally finds salvation when he lies down on a beach at twilight, depressed and tired, and is visited by a powerful goddess— Isis—who tells him he can regain his human shape by eating roses dedicated to her if he promises to serve her for the rest of his life.

We can quickly note some immediate parallels between the "master plot" of *The Golden Ass* and "Nausicaa." Both Lucius and Bloom find themselves despondent and weary on a beach in the darkening evening. Lucius, the ass, falls into a slumber and awakens to a redemptive vision of the goddess Isis, while Bloom views a more earthly Isis—a young woman he would rather idealize than see as she is—unveiling herself in the shadow of the Star of the Sea Chapel, dedicated to the Virgin Mary.

The first tension arising from a comparison of these texts results from a narratological difference regarding the possibility of closure: the earlier text provides a deus ex machina solution for its protagonist unavailable to Bloom. Just as Bloom cannot simply or literally go home to slay the suitors and reestablish his "kingdom" as Ulysses did, so he cannot transform himself back into a man by eating roses (although Gerty wonders "why you couldn't eat something poetical like violets or roses"—*U*13.229–30) or by subordinating himself to a goddess as Lucius does.

Other stories from *The Golden Ass* also echo in "Nausicaa." For example, at the start of the episode the two young boys—Master Tommy and Master Jacky—fight over "a certain castle of sand" referred to in the text as "the apple of discord" (*U*13.40–42), alluding to the apple of gold in the Judgment of Paris, a story retold at length in *The Golden Ass.* The Judgment of Paris concerns, appropriately, three goddesses and a man who must choose between them, mirrored in Bloom's consideration of the relative merits of the three "girl chums" who "had of course their little tiffs from time to time like the rest of mortals" (U13.93–94).

The most important and suggestive parallel between *The Golden Ass* and "Nausicaa," however, involves the story of Cupid and Psyche. *The Golden Ass* is our earliest source for this legend, which takes up approximately one-sixth of Apuleius' book.[4] This myth of ideal love provides an intriguing and suggestive "background" for the less-than-ideal relationship that Gerty Mac-Dowell and Leopold Bloom develop on Sandymount Strand. Earlier in *Ulysses,* when Bloom evades Boylan on the street, he ducks into the National Museum to inspect the statues of "shapely goddesses" to see whether they are more pure than human women, whether they have the necessary equipment for digestion and excretion (U8.920–32). Bloom's sexuality is so impaired by his sense of inadequacy, his fears of impotence, and his knowledge of Molly's affair with Boylan that he has become alienated from lovemaking and has taken refuge, as mentioned, in romanticized notions of women. "Nausicaa" demonstrates some of the bad effects of these tendencies through the episode's ironic relation to the myth of Cupid and Psyche, especially the motifs of seeing and not-seeing, knowing and not-knowing.

A schematic guide to *Ulysses* that Joyce gave to Carlo Linati lists the "eye" as one of the organs of the episode, "the projected mirage" as the "sense" or "meaning" of the episode, and "painting" as the art of "Nausicaa." The "Gorman-Gilbert schema" lists the "Virgin" as the "symbol" of this episode (Ellmann, *Ulysses,* Appendix). In "Nausicaa" we see first Gerty and then Bloom projecting "mirages" of the other, "painting" idealized pictures of the opposite sex by refusing to "see" correctly. Since the narration prior to the climax of the episode originates from Gerty's perspective, we note her participation in this idealization more fully; we do not know what goes on in Bloom's mind while he masturbates, entering his point of view only after he has finished.

Fritz Senn has pointed out that "the sentence that first announces Gerty contains just two verbs in its main clause, 'knew' and 'couldn't see'" ("Nausicaa" 291), and the episode is full of references to seeing and knowing. The legend of Cupid and Psyche as told by Apuleius provides subtle reinforcement for this motif. Our modern lovers cannot see each other clearly, partly because of the deepening twilight, partly because of their tendencies to idealize each other, nor do they want to know each other. Joyce's subtle allusions to the Cupid and Psyche story do more than simply provide an allusion to *The Golden Ass;* they reinforce and deepen the possible meanings that the reader can draw from the pervasive visual imagery in "Nausicaa."

Gerty sees Bloom through the lens of romance, painting him as "the gentleman in black" (U13.349), the "foreigner, the image of the photo she had of Martin Harvey, the matinée idol" (U13.416–17). Her ideas of love and romance form themselves through the interaction of reading and imagining, readings such as the poem she copies out of the newspaper entitled *"Art thou real, my ideal?"* (U13.645–46), a poem that causes Stephen Daedalus to experience "a sharp agony in the sensitive region" when Madden reads it to him in *Stephen Hero* (83). In forming her ideal of romantic love, Gerty casts herself unknowingly as Psyche, the young princess who becomes the lover of Cupid—of Love himself—but only on condition that she not see him. Her two jealous sisters (here perhaps adumbrated in Edy and Cissy), suspecting she is married to a god, convince Psyche that her nocturnal husband is actually a "most cruel serpent" (Apuleius 227). Seized with a desire to know the truth, to see her lover as he really is, the luckless Psyche lights a lamp after Cupid falls asleep that night and, amazed by seeing a beautiful god in her bed, accidentally pricks herself with one of his arrows, thereby falling in love with Love. She then spills oil from the lamp, burning his shoulder and awakening him. Cupid flies away, and Psyche must begin her quest to win him back.

Joyce's notes for "Nausicaa" reveal that images related to the Cupid and Psyche story formed part of his thoughts as he composed. His notes and notesheets refer to Cupid, Venus, lamps, burning, and the urge to see and know the beloved. Bloom, we learn, "dislikes to be seen in profile" and looks at Gerty "as a snake looks at its prey" (see appendix). Joyce went back through this episode in his typescript and placard revisions, adding elements that again hint at a correlation with *The Golden Ass*, and especially the myth of Cupid and Psyche. For example, in typescript he added to a description of Gerty's face the line, "her rosebud mouth was a genuine Cupid's bow, Greekly perfect" (U13.88–89). Soon after this, Joyce describes Gerty's "butterfly bow" (U13.157), neatly combining two traditional symbols related to Psyche (often referred to as a butterfly) and Cupid (the bow). Joyce describes a withering glance Gerty has given Edy Boardman in terms evocative of Cupid's arrows and Psyche's relations with her jealous sisters: "that shaft had struck home for her petty jealousy and they both knew that she was something aloof, apart, in another sphere, that she was not of them . . . " (U13.601–3). Again, alluding to Cupid's parents, Venus and Vulcan, we hear from Gerty's perspective: "If she saw that magic lure in his eyes there would be no holding back for her. Love laughs at locksmiths" (U13.652–53).

These references to *The Golden Ass* form only one strand in the web of motifs and allusions that Joyce weaves into "Nausicaa." References to lamps and lamplighters, for example, may also cause the reader to recall Maria Susanna Cummins's romance novel *The Lamplighter*,[5] just as references to goddesses and gold may participate as much in evoking the Virgin Mary as they do in alluding to Psyche, Venus, or Isis. All of these allusions, taken together, form a suggestive background for our modern Cupid and Psyche, Leopold and Gerty.

What, then, does this Apuleian background contribute to our reading of "Nausicaa"? Most immediately, it supplements the ironic contrast provided by the Homeric parallel. Bloom is no Odysseus and Gerty no Princess Nausicaa, nor are they Cupid and Psyche. We can more easily see Bloom's lame goddess as a parody of Madame Blavatsky's occultist text *Isis Unveiled* than as a parallel to Apuleius' redemptive vision of Isis. While Bloom may resemble Lucius' asininity, he is not rescued by a goddess on the beach at Sandymount, but is left to continue his wanderings.

The Golden Ass provides a mythic substrate that underscores the presence and importance of goddesses in this episode concerned with the effects of idealizing the object of one's desire. According to Arthur Power, Joyce once told him that "What makes most people's lives unhappy is some disappointed romanticism, some unrealizable or misconceived ideal. In fact you may say that idealism is the ruin of man . . ." (98). The myth of Cupid and Psyche as a subtext for *Ulysses* accentuates the effects of idealizing the other by providing a mythic counterpart—an intertextual "memory"—in which a woman becomes a goddess through love, in which a human being falls in love with Love itself (a fitting image for the voracious reader of romances), and, more important, in which love must exist without true knowledge or sight of the beloved. Gerty thinks of Bloom as her "dreamhusband" (U13.431), but this ideal image can only exist in an environment veiled, as "Nausicaa" is, by myopia and deliberate obscurity. As Bloom puts it when he sees Gerty get up and realizes she is lame, "See her as she is spoil all. Must have the stage setting, the rouge, costume, position, music" (U13.855–56). Just as Cupid flies away when he realizes Psyche has seen him and recognized him, so infatuation disappears when Bloom sees through the romantic idealizing that pervades this episode.

Joyce complicates and strengthens these echoes of *The Golden Ass* in "Nausicaa" by including an additional intertextual recollection of another, related story of love and redemption—the legend of Isis and Osiris—near the end of the episode, when Bloom sees a bat flying about in the twilight and thinks, "Ba. What is that flying about? Swallow? Bat probably. Thinks I'm a tree, so blind. . . . Metempsychosis. They believed you could be changed into a tree from grief. Weeping willow. Ba" (U13.1117–19). The "ba" was one of the parts of the soul in Egyptian religion,[6] and in Plutarch's retelling of the myth of Isis and Osiris in the *Moralia*—which Joyce had in his Paris library[7]—a chest containing the body of the murdered Osiris comes to rest under a tree which "enfolded, embraced, and concealed the coffer within itself." In the same story, Isis circles around and around this tree in grief in the form of a swallow (Plutarch 13).

As mentioned, "Nausicaa" takes place near a Catholic church dedicated to "Mary, Star of the Sea" (Gifford 384). As "Nausicaa" begins, in fact, we hear "the voice of prayer to her who is in her pure radiance a beacon ever to the stormtossed heart of man, Mary, star of the sea" (*U*13.7–8). Joyce would have known that "Star of the Sea" or "Stella Maris" is an epithet traditionally assigned to the Virgin Mary, and Joyce's schema lists the "symbol" of this episode as the Virgin. Joyce would also have realized, through his reading of Madame Blavatsky's *Isis Unveiled* and perhaps through his familiarity with Sir James Frazer's *The Golden Bough,* that both these authors and others accused Roman Catholicism of having used the imagery of the cult of Isis as a basis for the depiction of the Virgin Mary. Frazer, for example, asserts that "to Isis in her later character of patroness of mariners the Virgin Mary perhaps owes her beautiful epithet of *Stella Maris,* 'Star of the Sea,' under which she is adored by tempest-tossed sailors" (119). By juxtaposing the myth of Isis found in *The Golden Ass* with the cult of the Virgin Mary, Joyce adds yet another shade of complexity to the intertextual memories or resonances evoked by "Nausicaa." These allusions to Isis near the ending of "Nausicaa" imply that while the hero of the ancient romance can rely on the aid of a goddess and the ingestion of a bunch of roses to become a man once more, modern romance is more problematic. The goddess does not appear; the text subtly suggests her presence only to emphasize her absence.[8]

The tempest-tossed Leopold Bloom, then, finds himself unknowingly participating in a number of different plots, intertextual memories that help to form the cultural memory that inscribes us all in the various roles we play in daily life as Westerners. We find Bloom and Gerty not only ambiguously linked to the Homeric story of Odysseus and Nausicaa, but to the stories of Cupid and Psyche, Lucius and Isis, and perhaps even Isis and the Virgin Mary. Joyce has complicated the text of "Nausicaa" by supplementing the contemporary romances that dominate the language of the episode with an older romance hidden beneath the surface. The subtle presence of Isis and Mary in the episode provides a clever frame for Bloom's reliance on idealized images of women as goddesses and, at the same time, challenges the Catholicism dominant in the Irish setting of *Ulysses* with an older religion buried within the text. By "unveiling" these stories hidden in "Nausicaa," these allusions to *The Golden Ass* lead the careful reader to "remember" other possibilities and to consider new interpretations.

These echoes of *The Golden Ass* seem clearly ironic, localized as they are within an episode in which Bloom appears at his worst. Yet we can read this memory of the older text as a mockery not of what might be—unity, love, coherence—but of what *is* (e.g., Bloom's behavior in "Nausicaa"). The problems implied by such intertextual links throughout *Ulysses* are nevertheless deep, creating an ironic distance between the modern setting most immediately evident in the text and the ancient stories encoded more subtly within it. This technique, as we have seen, may strike readers either as a negative comment on the relative emptiness and absurdity of modern life in comparison to the richness of older traditions or—as Eliot would see it—as a suggestion of stability and hope under the apparent chaos and absurdity of daily life.

This layering and density of allusion—of intertextual memory—in *Ulysses* works on a deeper level than the simple mockery implied by the ironic technique of juxtaposing an older, closed plot such as *The Golden Ass* and the "Nausicaa" episode of *Ulysses* to emphasize the fragmentation or meaninglessness of life in Ireland in 1904. *Ulysses* is loaded with intertextual memories so subtle and obscure that no reader could be expected to catch all of them in one, two, three, or more readings, and certainly readers need not remember the stories of Lucius or Cupid and Psyche in order to form a clear sense of the relationship between Joyce's characters. Yet Joyce went to the trouble of burying this and many other obscure intertextual echoes and memories in the text of *Ulysses,* perhaps in an attempt to model the ways in which cultural narratives and cultural memory influence the structures and narratives of everyday life, or perhaps in the confidence that while readers might not recognize and remember these buried stories consciously while reading "Nausicaa," they would nonetheless sense and respond to the echoes of these myths, which would in turn subliminally shape their expectations and judgments as readers of *Ulysses*.

In the sense outlined above, intertextuality in *Ulysses* can be interpreted as mimetic, as a model of the way(s) memory "works" in our minds on various levels—personal as well as cultural—and perhaps on even deeper levels. Leopold Bloom is not aware that his actions fit into an Odyssean paradigm, and yet, by virtue of a broader design than he can grasp, this paradigm and the other models echoing throughout the text of *Ulysses* provide patterns or points of reference that structure and interpret his experiences without determining them.

The contrasts between the surface story of Bloom, Stephen, and Molly as it occurs in *Ulysses* and the stories buried in the text of *Ulysses* are thus both suggestive and problematic. While the relatively complete narrative structures provided by these parallel stories offer the hint or promise of closure for the characters, they may in the end simply emphasize the inappropriateness of closure and the inevitability of fragmentation in a modern text.

Joyce's manipulation of various historical traditions to create a dense and subtle subtext for *Ulysses* should finally be read as an ambivalent modern response to the realization that our lives are inevitably involved with and to some degree shaped by the various paradigms and stories that form our culture. Joyce's decision to cram the text of *Ulysses* with references not only to the popular writings of his own time (e.g., the romances Gerty reads) but also to older narratives may suggest both our intricate and often unconscious involvement in the various discourses that form our culture—that is, the inevitable presence of tradition and of narrative paradigms that give shape to our experiences—*and* the absence of any reassuring conviction that these older plots can any longer guarantee a final coherence or meaning in modern life. As Christine van Boheemen argues, Joyce's intertextuality in *Ulysses* is "ambivalent and unclear. Bloom is *both* different from *and* similar to the classical hero" (142; original italics).

The ambivalence and ambiguity of Joyce's use of tradition in *Ulysses* helps us formulate a response to the problems of modernism articulated in the introduction to his essay. Joyce's response to the modernist perception that the dominant paradigms and traditions of Western culture no longer had the power to define, control, or stabilize modern life was not to attempt to begin completely anew by severing all links to the past, nor was it a capitulation to Eliot's desire to somehow secure or moor the present moment in a mythic or traditional structure behind modern art.

Christine van Boheemen suggests that Joyce's intertextuality deliberately foregrounds "what all texts do unconsciously. All writing predicates itself upon previous structures, meanings, or texts. . . . Joyce's writing strategy proves emblematic of the intertextuality of all writing" (144). Joyce's intertextuality can be understood in the context of what Perry Meisel, in *The Myth of the Modern,* calls the modernist sense of "belatedness," of responding to the sense that the literary tradition one is working in is exhausted. In *Ulysses,* Meisel writes, we can see that Joyce's response to the accumulations of traditions and of other stories is to enter and embrace the situation rather than to repress or avoid it: "If there is an especially appropriate Joycean gloss for the problematic of modernism at large, it lies compact in Stephen's Miltonic remark . . . 'Dead breaths I living breathe'—the sense that one's life or one's art is the echo or repetition of another's" (139).

Joyce's intertextuality, then, is a way of coping with modernity—with the modern sense of the absurdity of life and with the modernist writer's sense of being inevitably already inscribed within a tradition of writing. In Joyce's construction of an intertextual memory—exemplified in the way he weaves the stories contained in older texts such as *The Odyssey* and *The Golden Ass* into the fabric of *Ulysses*—we can read both an awareness of the constant presence and influence of the past in daily life and of the ironic gap between our lives and the traditional stories that supposedly give them form and meaning.

Appendix   "Nausicaa" and *The Golden Ass*

I. Possible References to *The Golden Ass* in the Notes, Notesheets, Revisions, and Text of "Nausicaa"

From *Joyce's Notes and Early Drafts for* Ulysses, ed. Phillip F. Herring: (From Joyce's Notebook V. A. 2—Late notes for typescripts and galleys)—
p. 91 (Page 15 of notebook)—"Nausicaa":
Line 16: "Cupid"
Line 17: "you don't know how nice you looked"
Line 20: "Look daggers"

From *Joyce's* Ulysses *Notesheets in the British Museum*, ed. Phillip F. Herring:
126.49–50: ⟨Leo Dillon (16) Goddess Venus with all her belongings. Innocence⟩
131.48–50: Lamplighter's lintstock.
136.32: Aphrodite, poised hips unveiled for judgment
139.18: butterfly bow
142.95: the lamplight falls upon a face
142.108–114:
    lamp
    for the love of God!
    gazing far away into the distance
    downcast eyes
    I'm dying to know
    I'd give world to—
    LB dislikes to be seen in profile
150.29–30: His eyes burned into her as though to read her through & through
150.37–38: Maul in dark. Kiss & never tell.
151.71: Ass knows in whose face he brays.
153.9: wonderful eyes, but could you trust him
153.19: stole a look at him
154.40: soul in her eyes
158.43: brief cold blaze from her eyes
158.45: shaft strike home
158.59: as a snake looks at his prey
159.71: love laughs at locksmiths
159.80: Poor though the light was
160.125: light broke in upon him [him = her in text]

II. Echoes of *The Golden Ass* in "Nausicaa"
13.42: "The apple of discord was a certain castle of sand"
13.87–89: "her rosebud mouth was a genuine Cupid's bow, Greekly perfect." [Added in typescript].

13.93–94: "the girl chums had of course their little tiffs from time to time like the rest of mortals"

13.107: "eyes of witchery"

13.157–58: "a butterfly bow of silk to tone."

13.189: "Her very soul is in her eyes"

13.229–30: "often she wondered why you couldn't eat something poetical like violets or roses"

13.304: "scarce saw"

13.307: "never saw"

13.314–15: "when he sang *The moon hath raised* with Mr. Dignam" [Song goes: "The moon hath raised her lamp above, to light the way to thee my love." See Thornton 310].

13.361: "she was determined to let them see"

13.368: "she ventured a look at him"

13.411–17: "And while she gazed her heart went pitapat. Yes, it was her he was looking at, and there was meaning in his look. His eyes burned into her as though they would search her through and through, read her very soul."

13.437: "she just yearned to know all"

13.495–96: "Gerty could see without looking that he never took his eyes off of her"

13.504: "he had eyes in his head to see the difference for himself."

13.517: "He was eying her as a snake eyes its prey."

13.578: "A brief cold blaze shone from her eyes"

13.586–88: "Their eyes were probing her mercilessly but with a brave effort she sparkled back in sympathy as she glanced at her new conquest for them to see."

13.597–98: "she could give him [in this case, "Mr Reggy"] one look of measured scorn that would make him shrivel up on the spot."

13.601–3: "that shaft had struck home for her petty jealousy and they both knew that she was something aloof, apart, in another sphere, that she was not of them"

13.631: "lighting the lamp"

13.652–3: "If she saw that magic lure in his eyes there would be no holding back for her. Love laughs at locksmiths."

13.655: "There was the allimportant question and she was dying to know"

13.688–89: "she said she could see from where she was. The eyes that were fastened upon her set her pulses tingling. She looked at him a moment, meeting his glance, and a light broke in upon her."

13.697: "there was no-one to see only him"

13.730: "she wasn't ashamed and he wasn't either to look"

13.731: "he couldn't resist the sight"

13.744–47: "A fair unsullied soul had called to him . . ."

13.751: "the hiding twilight"

13.757: "one of love's little ruses"

13.762–64: "Their souls met in a last lingering glance and the eyes that reached her heart, full of a strange shining, hung enraptured on her sweet flowerlike face."

13.794: "Peeping Tom."

13.818–19: "You're looking splendid. Sister souls. Showing their teeth at one another."

13.832–33: "Kiss in the dark and never tell. Saw something in me."

13.836: "Didn't let her see me in profile."

13.839: "carry a bunch of flowers to smell"

13.855–56: "See her as she is spoil all."

13.872–73: "O, her mouth in the dark!"
13.902–3: "Caressing the little boy too. Onlookers see most of the game."
13.910: "picture of Venus"
13.911–13: "Never see them sit on a bench marked Wet Paint. Eyes all over them. Look under the bed for what's not there."
13.936–37: "Darling, I saw, you. I saw all."
13.1009–10: "Hm. Roses, I think. She'd like scent of that kind."
13.1058: "See ourselves as others see us."
13.1076: "A star I see. Venus?"

Notes

1   *Ulysses,* chap. 2, l. 377. Subsequent references to *Ulysses* will be provided parenthetically in the text in this format: (U2.377).
2   Perry Meisel argues that "by virtue of a Latin rather than properly Greek title, the novel gives us a graphic clue for its programmatic failure to complete Eliot's 'parallel' even on its face. If *Ulysses,* as Eliot claims, is a mythic replication of the *Odyssey,* why, then, is the book not called *Odysseus?*" (145). Christine van Boheemen also takes up this issue, arguing for the "ambivalent" nature of *Ulysses'* reference to the *Odyssey:* "Thus, this title, which points to the epic, also marks the text's revisionary difference from the classic narrative. The title as sign functions as an epitaph, marking the last remains of *The Odyssey.* In giving his novel the title *Ulysses,* Joyce incorporated Homer into his fiction as the paradoxical presence of a defunct absence" (145).
3   One anonymous reviewer in 1922 wrote that *Ulysses* "has nothing at all to do with Homer" (Deming 194), while Shane Leslie wrote in the *Quarterly Review* that "the great name of Ulysses is horribly profaned. We have only an Odyssey of the sewer" (Deming 207). Valéry Larbaud, on the other hand, claimed in 1922 that "the reader who approaches this book without the *Odyssey* clearly in mind will be thrown into dismay" (Deming 258).
4   Joyce owned an Italian version of this story excerpted from *The Golden Ass.* See Gillespie, *Catalogue* 33.
5   See Thornton 313–14.
6   See, for example, Breasted 55–56. The "ba" appears in *Finnegans Wake* as well ("Ba's berial nether," *FW* 415).
7   See Ellmann, *Consciousness* 123.
8   For more detail on the relation of this myth to "Nausicaa," see Rickard.

Works Cited

Apuleius. *The Golden Ass: Being the Metamorphoses of Lucius Apuleius.* Trans. W. Adlington (1566). Loeb Classical Library. Revised by S. Gaselee. Cambridge, Mass.: Harvard University Press, 1977.
Boheemen, Christine van. *The Novel as Family Romance: Language, Gender, and Authority from Fielding to Joyce.* Ithaca, N.Y.: Cornell University Press, 1987.
Breasted, James Henry. *Development of Religion and Thought in Ancient Egypt.* London: Hodder and Stoughton, 1912.
Certeau, Michel de. *The Practice of Everyday Life.* Trans. Stephen Rendall. Berkeley: University of California Press, 1984.

Cixous, Hélène. "Joyce: The (R)use of Writing." *Post-Structuralist Joyce: Essays from the French.* Ed. Derek Attridge and Daniel Ferrer. Cambridge: Cambridge University Press, 1984, 15–30.

Danto, Arthur C. "The Shape of Artistic Pasts: East and West," in *The Philosophical Uses of Historical Traditions.* Durham, N.C.: Duke University Press, 1993.

Deming, Robert H., ed. *James Joyce: The Critical Heritage.* Vol. 1: 1907–1927. London: Routledge and Kegan Paul, 1970.

Derrida, Jacques. "Two Words for Joyce." Trans. Geoff Bennington. *Post-Structuralist Joyce: Essays from the French.* Ed. Derek Attridge and Daniel Ferrer. Cambridge: Cambridge University Press, 1984, 145–59.

Eco, Umberto. *The Aesthetics of Chaosmos: The Middle Ages of James Joyce.* Trans. Ellen Esrock. University of Tulsa Monograph Series, no. 18. Tulsa: University of Oklahoma, 1982.

Eliot, T. S. "*Ulysses,* Order and Myth," in *Selected Prose of T. S. Eliot.* Ed. Frank Kermode. New York: Harcourt Brace Jovanovich, 1975.

Ellmann, Richard. *The Consciousness of Joyce.* New York: Oxford University Press, 1977.

———. *Ulysses on the Liffey.* New York: Oxford University Press, 1972.

Frazer, James G. *Adonis, Attis, Osiris: Studies in the History of Oriental Religion,* part 4, vol. 2, of *The Golden Bough: A Study in Magic and Religion.* 3d ed., 1913. London: Macmillan, 1980.

Gifford, Don, and Robert J. Seidman. *Joyce Annotated: Notes for James Joyce's* Ulysses. Revised and expanded ed. Berkeley: University of California Press, 1988.

Gillespie, Michael Patrick. *James Joyce's Trieste Library: A Catalogue of Materials at the Harry Ransom Humanities Research Center, the University of Texas at Austin.* Austin: Harry Ransom Humanities Research Center, 1986.

———. "Sources and the Independent Artist." *James Joyce Quarterly* 20 (Spring 1983): 325–36.

Herring, Phillip F., ed. *Joyce's Notes and Early Drafts for* Ulysses. Charlottesville: University Press of Virginia, 1977.

———, ed. *Joyce's* Ulysses *Notesheets in the British Museum.* Charlottesville: University Press of Virginia, 1972.

Joyce, James. *Finnegans Wake.* London: Faber and Faber, 1939.

———. *Letters of James Joyce.* 3 vols. Ed. Stuart Gilbert, vol. 1, and Richard Ellmann, vols. 2 and 3. New York: Viking Press, 1966.

———. *Stephen Hero.* Ed. Theodore Spencer. New ed. New York: New Directions, 1963.

———. *Ulysses: A Critical and Synoptic Edition.* Ed. Hans Walter Gabler et al. New York: Random House, 1986.

Jung, Carl Gustav. *Ulysses: A Monologue.* Trans. W. Stanley Dell. Brooklyn, N.Y.: Haskell House, 1977.

MacCabe, Colin. *James Joyce and the Revolution of the Word.* London: Macmillan, 1978.

Meisel, Perry. *The Myth of the Modern: A Study in British Literature and Criticism After 1850.* New Haven, Conn.: Yale University Press, 1987.

Plutarch. *Plutarch's Morals: Theosophical Essays.* Trans. C. W. King. London: G. Bell, 1898.

Power, Arthur. *Conversations with James Joyce.* New York: Harper and Row, 1974.

Rickard, John S. "Isis on Sandymount." *James Joyce Quarterly* 20 (Spring 1983): 356–58.

Senn, Fritz. "Nausicaa." *James Joyce's* Ulysses: *Critical Essays.* Ed. Clive Hart and David Hayman. Berkeley: University of California Press, 1974, 277–311.

Thornton, Weldon. *Allusions in 'Ulysses.'* Chapel Hill: University of North Carolina Press, 1968.

Stanley Rosen

Plato's

Quarrel

My topic in this essay is the quarrel between   with the
philosophy and poetry in Plato, especially in
the *Republic*. I want to suggest the close rela-   Poets
tionship between two puzzling features of the
Republic, the first of which is the problematic
nature of the city sketched there. I refer not merely to many objections that
the modern reader would raise against that city's nature, but to reservations
of Glaucon and Adeimantus, Socrates' two main interlocutors. These reservations touch on such central issues as the blessedness or happiness of the
city's residents, the apparent injustice in the need to force the philosophers
to rule, and the very possibility of the city. The second feature is the quarrel
between philosophy and poetry referred to in Book Ten, which is enacted in
the dialogue by the expulsion of the mimetic poets from the city. Once again,
we note, but do not restrict ourselves to, the dissatisfaction felt by modern
readers with Socrates' treatment of poetry. Internal evidence also makes the
strict censorship of poetry ambiguous.

Let me begin by indicating the most important passages from the *Republic*
that cause internal difficulties on these points. The question whether the
guardian or ruling class can be happy is introduced at IV. 419a1ff. Here,
Socrates asserts that his concern is with the happiness of the city as a whole,
not with that of a class of citizens. At V. 465d5ff, Socrates claims that the
guardians will be happier than Olympian victors in existing cities because
they have no private property or family, women and children—with certain
technical restrictions to avoid incest—being held in common.

Socrates claims that individual guardians will treat the class to which they
belong as their family. For each guardian, "mine" will be synonymous with
"ours" (V. 462c7ff and 463c3–8); he also says that we take the best care of
what we love most, and we love most what we identify with our own
interests (III. 412d2ff). The problem here is twofold. First, it will be necessary to expunge every vestige of private love from members of the guardian
class in order to make them into members of a unity having common

pleasure (V. 462a9ff, 464d4f). To say the least, it is implausible to assume that this can be done. The sensations of each body are its private property, so to speak, and the same must be said of the attendant pleasures. The question, then, is whether these private pleasures do not guarantee private attachments between sexual partners.

The implausibility is suggested by Socrates himself in his remarks concerning the great difficulty in controlling eros as well as breeding (V.458c6ff for erotic necessity; 459c8ff for the need for medicinal lying in connection with mating and reproduction; VIII. 546a2: the city decays through failure to control breeding). But second, even if the education imposed by the philosopher-kings is successful in replacing private by common pleasures, the result will be to divide the city into half, or in other words to multiply it, since the guardians will be sharply separated from the workers, to whom the communal way of life does not apply. The guardians will identify with their fellow guardians, but not with the city, which will become two cities, as Aristotle points out in the *Politics*. The happiness of the guardians depends on conditions that, if obtained, must dissolve the city, or turn it into an armed camp.

The possibility of the city turns on the philosopher-king, but the genuine philosopher will refuse to govern unless compelled to do so (VII. 517c7ff; 519c1ff). Socrates claims that it is just to compel the genuine philosopher who is a child of the just city and therefore owes it his service. The just city therefore requires that the philosopher be constrained to live a worse life, i.e., that of political authority, and so to sacrifice involuntarily the better life, i.e., that of philosophy (VII. 519d8ff; 520a6ff).

I note a related passage concerning the founding of the city. Socrates says that the philosopher-kings will initially send everyone over the age of ten out into the countryside in order to begin with relatively uncorrupted citizens. It takes little imagination to realize that the philosopher-kings will have to use violence, and perhaps mass murder, to carry out this initial step. The just city, as in Machiavelli's teachings, begins in what looks like injustice, or, if justice does not begin until the city is established, certainly in cruelty and violence of a comprehensive sort.

Socrates makes a variety of not entirely compatible remarks about the possibility of the just city. The most important are these: at V. 472b7ff and again at 473a1ff, he notes that we have looked for a paradigm of justice to copy as closely as possible, but not to show that it is possible for the paradigm itself to come into existence. Hence, he declines to be asked whether what the speakers have accomplished in discourse is possible in deed. His final observation on this topic is at VII. 540d1ff, where he says that if the city they have described is impossible, then their speech has been mere wishing or daydreaming; but, he claims, it is possible, although very hard, for the city to come into existence.

This possibility, again, depends on the coincidence that a philosopher become a king or an existing king be a philosopher by nature. The problem is that since no philosopher in an existing city will choose to be a king, and since prior to the founding of the just city there is no one to force this choice, it seems as if it is impossible, and not just difficult, for the city to come into existence. Should a king be born with the nature of a philosopher, on Socratic premises he would abdicate and devote himself to philosophy rather than attempt to establish a new city. One must also ask how the philosopher, even if he should wish to be a king, would be able to remove everyone over the age of ten from the city. Certainly, no existing police force would administer its own expulsion, and prior to the foundation of the city there are no guardians to do it.

Let me summarize. On the basis of internal evidence, it is at least dubious whether the city founded in speech by Socrates and his interlocutors is just or possible, and if it is just and possible, it remains doubtful that the two highest classes, the philosophers and the guardians, are happy. This being so, it is doubtful that Socrates has shown the just life to be the happiest for the individual human being. The only happy class in the just city seems to be that of the workers, who live very much as do most citizens in actual cities, i.e., as unjustly as possible. In slightly different terms, the so-called just city may not be just, but whether or not it is just, it certainly seems to be irrelevant to the question of what kind of life to live in existing or corrupt cities.

I turn to the second puzzle concerning the *Republic,* namely, the sharp criticism of poetry and the expulsion of the mimetic poets from the city. In the case of the first puzzle, Socrates' argument seems to be incoherent or self-contradictory. In the case of the second, the problem is somewhat different. Despite a number of confusing peripeties, there are, I think, no incoherences in Socrates' criticism of poetry. The difficulty arises from another angle, namely, that the Platonic dialogues in general, and the *Republic* in particular, are examples of mimetic poetry. This has led many modern readers of the *Republic* to wonder whether Plato shares the criticism of mimesis assigned to Socrates, and if he does, whether he is not being inconsistent with his own practice. There is also a question as to whether Socrates' criticism of poetry is just.

Let us look once more at some internal evidence. As I have written extensively on the details of the Socratic criticism of poetry, I will not repeat them here. Suffice it to say that mimetic poetry is associated with the tyrannical Eros or with the rule of pleasure, which is the defining characteristic of the tyrant; there is also a link between the innovativeness of poetry and the excessive love of freedom that characterizes democracies and causes them to deteriorate into tyrannical regimes (IX. 573b6ff; X. 607a5–8, c4–5). Socrates also criticizes the poets for their lack of knowledge, or separation from the Ideas; but this line of criticism is based on the obviously erroneous thesis that poetry is the imitation of things or of technical knowledge, whereas it is rather, if imitative at all, then, as Aristotle points out in the *Poetics,* the mimesis of action. In Platonic language, poets copy (and of course interpret) the soul. That they possess an expertise in this understanding is verified by Socrates himself, who in the *Republic* often quotes Homer and other poets as authorities on human nature.

It is appropriate, therefore, to limit ourselves to the political function of imitation. In my opinion, the most overlooked example of the difficulty in question arises when justice is defined by Socrates as "minding one's own business" or "doing one's own work" (III. 433a4–b4; IV. 441d5ff). The image of the Idea of justice is that each man practice the single art for which he is best suited by nature; accordingly, injustice is defined as *polypragmosyne,* or minding everyone's business (IV. 443c4ff, 444b1–8). It is, however, perfectly obvious, or should be, that Socrates, in founding the city, minds everyone's business, or in other words imitates all types of human being, that is to say, the city as a whole. Thus, Plato in the *Republic* practices a form of poetry that is even more comprehensive than that of Homer. In so doing, he is either guilty of *polypragmosyne* or else claims implicitly to possess technical knowledge of every fundamental aspect of human existence.

If the philosopher were to follow the "one man, one *techne*" principle, he or she would mind his or her own business, and hence not rule at all. This is exactly what philosophers do in actual cities, according to Socrates. Hence, it is only in the "just city" that philosophers are forced to practice *polypragmosyne* or injustice. This injustice may not be quite as extensive as that of the lawgiver or founding father, but it is extensive enough.

To restate this issue in terms of poetry, the founding fathers, and by extension the philosopher-kings and guardians, are the true mimetic poets who copy the paradigm of justice, the city laid up in speech or the heavenly paradigm (IX. 592a1ff, 592b2). Frequently throughout the dialogue, Socrates employs the verb *plattein,* which may be translated as "to make imaginatively," "to shape," and almost as "to create," to describe the activities of the founders of, as well as of the rulers within, the city. We produce the city (II. 374a5); by the use of myths (including medicinal and noble lies) we shape the souls of the citizens (II. 377b6; 377c3); the philosopher produces not only himself, but temperance, justice, and all of demotic virtue by looking to the Ideas (500d4–8); we are painters of the city, for which we require a clean canvas (500e2–4; 501a1ff); we have produced an image of the soul in speech (IX. 588b10ff). As the demiurge of the city, the philosopher is a comprehensive mimetician; accordingly, he is a tyrant of a more comprehensive sort than the poet, because his Eros is stronger than the poet's.

A similar list of passages could be cited in which Socrates uses expressions such as "telling myths" to make explicit the poetic, mimetic, or constructive nature of his activity in the *Republic*. It is also evident that the basic education of the guardian class, from which the philosopher-kings are chosen, is musical; it sinks into the soul like a dye, or paints the correct shape of the citizen on the canvas of the city (III. 401d5ff, 404e4f). On two occasions Socrates says he is not a poet (II. 378e7 and III. 393d8), but in both passages it is explicit that he means only that he does not write in meter and that his "poem" is a city, not a traditional work of art.

So much for the passages that establish our two puzzles. I want next to restate the issue of poetry more specifically in terms of the relation between philosophy and politics. As is well known, Aristotle offers as one of his three definitions of the human animal that it is by nature political (the other two: it possesses *logos* and is the imitative animal). According to this definition, politics is the perfection of human existence; even philosophy depends on the city. The city follows from human nature, which may be described as "at home" in the cosmos in the sense that nature provides the paradigm (the natural order) which human beings imitate to achieve a life in accord with natural ends.

This view is not contained in Plato. It is true that Socrates regularly appeals to nature in the *Republic* while constructing his just or beautiful city. But the only natural city is precisely the city laid up in speech, the heavenly paradigm; all actual cities are sick or unnatural. In the decisive case, none of the actual cities corresponds to the life that is best by nature, namely, the philosophical life (VI. 497b1f). The philosopher cannot live a fully philosophical life in any existing city (VI. 497a3f). I should also note that Socrates' appeals to nature, even in the act of constructing the just city, are not always without irony. Perhaps the most obvious example is his attempt to prove that the possibility of combining ferocity toward strangers and gentleness toward friends, essential in the nature of the guardian class, is established by citing the nature of the dog who barks at strangers and is gentle to friends (II. 375a2ff).

Politics is regularly presented in the Platonic dialogues as a productive art, analogous to weaving, which makes blankets and clothing to protect human beings against the natural elements. As we have seen from the evidence in the *Republic*, politics is for Plato a kind of poetry; in the best case, it is employed by the philosopher for the production, or at least the modification, of citizens. This productive activity is required because the human animal is *not* at home in the cosmos; nature is hostile at least as much as it is friendly to human existence. Accordingly, human beings must take steps to secure themselves in a cosmos that requires radical construction, in the decisive instance of a revolutionary new city; what the Stoics call the life in accord with nature is not possible for human beings. To make the same point in another way, whereas Aristotle distinguishes three kinds of arts, theoretical, practical, and productive, there is no distinct praxis in Plato, i.e., no distinct practical virtue. Political virtue is a mixture of theory and production.

We can now understand the quarrel between philosophy and poetry as in principle political. Poetry in the conventional sense reconciles human beings to their tragic status in the cosmos; philosophy, or more precisely philosophic poetry, attempts to remake human beings in such a way as to balance the tragic and the comic elements in our existence. Furthermore, whereas for Aristotle the species-form is actualized within the intellect of the knower, and so is present within the domain of genesis, according to Plato the Ideas are in a hyperuranian place, and can be seen only intermittently, or described in mythical and metaphorical language.

The philosopher does not imitate nature but rather the Ideas. I cannot enter now into the difficult question of what Plato meant by the Ideas. Suffice it to say that they are referred to in the *Phaedo* as the most secure hypothesis or basis for attempting to understand anything in the world of genesis. In the *Republic* the capacity of the philosopher-kings to rule with wisdom is contingent on possessing the science of dialectic, i.e., knowledge of Ideas, and, in particular, the Idea of the Good, the first principle of the Ideas, and so of the whole of Being.

Socrates never says in the *Republic* that there is in fact knowledge of the Idea of the Good, nor does he offer any "proof" that the Ideas exist. He asserts that without knowledge of the Good, nothing is worth anything (VI. 505a4ff). We do not receive knowledge of the Good in the *Republic* but only metaphors or images about the Good, of which the most famous is the sun. Neither do we receive any instance of dialectic, or knowledge of the Ideas; instead, we are told what it would be like in a passage of unusual brevity and obscurity: namely, knowledge of Ideas on the basis of knowledge of other Ideas (VI. 510b4ff). On balance, it is fair to say that in the *Republic,* Socrates' account of the Ideas, the Good, and dialectic is poetic, not dialectical or philosophical in the advertised sense (cf. VI. 504b1ff and 506d8ff).

I will not go so far as to say that the "theory" of Ideas is in fact a philosophical poem. I will say, however, that the presentation of the Ideas in the *Republic* is poetic; the crux of the refutation of poetry, or let us say of the demonstration of the superiority of philosophy to poetry, is itself poetic. There cannot be any doubt about the fact that in the *Republic,* to speak only of this dialogue, Plato presents philosophy in a poetic form or image. And this means, in turn, that philosophy is subordinate to poetry in a crucial respect.

Outside or prior to the foundation of the city ruled by philosophers, poetry must be employed in order to present the problem of the quarrel between philosophy and poetry. This quarrel has nothing to do with the use of meter rather than prose; it has to do with our response to man's status in a hostile cosmos. Inside the philosophical city, poetry is required to produce citizens.

This concludes the first stage in my discussion of the quarrel between philosophy and poetry in Plato. But we are far from having concluded our investigation. For we must turn to a question at least as difficult as those that have occupied us. Why does Plato present us with a poem that is both internally incoherent and evidently unappealing to those who would be expected to take a leading role in the city it celebrates?

We will make no progress in understanding this question if we follow the usual procedure of self-styled Platonists who attempt to convince us that there are no problems in the *Republic* of the kind whose existence I have demonstrated. Philosophers are usefully defined as those who see things as they are. The city described in the *Republic* is, to put it bluntly, obnoxious. It is neither just nor filled with happy citizens, at least in the two highest classes; and in saying this, I am not merely adopting the prejudices of the moderns, or falling short of the exalted virtue of the ancients.

The evidence I have accumulated was indispensable to persuade that either Plato is a thoughtless and incompetent writer, or else he must be aware of the problems raised by his political recommendations in the *Republic*. It will do no good to say that Plato was a typical Greek, a male chauvinist pig, an elitist and a reactionary. On none of these grounds could one arrive at the city founded by Socrates. In fact, the opinions assigned to Socrates are not typically Greek, as Socrates explicitly notes. Furthermore, they are not those of a male chauvinist, since women of outstanding natures are put on an equal level with the male guardians and philosophers. Socrates' doctrines are not reactionary but revolutionary. They are in fact elitist, but this does not go to the core of the matter, since not all elitist doctrines advocate the rule of philosophers.

What I propose is to develop a plausible way of viewing the *Republic*, a way that will make sense out of Plato's overall procedure and thereby lead us to a reasonable hypothesis as to why Socrates argues as he does. I will make no attempt to prove that Plato writes in accord with my hypothesis. And I will certainly not try to convince that the city founded by Socrates is in fact just, blessed, and the fulfillment of the philosopher's resolution of the human predicament. The reader is free to believe that Plato was a poor philosopher or an elitist swine. My hypothesis is not a proof, but an alternative reading.

In constructing my case, I must restrict myself to the question of the ostensible quarrel between philosophy and poetry. We take our bearings by the fact that, in the *Republic,* Socrates advocates the censorship of art, or the entire subordination of poetry, i.e., mimesis, to political ends. In modern terminology, there is no freedom of speech in Socrates' city. Let us now ask ourselves a difficult question: Why are we in favor of freedom of speech and, hence, of innovation? I am not asking whether we like or desire freedom of speech. I am asking how we justify this desire. I take it as an empirical fact that freedom of speech, and so artistic innovation, is pleasant. But pleasure is not a philosophically respectable reason since, as Plato pointed out, there are noble and base pleasures. The turn to pleasure as the criterion for virtue, and so for justice, is in fact, whether we admit it or not, a repudiation of philosophy. This is why postmodern defenses of radical difference are closely associated to the claim that philosophy is dead, or that we live in a post-philosophical epoch.

The antiphilosopher, as I shall call him, asserts that there are no natural standards of nobility and baseness, and so, no criteria for restricting the speech of others but only the use of violence. Since there are no natural standards, all speech is innovative. The point here is quite different from Plato's critique of mimesis. Whereas Socrates claims that the imitations of ordinary poets are defective because copies of generated rather than of eternal paradigms, the modern, and of course the postmodern, defender of poetry insists that, since there are no originals or paradigms, all discourse is innovative or creative.

In other words, since there are no silent originals to which speech refers, all speech is original. The antiphilosophical thesis is thus, in fact, that there are no images but *only* originals. There are, in the contemporary jargon, nothing but signs. The antiphilosopher accordingly claims that it is unjust to restrict any speech. But this is an entirely unconvincing argument, even if we may find it emotionally pleasing. If the referent of every sign is another sign, there cannot be an independent standard of significance. And if there are no standards, there can be no injustice. It will then be true that the restriction of freedom of speech, or the censorship of art, is violent. But violence is neither just nor unjust, on the premise of the defender of freedom who denies natural standards. The violent man is as free as the pacifist to create an original or paradigm according to which might makes right. Some have called this the will to power.

The point here is just this: there is no good argument for defending freedom of speech other than an appeal to our ignorance. To make a long story short, we claim that we do not know enough, or anything, to justify stifling the speech of others, or imposing our views on them. But if we are ignorant, we cannot defend ourselves against those who purport to possess natural or supernatural standards for the regulation of speech, and so of art. Differently stated, the only way in which we can defend ourselves against such claims is by force, by violence, not by reason.

Some will want to object that there is empirical evidence to support the thesis that restriction of free speech leads to tyranny. I do not deny this; tyranny is also a natural consequence of the rejection of natural or supernatural standards for nobility and baseness. Tyranny, in one form or another, is a consequence of all consistently and rigorously applied political programs. So far as I can see the only plausible defense of free speech is that we like it, i.e., that it is pleasant, and that we will fight to preserve it. But this means that we accept the premise of those who contend that might makes right.

What I have just said may seem peremptory. Can it not be maintained that there is a rational paradigm for human existence that includes freedom of speech and art? My point is that such a paradigm is the expression of a standard, and that the imposition of a standard entails restrictions on speech and action. All philosophical defenses of freedom based on rational paradigms define freedom in such a way as to exclude at least some speech.

To take the extreme case, in a totally free society, we would have to exclude the speech of censorship, as well as the action that leads to the suppression of freedom as defined by our paradigm. Total freedom is an empty phrase—a signifier without a referent (I almost said). The sign is variously interpreted by representatives of various theoretical positions. As is immediately obvious to anyone with any experience of the contemporary intellectual and university world, censorship is enforced by those who never cease to speak of tolerance, by which they mean tolerance for currently fashionable views, or in other words subservience to the will to power. The iron fist in a velvet glove remains a fist, even if the velvet is what some would charmingly refer to as "argument."

The rational paradigm for freedom is in fact a rational paradigm for the restriction of freedom. I am not claiming that there are no empirical differences among these paradigms, or that some are not preferable to others. My point is theoretical, not practical. The assertion of a philosophical paradigm of freedom amounts to the claim that we are in possession of natural criteria for just and unjust speech, and so, as a corollary, for noble and base art. If the claim is merely on behalf of some conventional or historically justified paradigm, this is finally equivalent to the thesis that might makes right, i.e., that what happens, or what the majority believe to have happened, is right. The censorship of art and the restriction of free speech then becomes a moral imperative: a matter of justice. And what we mean by justice is backed up by our appeal either to the natural criteria or to their historical, and so conventional, simulacra.

The political articulation of any appeal to a standard of freedom, whether natural or historical, would look, if we thought it through to the end, very much like the city founded in the *Republic* by Socrates. Again, I am restricting myself to broad and essential considerations and disregarding the details. Let me alert the reader at once to my purpose in calling attention to this resemblance. It is not at all to persuade that Plato's *Republic* is after all a splendid political paradigm. It is rather to suggest that justice, as a goal of coherent, intense, single-minded effort by rational human beings, is impossible; or let us say that the results of such an effort are not only undesirable but obnoxious. We ought *not* to think our political principles through to the end. If we were to do so, we would end up, if we were incompetent, in a tyranny of pseudo-philosophers or ideologists, and if we were competent, in the city of Plato's *Republic*.

I am therefore in sympathy with the view, which I first heard enunciated many years ago by Leo Strauss, that the *Republic* is a political satire, very much as Spinoza claims is the case with Machiavelli's *Prince*. On this view, the political message of the *Republic* is that the single-minded pursuit of justice is unjust. Strauss is today widely regarded as a conservative, thanks in large part to his own exoteric rhetoric, but also to the low level of intelligence that has been addressed to the study of his writings. In fact, Strauss, like all genuine Platonists, was a revolutionary on behalf of philosophy; in this sense, his primary loyalty was not to politics at all.

This is not to say that I agree with the political tactics Strauss devised on behalf of philosophy. To explain this point would take me too far afield; I must refer, instead, to my writings in *Hermeneutics as Politics* and elsewhere. In the terms of the present essay, the question is one of the role to be assigned to poetry. As I have indicated, Plato cannot be understood from an Aristotelian perspective. It is already obvious from the difference between a Platonic dialogue and an Aristotelian treatise that poetry has a higher role in Plato than it does in Aristotle. Strauss was aware of this difference but muffled its consequences in exoteric Aristotelian rhetoric because of a mistaken view of the exigencies of the contemporary historical and political situation.

But this is by the way. The *Republic*, I suggest, taken as a political analysis, is in fact a reductio ad absurdum. The genuine political teaching would have to be reconstructed from the rubble of that reductio, and such a reconstruction would involve the rethinking of the philosophical role of poetry. It is poetry, not philosophy, that makes citizens. Accordingly, it is the task of philosophy to *make poetry*. This crucial point is plain enough in the explicit argument of the *Republic,* and it is not dissolved by the failure of that argument. It is sustained by the process of thinking through what we must do to ensure a perfectly just society.

And this brings me back to the coincidence between such a requirement and the main characteristics of Socrates' founding of the just city. Perfect justice requires giving to each person precisely what that person deserves. To carry out this definition, the following is necessary. First, we must know exactly what each person deserves. This in turn requires that human beings have natures such that we can assign to them what is best for each. I say "we," but of course what is required is that the rulers possess this knowledge. Perfect justice requires perfect rulers, or let us say the selection of the most outstanding human beings for leadership, to which they will succeed on completing a long and rigorous education of body and soul. If all human beings were perfect, no government of the sort considered by political thinkers would be necessary. As at least some anarchists have understood, complete equality among human beings would make government either unnecessary or impossible.

The rulers must have control over all aspects of political life so as to guarantee that justice will prevail; in an alternative formulation, they must be able to stifle injustice before it appears. The combination of knowledge and power must be used to preserve the true knowledge on which the city is based, and so to exclude all innovation, which must be error. This entails regulation not only of the intellectual and artistic life of the city, but of its economic structure, the assignment of persons to occupations, and the regulation of social and sexual relations among individuals.

I interrupt this sketch to note, as I trust is obvious, that it coincides with Socrates' own procedure with one exception. Socrates restricts his supervision of the private and especially the sexual relations of the citizens to the members of the guardian class. As I pointed out, this differentiation between guardians and workers leads inevitably to the dissolution of the unity of the city. It would seem that the modern universal homogeneous world-state, as advocated by Alexandre Kojève, is more consistent here in that it at least makes possible the supervision of all citizens, workers as well as soldiers and philosophers.

Why does Socrates distinguish between the erotic regulation of the guardians and the erotic freedom of the workers? A complete consideration of this problem would take us into the depths of Socrates' analogy between the city and the soul, and so into his analogy between the three main parts of the soul and the three kinds of human being. I must restrict myself to the suggestion that there is no such analogy, as is plain from the fact that it is not cities which are philosophers, soldiers, or workers, but individuals.

Differently stated, Socrates wishes to draw a political analogy from the rule within the individual soul of the intellect over the spirited element and the desires. This shows, incidentally, that his procedure is circular, since he introduces the analogy between the city and the soul on the grounds that it is easier to see the city, and so to infer the nature of the soul from the nature of the city. In fact, Socrates infers the structure of the city from the nature of the soul.

But just as the philosopher contains a spirited element as well as desires, so too the members of the two lower classes contain intellects, and, in fact, all three of the spiritual components. The philosopher is as likely to be subjected to sexual eros, which is a desire, as is the guardian to be moved by theoretical eros. It is all very well to say that eros can be restrained by intellectual effort. But what must be restrained certainly exists. In fact, the most pressing problem of the philosopher-kings is to regulate eros in the top two classes. But since eros is a desire, and the worker class corresponds to the desiring part of the soul, if the analogy held between city and soul, there would either be no eros in the rulers and guardians, or not enough to pose a problem. It is thus clear that the analogy is misleading at best and nonexistent at worst.

Let me underline this crucial point. The restriction of intellectual activity to the philosopher must be understood, no doubt, to mean that the philosopher will entirely regulate the cognitive processes of the guardians. But Socrates inconsistently deprives the guardians of sexual eros by identifying them with the spirited element of the individual soul, and at the same time making clear that their very powerful eros must not only be controlled or suppressed, but will inevitably lead to the dissolution of the city.

The eros of the guardians is the Achilles' heel of the city in the *Republic*. It leads not to unity but to multiplicity, and so to destruction. We can avoid this problem by the simple expedient of jettisoning the analogy between the city and the soul. But as soon as we jettison this analogy, Socrates' entire procedure for determining whether the just or the unjust life is happier or more blessed becomes irrelevant. The instability of the guardians is thus a clue presented to us by Plato as to the rhetorical nature of Socrates' entire argument.

This reconsideration of the problem of eros has led us to see the poetic or constructive nature of Socrates' discursive city. One could make the same point by saying that, as a reductio, the city is a technical artifact, not a serious political proposal but an instrument designed to assist us in thinking seriously about politics. In a way very similar to the procedure of contemporary philosophers of science, Socrates is a model-builder.

The city in the *Republic* is a model of the political consequences of the hypothesis that justice is the highest political value, or that everything in human life must be subordinated to the attainment of justice. What the model shows us is that the result of this effort is injustice. Given the radically unjust nature of all existing cities, the political message of the *Republic* is that there is no solution to the political problem: no *final* solution, to use a terrifying expression from our contemporary experience.

All reasonable solutions are interim solutions. If this conclusion were developed in detail, it would seem to lead to a defense of prudence or practical intelligence, and so perhaps to Aristotle rather than to Plato. I think that this is what in fact happens if our intentions are political rather than purely theoretical. Plato is always extreme, even when, as in the *Statesman,* he defends *phronesis,* or what might be translated as practical intelligence.

It was also a thesis of Leo Strauss that there is no fundamental political difference between Plato and Aristotle. This thesis is easily misunderstood if we take the *Republic* as a blueprint for politics, rather than as a reductio, or in still different terms, as a poetical instrument in the radical theoretical consideration of the nature of the human soul. Aristotle's separation of practice from both theory and production is a mark of prudence, and hence of conservatism, not simply in the political, but also in the theoretical sense.

This conservatism separates poetry as well as pure theory or "metaphysics" from politics. It is therefore unnecessary for Aristotle to criticize mimetic poetry as Plato does. For Aristotle, there is no quarrel between philosophy and poetry because the two are expressions of distinct human faculties, both of which are in turn distinct from the faculty of practical intelligence, and so from political life. In Plato, however, the quarrel arises from the radical understanding of philosophy as a unity of theory and practice. This unity is in a sense disguised by the treatment of the separate parts of the soul and the discussion of the philosophical education and activity in the middle books of the *Republic.* But the disguise, if that is the right term, falls away as soon as we read the *Republic* as a whole, or for that matter, virtually any Platonic dialogue.

As the unity of theory and practice, that is to say, as the right way of life, philosophy is inseparably united with poetry. The quarrel between them is fraternal or "political" in the metaphorical sense that, like Romulus and Remus, they struggle for the throne. Whereas this struggle need not end in fratricide, it does so with sufficient frequency to show that the aforementioned unity of human existence is deeply flawed. Each of us must attempt to repair this flaw or fissure within our nature by means of constructions that, unfortunately, reproduce the dualism between philosophy and poetry. This is why Plato leaves it unresolved whether human existence is a tragedy or a comedy. In so doing, he silently affirms Socrates' contention at the end of the *Symposium* (223d3ff) that the same man can excel at the writing of tragedies and comedies, and thereby contradicts his denial of this point in the *Republic* (III. 395a4).

Selected Bibliography

for Further Reading

Alexander, Peter. "History of Philosophy: The Analytical Ideal." *The Aristotelian Society, Supplementary Volume* 62 (1988): 191–208.

Allan, George. *The Importance of the Past*. Albany: State University of New York Press, 1985.

———. *Realizations of the Future*. Albany: State University of New York Press, 1990.

Armstrong, A. M. "Philosophy and Its History." *Philosophy and Phenomenological Research* 19 (1958): 447–65.

Ayers, Michael. "Substance, Reality, and the Great Dead Philosophers." *American Philosophical Quarterly* 7 (1970): 38–49.

Bann, Stephen. "Towards a Critical Historiography: Recent Work in Philosophy." *Philosophy* 56 (1981): 365–86.

Baynes, Kenneth, James Bohman, and Thomas McCarthy, eds. *After Philosophy: End or Transformation?* Cambridge, Mass.: MIT Press, 1988.

Blau, J. L. "The Philosopher as Historian of Philosophy." *Journal of the History of Philosophy* 10 (1972): 212–15.

Brann, Eva T. H. *The World of the Imagination: Sum and Substance*. Lanham, Md.: Rowman and Littlefield, 1990.

———. *The Paradoxes of Education in a Republic*. Chicago: University of Chicago Press, 1979.

Cassirer, Ernst. *The Problem of Knowledge: Philosophy, Science, and History Since Hegel*. Trans. William H. Woglom and Charles W. Hendel. New Haven, Conn.: Yale University Press, 1950.

Cohen, Lesley. "Keeping the History of Philosophy." *Journal of the History of Philosophy* 14 (1976): 383–90.

Collingwood, R. G. *An Autobiography*. London: Oxford University Press, 1939.

———. *Essay on Metaphysics*. London: Oxford University Press, 1940.

———. *The Idea of History*. Oxford: Clarendon Press, 1946.

Copleston, Frederick. *On the History of Philosophy and Other Essays*. Totowa, N.J.: Barnes and Noble, 1979.

Curley, Edwin. "Dialogues with the Dead." *Synthese* 67 (1986): 33–49.

D'Amico, Robert. *Historicism and Knowledge*. New York: Routledge, 1989.

Daniel, Stephen H. "Metaphor in the Historiography of Philosophy." *Clio* 15 (1986): 191–210.

Danto, Arthur C. *Analytical Philosophy of History*. Cambridge: Cambridge University Press, 1965.

———. *Connections to the World*. New York: Harper and Row, 1989.

———. *Mysticism and Morality*. New York: Columbia University Press, 1988.

———. *Narration and Knowledge*. New York: Columbia University Press, 1985.

———. *The Philosophical Disenfranchisement of Art*. New York: Columbia University Press, 1986.

————. *The Transfiguration of the Commonplace: A Philosophy of Art.* Cambridge, Mass.: Harvard University Press, 1981.

Dauenhauer, Bernard P., ed. *At the Nexus of Philosophy and History.* Athens: University of Georgia Press, 1978.

Dombrowski, Daniel A. *Plato's Philosophy of History.* Washington, D.C.: University Press of America, 1981.

Dupré, Louis. "Is the History of Philosophy Philosophy?" *Review of Metaphysics* 42 (1989): 463–82.

Ehrlich, Walter. "Principles of a Philosophy of the History of Philosophy." *Monist* 53 (1969): 532–62.

Faurot, J. H. "What Is History of Philosophy?" *Monist* 53 (1969): 642–55.

Feibleman, James K. "The History of Philosophy as a Philosophy of History." *Southern Journal of Philosophy* 5 (1967): 275–83.

Foucault, Michel. *The Order of Things: An Archeology of the Human Sciences.* New York: Random House, 1970.

Frede, Michael. "The History of Philosophy as a Discipline." *Journal of Philosophy* 85 (1988): 666–72.

Galgan, Gerald J. "What's Special About the History of Philosophy?" *American Philosophical Quarterly* 24 (1987): 91–96.

Gerber, William. "Is There Progress in Philosophy?" *Journal of the History of Ideas* 34 (1973): 669–73.

Goodman, Nelson, and Catherine Elgin. *Reconceptions in Philosophy and Other Arts and Sciences.* Indianapolis: Hackett, 1988.

Graham, Gordon. "Can There Be History of Philosophy?" *History and Theory* 21 (1982): 37–52.

Gueroult, Martial. "The History of Philosophy as a Philosophical Problem." *Monist* 53 (1969): 563–87.

Guthrie, W. K. C. "Aristotle as Historian," in David J. Furley and R. E. Allen, eds., *Studies in Presocratic Philosophy.* London: Routledge and Kegan Paul, 1970, 239–54.

Hare, Peter H., ed. *Doing Philosophy Historically.* Buffalo, N.Y.: Prometheus Books, 1988.

Hartle, Ann. *Death and the Disinterested Spectator: An Inquiry into the Nature of Philosophy.* Albany: State University of New York Press, 1986.

Hesse, Mary B. "Vico's Heroic Metaphor," in R. S. Woolhouse, *Metaphysics and Philosophy of Science in the Seventeenth and Eighteenth Centuries.* Dordrecht: Kluwer, 1988.

Holland, A. J., ed. *Philosophy, Its History, and Historiography.* Dordrecht: Reidel, 1985.

Horowitz, Maryanne. "Complementary Methodologies in the History of Ideas." *Journal of the History of Philosophy* 12 (1974): 501–9.

Iggers, George G. *The German Conception of History: The National Tradition of Historical Thought from Herder to the Present.* Middleton, Conn.: Wesleyan University Press, 1983.

Irwin, Terence. *Aristotle's First Principles.* Oxford: Clarendon Press, 1988.

Jordan, Mark. "History in the Language of Metaphysics." *Review of Metaphysics* 36 (1983): 849–66.

Joy, Lynn Sumida. *Gassendi the Atomist, Advocate of History in an Age of Science.* London: Cambridge University Press, 1987.

Joynt, Carey B., and Nicholas Rescher. "The Problem of Uniqueness in History." *History and Theory* 1 (1961): 150–62.

Kelley, Donald R. "Horizons of Intellectual History: Retrospect, Circumspect, Prospect." *Journal of the History of Ideas* 48 (1987): 143–69.

————. "Vico's Road: From Philology to Jurisprudence and Back," in Giorgio Tagliacozzo and

Donald Phillip Verene, eds., *Giambattista Vico's Science of Humanity*. Baltimore: Johns Hopkins University Press, 1976.

King, Preston, ed. *The History of Ideas: An Introduction to Method*. Totowa, N.J.:Barnes and Noble, 1983.

Klibansky, Raymond, and Herbert James Paton, eds. *Philosophy and History*. New York: Harper and Row, 1963.

Kristeller, Paul Oskar. "Philosophy and Its Historiography." *Journal of Philosophy* 82 (1985): 618–25.

Kuklick, Bruce. "Studying the History of American Philosophy." *Transactions of the C. S. Peirce Society* 18 (1982): 18–33.

Kuntz, Paul Grimley. "The Dialectic of Historicism and Anti-Historicism." *Monist* 53 (1969): 656–69.

Lovejoy, Arthur O. "The Historiography of Ideas," in Arthur O. Lovejoy, *Essays in the History of Ideas*. Baltimore: Johns Hopkins University Press, 1948, 1–13.

Lucas, George R., Jr. *The Rehabilitation of Whitehead*. Albany: State University of New York Press, 1989.

———. *Whitehead und der deutsche Idealismus*. Frankfurt and Bern: Peter Lang, 1990.

MacIntyre, Alasdair. *After Virtue*. 2d ed. Notre Dame, Ind.: University of Notre Dame Press, 1984.

———. "Epistemological Crises, Dramatic Narrative, and the Philosophy of Science." *Monist* 60 (1977): 453–72.

———. *First Principles, Final Ends, and Contemporary Philosophy*. Milwaukee: Marquette University, 1990.

———. *A Short History of Ethics*. New York: Macmillan, 1966.

———. *Three Rival Versions of Moral Enquiry: Encyclopedia, Genealogy, and Tradition*. Notre Dame, Ind.: University of Notre Dame Press, 1990.

———. *Whose Justice? Which Rationality?* Notre Dame, Ind.: University of Notre Dame Press, 1989.

Makin, Stephen. "How Can We Find Out What Ancient Philosophers Said?" *Phronesis* 33 (1988): 121–32.

Mandelbaum, Maurice H. *Philosophy, History, and the Sciences: Selected Critical Essays*. Baltimore: Johns Hopkins University Press, 1984.

———. *The Problem of Historical Knowledge*. New York: Harper and Row, 1967.

Mash, Roy. "How Important for Philosophers Is the History of Philosophy?" *History and Theory* 26 (1987): 287–99.

Morgan, Michael L. "Authorship and the History of Philosophy." *Review of Metaphysics* 42 (1988): 327–55.

———. "The Goals and Methods of the History of Philosophy." *Review of Metaphysics* 40 (1987): 717–32.

Nehamas, Alexander. "What an Author Is." *Journal of Philosophy* 83 (1986): 685–91.

Neville, Robert Cummings, ed. *New Essays in Metaphysics*. Albany: State University of New York Press, 1987.

Neville, Robert Cummings. *The Puritan Smile*. Albany: State University of New York Press, 1988.

———. *The Reconstruction of Thinking*. Albany: State University of New York Press, 1982.

———. *The Recovery of the Measure: Interpretation and Nature*. Albany: State University of New York Press, 1989.

O'Hear, Anthony. "The History That Is in Philosophy." *Inquiry* 28 (1985): 455–66.

Olafson, Frederick A. *The Dialectic of Action: A Philosophical Interpretation of History and the Humanities*. Chicago: Chicago University Press, 1979.

Passmore, John Arthur. "The Idea of a History of Philosophy." *History and Theory* 5 (1965): 1–32.

Popkin, Richard H. "Philosophy and the History of Philosophy." *Journal of Philosophy* 82 (1965): 625–32.

Popper, Karl. *The Poverty of Historicism*. London: Routledge and Kegan Paul, 1957.

Power, Lawrence H. "On Philosophy and Its History." *Philosophical Studies* 50 (1986): 1–38.

Putnam, Hilary. *Reason, Truth and History*. Cambridge: Cambridge University Press, 1981.

Rajchman, John, and Cornel West, eds. *Post-Analtic Philosophy*. New York: Columbia University Press, 1985.

Randall, John Herman, Jr. *How Philosophy Uses Its Past*. New York: Columbia University Press, 1963.

Rauche, G. A. "Systematic Aspects of the History of Philosophy." *Man and World* 6 (1973): 63–78.

Ree, Jonathan, Michael Ayers, and Adam Westoby, eds. *Philosophy and Its Past*. Atlantic Highlands, N.J.: Humanities Press, 1978.

Rorty, Richard, J. B. Schneewind, and Quentin Skinner, eds. *Philosophy in History: Essays on the Historiography of Philosophy*. Cambridge: Cambridge University Press, 1984.

Rosen, Stanley. *The Ancients and the Moderns: Rethinking Modernity*. New Haven, Conn.: Yale University Press, 1989.

――――. *Hermeneutics as Politics*. London: Oxford University Press, 1987.

――――. *The Limits of Analysis*. New Haven, Conn.: Yale University Press, 1980.

――――. *Plato's Sophist: The Drama of Original and Image*. New Haven, Conn.: Yale University Press, 1983.

――――. *Plato's Symposium*. 2d ed. New Haven, Conn.: Yale University Press, 1987.

――――. *The Quarrel Between Philosophy and Poetry*. Methuen, N.J.: Routledge, 1988.

Schmitz, Kenneth L . "The History of Philosophy as Actual Philosophy." *Journal of Philosophy* 85 (1988): 673–78.

Schneewind, J. B. *Backgrounds of English Victorian Literature*. New York: Random House, 1970.

――――. *Sidgwick's Ethics and Victorian Moral Philosophy*. Oxford: Oxford University Press, 1977.

Shapiro, Gary. "Canons, Careers and Campfollowers: Randall and the Historiography of Philosophy." *Transactions of the C. S. Peirce Society* 23 (1987): 31–43.

Skinner, Quentin. "Hermeneutics and the Role of History," *New Literary History* 7 (1975): 202–32.

Smart, Harold Robert. *Philosophy and Its History*. LaSalle, Ill.: Open Court, 1962.

Smith, John E. *The Spirit of American Philosophy*. Albany: State University of New York Press, 1983.

Stambovsky, Phillip. "Metaphor and Historical Understanding." *History and Theory* 27 (1988): 125–34.

Strauss, Leo. "On Collingwood's Philosophy of History" and "Political Philosophy and History," in Preston King, ed., *The History of Ideas*. Totowa, N.J.: Barnes and Noble, 1983.

Tuttle, Howard N. "The Negation of History." *Southwest Philosophical Studies* 7 (1982): 1–15.

Verene, Donald Phillip. "Imaginative Universals and Narrative Truth," and Alasdair MacIntyre, "Imaginative Universals and Historical Falsification: A Rejoinder." *New Vico Studies* 4 (1988): 1–30.

――――. *The New Art of Autobiography*. London: Oxford University Press, 1991.

————, ed. *Vico and Joyce*. Albany: State University of New York Press, 1987.

————. *Vico's Science of Imagination*. Ithaca, N.Y.: Cornell University Press, 1981.

Vico, Giambattista. *The Academies and the Relations Between Philosophy and Eloquence*. Trans. Donald Phillip Verene. Ithaca, N.Y.: Cornell University Press, 1990.

————. *The Autobiography of Giambattista Vico*. Trans. Max Harold Fisch and Thomas Goddard Bergin. Ithaca, N.Y.: Cornell University Press, 1944.

————. *The New Science of Giambattista Vico*. Trans. Thomas Goddard Bergin and Max Harold Fisch. Ithaca, N.Y.: Cornell University Press, 1986.

————. *On the Most Ancient Wisdom of the Italians*. Trans. L. M. Palmer. Ithaca, N.Y.: Cornell University Press, 1990.

————. *On the Study Methods of Our Time*. Trans. Elio Gianturco. Ithaca, N.Y.: Cornell University Press, 1990.

Wiener, Phillip P. "The Logical Significance of the History of Thought." *Journal of the History of Ideas* 7 (1946): 366–73.

————. "Some Problems and Methods in the History of Ideas." *Journal of the History of Ideas* 22 (1961): 531–48.

Yolton, John W. "Is There a History of Philosophy? Some Difficulties and Suggestions." *Synthese* 67 (1986): 3–21.

————. "Some Remarks on the Historiography of Philosophy." *Journal of the History of Philosophy* 23 (1985): 571–78.

Index

Nichomachean Ethics (Aristotle), 111
Nietzsche, Friedrich Wilhelm, 115; and death
of God, 155; engagement by, 117
Novum Organum (Bacon): influence of, on
Vico, 50

Oakeshott, Michael, 23, 27
Obligation: in ontological covenant, 157
"Ode on a Grecian Urn" (Keats), 174–75; fig-
ures in, 168–69; modes of silence in, 167,
173–74; scenes in, 168–69; symmetry in,
172; and tradition, 172; world of, 169. *See
also* Grecian urn
"Ode to Autumn" (Keats), 172
"Ode to Melancholy" (Keats), 172
Odysseus and Nausicaa, 205
Odyssey (Homer), 207; and *Ulysses,* 198–200
Ogarev, Nicholas P., 180
On Generation and Corruption (Aristotle), 44
On Man, His Mortality and Immortality
(Radishchev), 177
On the Law of War and Peace (Grotius), 93
Ontological covenant. *See* Covenant, on-
tological
Optics (Euclid), 139
Opyt nauki iziashchnogo (Galich). *See An Es-
say on the Science of the Beautiful*

Painting: and poetry, 172; progress in, 129–
30
Paris Hippocratics, 142. *See also* Art
Parochial interpretations, 31
Parochial tradition, 31, 32, 37; biblical, 32–33
Past: as function of present, 131; influence of,
on narrative, 132. *See also under history*
Paul, Saint, 86, 162
Peirce, C. S.: semiotics of, 21
Pelagianism, 93
Perception: and memory, difference between,
125
Périon, Joachim: mistranslation of Aristotle
by, 141
Petter, Stephen, 112
Permissiveness: and tradition, 30
Phaedo (Plato), 47, 107
Phaedrus (Plato), 171
*Phänomenologie des Geistes. See Phenomenol-
ogy of Spirit*
Phantasia, 116
Phenomenology of Spirit (Hegel), 41, 50; as
basis for Ibsen's work, 48; circles in, 43;
consciousness in, 52; knowledge in, 44;
prudence in, 51; recollection, 44

Philosopher-king: as poet, 215–16; reluctance to rule, 213
Philosophers: disagreements among 80–81;
memory for, 49; as poets, 215–16; in *Republic,* 214, 215; wisdom for, 49
Philosophical disagreements: interminable,
73; kinds of, 70; sources of, 69, 71; systematic, 71; targets of, 70. *See also* Conflict of
systems
Philosophical history: genres for studying, 2–
3
Philosophical imagination, 1; and cultural
memory, 2, 6, 9; defined, 5; and history of
philosophy, 6–9; necessity of, 78
Philosophical issues: in other disciplines, 71;
relevance of history of philosophy to, 84
Philosophical memory, 6; defined, 6; narration as goal of, 5–6. *See also* Memory
Philosophical movements, 114. *See also* Engagement
Philosophical questions: abandoned, 112;
disagreements about, 67; about morality,
67; nonphilosophers' need to raise, 80;
philosophical systems as response to, 74;
posed from within a system, 72; progress
in, 67–68
Philosophical systems: characteristics of, 73;
circularity involved in, 74–75; competition among, 78–79; encounters between,
7–8; establishing superiority of, 145; evaluation of, 145; internal problematic of,
77–78; internal representations of rivals
in, 78, 79–80; justification of, 77; questions in, 72; rational adequacy of, 7, 8, 76;
as responses to philosophical questions,
74; stages in, 79
Philosophical tradition: as ahistorical, 7; historicism, 7
Philosophy: academic, justification for, 66,
67; agreements in, 69; of art history, 129;
as correction for religion, 149; and cultural
memory, 3–6; definition of, 40–41, 149;
disagreements in, 69, 80–81; as a discipline, 10; discipline-history of, 6; as divine
passion, 115–16; engagement in, 117; as
an everyday activity, 66; external utility of,
65–66; forgetting in, 47–48; and historiography, 6; as history, 115; as imagination, 40, 54; as ingenuity, 55; jurisprudence as, 52; justification for, 65, 66, 81–
82, 118; lack of progress in, 66; as memory, 5, 49, 54; as narrative, 49; necessity of
poetry to, 46–47; as poetry, 217–18, 224;

Contributors

George Allan is dean of the college and professor of philosophy at Dickinson College in Carlisle, Pennsylvania. He has published articles on Hegel, Whitehead, and Croce, as well as essays devoted to the philosophy of history, philosophy of culture, and education. He recently published two books, *The Importances of the Past* and *The Realizations of the Future.*

Eva T. H. Brann is dean of the college and tutor at St. John's College in Annapolis, Maryland. She is a regular contributor to the *St. John's Review,* and she lectures frequently throughout the country. Her books include *Late Geometric and Protoattic Pottery: The Athenian Agora* (1962), *The Paradoxes of Education in a Republic* (1979), and *The World of the Imagination: Sum and Substance* (1991).

Patricia Cook is assistant professor of philosophy at Loyola College in Maryland. She recently received her doctoral degree in philosophy at Emory University with the dissertation "Forgetting: An Inquiry through Plato's Dialogues." She served as assistant director for the 1990 National Endowment for the Humanities Summer Institute, and has published articles and reviews on Kant, Vico, Descartes, and the pre-Socratic philosophers.

Arthur C. Danto is Johnsonian Professor of Philosophy at Columbia University and is art critic for *The Nation.* A past president of the American Philosophical Association, he is author of numerous articles and many books, including *Nietzsche as Philosopher, Narration and Knowledge, The Philosophical Disenfranchisement of Art, Mysticism and Morality,* and *The Transfiguration of the Commonplace.*

Lynn S. Joy is associate professor of philosophy and associate professor of history at the University of Notre Dame. She is author of *Gassendi the Atomist: Advocate of History in an Age of Science.* More recently, she has written on the philosophical problems that informed Renaissance humanism and science, and she is working on a history of Renaissance philosophy that focuses on the conflicts among rival philosophical traditions from Ockham to Descartes.

George L. Kline retired in 1991 as the Milton C. Nahm Professor of Philosophy and chairman of the department of Russian at Bryn Mawr College. He has published numerous books and more than one hundred scholarly articles on the thought of Spinoza, Vico, Hegel, Marx, Whitehead, Sartre, Lukacs, and Kolakowski, and he is an internationally recognized authority on the history of Russian philosophy. He has translated scores of books, articles, and poems, and is the premier translator of the poetry of Nobel Laureate Joseph Brodsky.

George R. Lucas, Jr. is currently assistant director for research at the National Endowment for the Humanities in Washington, D.C., and philosophy series editor of the State University of New York Press. He served as director for the National Endowment for the Humanities Summer Institute, "The Philosophical Uses of Historical Traditions," in 1990. His books include *The Rehabilitation of Whitehead, Poverty, Justice, and the Law, Lifeboat Ethics,* and *Hegel and Whitehead.*

Alasdair MacIntyre is McMahon/Hank Professor of Philosophy at the University of Notre Dame. His books include *A Short History of Ethics* (1966), *After Virtue* (1981), *Whose Justice? Which Rationality?* (1989), and *Three Rival Versions of Moral Enquiry: Encyclopaedia, Genealogy, and Tradition* (1990).

Robert Cummings Neville is dean of the School of Theology and professor of philosophy and religion at Boston University. He is the author of many articles and books, including *Soldier, Saint, Sage, God the Creator, The Cosmology of Freedom, The Tao and the Daimon: Segments of a Religious Inquiry, The Reconstruction of Thinking, The Puritan Smile: A Look Toward Moral Reflection, The Recovery of the Measure: Interpretation and Nature, Behind the Masks of God, A Theology Primer,* and, most recently, *The Highroad around Modernism.*

John S. Rickard is assistant professor of English at Bucknell University. He is completing a book entitled *Joyce's Book of Memory: The Mnemotechnic of Ulysses.* He has written on James Joyce, Yeats, and modern Irish literature.

Stanley Rosen is Evan Pugh Professor of Philosophy at Pennsylvania State University and has lectured and taught all over the world. His books include *Hermeneutics as Politics, The Ancients and the Moderns, G. W. F. Hegel: An Introduction to the Science of Wisdom, Plato's Sophist, The Limits of Analysis, Plato's Symposium, The Quarrel Between Philosophy and Poetry, Nihilism: A Philosophical Essay,* and a book of poetry, *Death in Egypt.*

J. B. Schneewind is professor of philosophy at Johns Hopkins University. He codirected a summer institute on Kantian ethical thought in 1983, sponsored by the National Endowment for the Humanities and the Council for Philosophical Studies. He is the author of *Backgrounds of English Victorian Literature* and *Sidgwick's Ethics and Victorian Moral Philosophy* and is editor of an anthology *Moral Philosophy from Montaigne to Kant.*

Donald Phillip Verene is Charles Howard Candler Professor of Metaphysics and Moral Philosophy and director of the Institute for Vico Studies at Emory University. He was recently Visiting Fellow at Pembroke College, Oxford. Among his published works are *Symbol, Myth, and Culture: Essays and Lectures of Ernst Cassirer 1935–1945* (1979), *Vico's Science of the Imagination* (1981), *Hegel's Recollection: A Study of the Images in Hegel's Phenomenology of Spirit* (1985), *Vico and Joyce* (1987), and *The New Art of Autobiography: An Essay on the "Life of Giambattista Vico Written by Himself"* (1990).

Library of Congress Cataloging-in-Publication Data
Philosophical imagination and cultural memory : appropriating historical traditions /
edited by Patricia Cook.
Includes bibliographical references and index.
ISBN 0-8223-1307-3 (cloth). — ISBN 0-8223-1322-7 (pbk.)
1. History—Philosophy.   2. Imagination (Philosophy)   I. Cook, Patricia, 1958–
D16.9.P416   1993
901—dc20   92-34703 CIP